Law in popular belief

MANCHESTER
1824

Manchester University Press

Law in popular belief
Myth and reality

Edited by *Anthony Amatrudo* and *Regina Rauxloh*

Manchester University Press

Published by Manchester University Press
Altrincham Street, Manchester M1 7JA
www.manchesteruniversitypress.co.uk

British Library Cataloguing-in-Publication Data is available

ISBN 978 0 7190 9783 6 hardback
ISBN 978 1 5261 2506 4 paperback

First published by Manchester University Press in hardback 2017

This edition first published 2020

Typeset by Out of House Publishing

To my loved ones
(Regina)

Contents

Notes on contributors

Anthony Amatrudo is an Associate Professor of Criminology at Middlesex University, UK. He is also a consultant to the Cabinet Office on legal understanding and a member of the Good Law Review. His work deals increasingly with issues drawn from political theory. His most recent book is *Human Rights and the Criminal Justice System* (Routledge, 2015) and he is currently editing a special edition of the Onati Socio-Legal Series on group offending.

Matthew R. Draper is an Associate Professor of Behavioral Sciences at Utah Valley University, USA. He completed his doctoral work in counselling psychology at the University of Texas at Austin. Before working at Utah Valley he served as Director of Clinical Training and Mental Health Counseling Program Director at Indiana State University. His clinical work entails serving marginalised members of society, particularly his work in a supermaximum security prison as well as local jails. His teaching specialisation is in the areas of psychotherapy theory and practice, the history of psychotherapy and philosophy of the behavioural sciences. His research and scholarship entails careful examinations of the philosophy and practice of psychotherapy, particularly the moral philosophy of psychotherapy, from a broadly phenomenological hermeneutic and dialogic frame. He also examines how these ideas relate to working with marginalised and underserved groups such as the currently and formerly incarcerated.

Robert Jago MPhil is a Senior Lecturer in Law at Royal Holloway, University of London, UK. He has extensive experience of research in the field of criminal justice and has considered the umbrella term 'exclusion' to consider the land rights of gypsies along with the allocation of medical resources in *The Politics of the Common Law* (Routledge, 2013 – with A. Gearey and W. Morrison). He has written on grand corruption and asset recovery along with incidences of petty corruption in the developing world (with I. Carr) and his current research is looking at the interaction between law and regulation with a particular interest in health care professions.

Paul Johnson is Professor in Sociology at the University of York, UK. His research is concerned with a number of broad questions about the relationship between law, human rights, sexual orientation and intimacy. He has a general interest in the role and purpose of law in promoting and protecting particular kinds of sexuality and human relationships. Recent research has focused on the jurisprudence of the European Court of Human Rights in respect of sexual orientation, resulting in *Homosexuality and the European Court of Human Rights* (Routledge, 2013), the first book-length study devoted entirely to this aspect of the Court's work. Other publications include the monographs *Love, Heterosexuality and Society* (Routledge, 2005) and *Genetic Policing* (Willan Publishing, 2008 – with Robin Williams), and the edited collection *Policing Sex* (Routledge, 2012 – with Derek Dalton). His monograph *Law, Religion and Homosexuality* (Routledge, 2014 – with Robert Vanderbeck) explores how religion has shaped, and continues to shape, law that regulates the lives of gay men and lesbians.

Ronnie Lippens is Professor of Criminology at Keele University, UK. His research interests include theoretical and critical criminology, organisational criminology and visual criminology. He has published prolifically on these topics in a wide variety of venues, both in English and in Dutch. His research and writing usually straddle disciplines and perspectives in the humanities and the social sciences. He has, latterly, been working on a number of themes in visual criminology, in particular on 'prophetic painting'. In this recent work the overall focus is on how, and to what extent, art (painting especially) is able to announce or indeed foreshadow emerging forms of life and their corresponding forms of governance before traces of the latter appear in more conceptual works such as academic treatises or political tracts. He is also the author of what is probably the slimmest textbook in the criminological domain, that is, *A Very Short, Fairly Interesting and Reasonably Cheap Introduction to Studying Criminology* (Sage, 2009).

David Polizzi is an Associate Professor of Criminology at Indiana State University, USA. He holds an MA in International Affairs with a concentration on American Foreign Policy and Latin American Politics from the American University in Washington, DC and an MA in Humanistic Psychology from West Georgia College. He completed his doctoral work in clinical psychology at Duquesne University and works as a licensed substance abuse counsellor in addition to his many university duties. He has over twenty years' experience working as a psychotherapist, which entailed extensive work in both prisons and jails both in the state of Pennsylvania as well as Indiana. In addition, he has extensive experience of working in the field of addictions, both inside and outside of the correctional system. Inspired by his many years working in corrections and with addictions he works to advocate for the needs of the currently and formerly incarcerated through his research and scholarship. His scholarship entails a thoroughgoing phenomenological hermeneutic of many issues relative to criminology, psychology and psychotherapy, which prompted him to found the *Journal of Theoretical and Philosophical Criminology*, for which he currently serves as editor.

Regina E. Rauxloh studied for her first law degree in Germany before moving to the UK in 1999. She received her LLM (in Law and Development) and her PhD from the University of Warwick, UK. She worked as a Senior Lecturer at the University of Surrey, UK, and is now Associate Professor in Law at the University of Southampton, UK. Her research interests lie in international criminal law, criminal procedure law, the law of armed conflict and comparative law. She has published work on corporate criminal responsibility in international criminal law, human trafficking, multinational corporations in international criminal law, drone warfare, comparative procedural law and regionalism. She has presented her work in New Zealand, the USA, South Korea, Germany, Greece, France and the UK. Her monograph *Plea Bargaining in National and International Law* came out in 2012 and she co-edited the volume *Precision Strike Warfare and International Intervention: Strategic, Ethico-Legal and Decisional Implications* (Routledge, 2014 – with Mike Aaronson, Wali Aslam and Tom Dyson).

Lizzie Seal is Senior Lecturer in Criminology in the Sociology Department at the University of Sussex, UK. Her research interests include gender representations of women who kill, cultural criminology and capital punishment. She has published *Women, Murder and Femininity: Gender Representations of Women Who Kill* (Palgrave, 2010) and, with Maggie O'Neill, *Transgressive Imaginations: Crime, Deviance and Culture* (Palgrave, 2012). Her monograph *Capital Punishment in Twentieth-Century Britain: Audience, Justice, Memory* was published in 2014. She is on the editorial board of the *British Journal of Criminology* and is a member of the Howard League's Research Advisory Group.

Matthew R. Smith is a Barrister-at-Law, based at Park Square Barristers in Leeds, UK, where his practice concentrates upon aspects of fraud and commercial litigation. He holds a degree from Durham University in Economics and Law and an MPhil in Criminology from the Institute of Criminology at Cambridge University. Since then he has undertaken a wide variety of criminal and civil work at the Bar and has a particular interest in criminal and civil justice under the current regime of budget cuts. He lectures regularly to lawyers, civil servants and the insurance industry.

Colin Sumner is Professor and Head of the School of Sociology and Philosophy at University College Cork, Ireland. He has written two major monographs, *Reading Ideologies: Investigation into the Marxist Theory of Ideology and Law* (Academic Press, 1979) and *The Sociology of Deviance: an Obituary* (Open University Press, 1994), and edited several innovative collections including: *The Blackwell Companion to Criminology* (Wiley-Blackwell, 2004); *Crime, Justice and Underdevelopment* (Ashgate, 1982); *Censure, Politics and Criminal Justice*, and *Violence Culture and Censure* (Open University Press, 1990). He is a co-founder of the journal *Theoretical Criminology*. He currently teaches sociology of crime and deviance, social theory and sociology of the media and has been Programme Director of the MA in Criminology and the BA in Criminology since September 2014.

David Wilson is Professor of Criminology at Birmingham City University (BCU), UK, and a former prison governor. He received his PhD from Cambridge University in 1983 and then joined HM Prison Service as Assistant Governor at HMP Wormwood Scrubs. He also worked at HMPs Grendon and Woodhill – experiences that brought him into contact with many recent British serial killers. He resigned from the prison service in 1997 and took up his appointment at BCU. He has written fifteen books – including *A History of British Serial Killing* (Sphere, 2011), and is editor of the *Howard Journal of Criminal Justice*, one of the leading criminology journals in the country. He is the Vice Chair of the Howard League for Penal Reform, Vice President of New Bridge, and Chair of the Friends of Grendon. He is a noted commentator and broadcaster about crime generally and prisons specifically and his Channel 5 series *Banged Up* was nominated for an RTS Award in 2010. In 2012, he was made a National Teaching Fellow. His most recent book *Pain and Retribution: A Short History of British Prisons* was published by Reaktion Books in 2014.

Acknowledgements

I would like to acknowledge the help, inspiration and support of the following people: Professor Hans-Jorg Albrecht, Jake and Dinos Chapman, Professor Robert Fine, Dr Volker Grundies, Professor Robert Reiner, Dr Magnus Ryan and Professor George Steiner FBA. I also wish to acknowledge the help and assistance of St Edmund's College, Cambridge, the Institute of Criminology at the University of Cambridge and the Max-Planck-Institut für Europäische Rechtsgeschichte in Frankfurt am Main and Max-Planck-Institut für Ausländisches und Internationales Strafrecht in Freiburg for their collegial support.

(Anthony Amatrudo)

I am greatly thankful for the many helpful suggestions by Emma Hardy and Claire Griffith and especially for the valuable advice from Prof David Gurnham.

(Regina E. Rauxloh)

Anthony Amatrudo and Regina E. Rauxloh

Introduction

Law and its representation take up a great deal of our time as readers of newspapers, consumers of broadcast media and of popular fiction. Indeed, it is hard to identify any area of everyday life and social interaction which is not governed to some degree by law. The law as understood by lawyers, lawmakers and legal scholarship is very different, nonetheless, from how it is understood, and represented, to the wider public. This gap is usually not addressed in technical terms but in terms of the way in which the media necessarily distorts the law, being unable, or unwilling, to address all aspects of an issue, and often leaving aside not only important details but also *underlying* issues, such as power and ownership. It is this gap between the law as it is known by lawyers on the one hand and the popular understanding of it on the other that this volume aims to explore from a number of angles. The aim of this volume is to explore the relationship between law and its public perceptions by drawing on the experience and expertise of well-known practitioners, scholars and theorists. It critically assesses the public's level of legal, psychological and social awareness in relation to their knowledge of law and deviant behaviour. The authors look at a number of themes that are central to examining the ways in which myths about law are formed, the ways in which epistemological deficits allow this process to operate and how there is inevitably a constitutive power aspect to this myth making. In addressing contemporary issues concerning the relationship between law and popular beliefs, this book is a contribution to public criminology. There have been few works that have brought together such a diverse group of writers, practising lawyers and academics from law, sociology, criminology and social studies and conducted this analysis on such a broad canvas.

Although the chapters take very different approaches to this expansive area, there are a number of links between the individual contributions to this volume. The book is, therefore, divided into three parts. Part I, 'Perception shaped by traditional media', explores how public beliefs about the law are not formed by primary sources such as legislation, court cases or police reports but rather by its representation in the media, be it in news reporting or in popular culture. Part II, 'Perception shaped by other means', goes beyond traditional media and examines other vehicles of communication in which the public is being fed certain impressions of the law. Part III, 'Perception of those at the fringe of society', examines how those people at the margins of society are perceived by mainstream public perception and what role law plays in the identification of 'us' and 'the other'.

Part I: Perception shaped by traditional media

In his chapter 'Criminology through the looking glass', Colin Sumner draws upon a lifetime of academic commitment to developing criminological theory, notably in relation to the development and operation of social censures in mature Western economies. In his essay, he questions the underlying assumptions of popular notions of crime. He notes that while 'the rich get richer and the poor get prison', as Reiman's famous book title suggests (1995), society's perception and condemnation is in reverse to the social harm caused. The crimes of the poor and young cause the least social harm and yet receive the greatest social censure, whereas the crimes of the rich are the ones that cause the greatest harm to society but receive, nevertheless, the weakest social censure. This paradox perception of the effect of crime reminds one of a through-the-looking-glass Jabberwocky poem, whose reverse message can only be read by holding it up to the mirror. Sumner's chapter assesses whether this strange criminology can be explained by the analysis of mimesis and the mimetic double bind in the work of René Girard, or whether the phenomenon is better seen as an inevitable reflection of the roots of dominant social censures within dominant and contradictory social relations. This chapter makes a head-on assault upon criminological convention, which typically ignores the major effects of major economic, historical and social transformations in favour of an overemphasis on the more mundane forms of crime. Sumner shows how the manufacture and reformulation of the social censures what people come to understand as important are simply the end result of a process of ideological machination that gives the public a reason to see crime as the powerful want them to see it. The author consequently asks serious questions about the history of criminology. Why did criminology come to be part of the process of equating crime with the working classes? Why did criminology come to see crime as an aspect of poverty? Why did it come to see its project as tied to the control of the poor and largely overlook the bigger crimes and especially those of the powerful?

Anthony Amatrudo's chapter, 'What do they know of law who only cop shows know?', explores how it is not the law, as such, but only representations of it that affect behaviour. He maintains that citizens come to act in terms of what they *believe* the law is and not necessarily as it actually is. The chapter shows how the public's knowledge of the law is drawn increasingly from a range of traditional and modern media with an increasingly important role for the Internet. People download, view and ingest alleged information about law in an *ad hoc* and unsystematic manner. Amatrudo shows how this works in the matter of victims' interests. The now established victims' rights discourse embedded in journalistic practice and media generates legal narratives that tend to play down the rights of defendants and undermine important legal principles that safeguard the efficacy of the trial process. Thus, the attempts of the law to balance crime control and due process are not reflected in the popular belief about the aims and objectives of criminal law. As the general public learns about the law through the media, not surprisingly, a diet of victim-centred news coverage over time has tended to make the general public more overtly retributive in their thinking. Moreover, the media often prefers to highlight the *sensational* and show the world as, for example, far more violent than it actually is. This includes presenting lower police detection rates than is actually the case and the misrepresentation of the racial make-up of offenders. Amatrudo shows that while there is extensive media coverage of crime there is little consideration of legal principles and procedures, and the need for procedural safeguards and due process. The notion that law is a technical and elaborate system of knowledge is entirely absent in the simplified portrayal of crime in both news and drama. An example of this is the so-called *CSI*-effect: the fact that recently citizens, notably jurors, hold to high levels of proof in relation to forensic evidence and how this obsession with and unrealistic trust in forensic evidence has had the effect of undermining the jury process.

Matthew R. Draper, a psychologist and David Polizzi, a clinical psychotherapist, both have clinical practices but also teach criminal justice. In their chapter 'Regurgitating the media image: towards a phenomenology of visible in criminal justice', they address the problematic nature of the social construction of crime for law enforcement and jurisprudence. After highlighting many of the consequences to which these constructions lead, they offer an ethic of phenomenological reduction of crime and the incumbent legal processes as a solution. They do so by drawing upon the work of Jean-Luc Marion, Claude Romano, Werner Marx, James Mensch and Immanuel Levinas in order to understand a new potential for exploring the complex nature of crime and its resulting legal processes. The reduction, in this case, entails an ethical argument to reduce what is given to those experiencing these processes and to us as observers. In the case of the one accused of crime, a reduction of their experience often breaks free the understanding of the good-guy and bad-guy portrayals in media. Likewise, a reduction of the experience and activity of law-enforcement and jurisprudence professionals highlights their professional, personal and interpersonal complexities as they do their jobs. Finally, they propose that this phenomenological ethic (by which they mean a form of ethics that prioritises the face-to-face and the empathetic and champions our shared humanity), when taken up by the media, would actually not only increase the portrayals of these processes in a more authentic manner, but increase the potential for sharing the dramatic stories of the criminal, law enforcement and legal professionals. This would serve to further their agenda of telling marketable and engaging stories by highlighting the incredible personal and interpersonal complexities of the people caught up in these experiences. For Draper and Polizzi, the issue that is most important in criminological study is the adoption of a more compassionate and humanitarian ethic. They argue that only when criminologists, police officers and others engaged in the criminal justice system adopt such an ethic will true understanding follow. Draper and Polizzi maintain that only when this ethic is adopted will there be no more need for the media and other forms of manipulation; rather there will be a richer, more complex and thorough understanding. Moreover, it will be set in more human terms.

Part II: Perception shaped by other means

In her chapter '"Kony is so last month" – lessons from the social media stunt "Kony 2012"', Regina E. Rauxloh explores how myths and public beliefs are created by social media campaigns. While there are a number of examples in recent history where political change is claimed to have been facilitated by social media (such as the so-called Arab Spring), this chapter uses the case study of the YouTube clip 'Kony 2012' to show potential pitfalls. This video, which attracted over 100 million viewers within a week, depicts the armed conflict in Uganda, the crimes of Joseph Kony, with special emphasis on the recruitment of child soldiers, and campaigns for military intervention by foreign forces in order to secure the arrest of Kony and prosecute him before the International Criminal Court. After introducing the organisation Invisible Children, who created this video and the factual background of the armed conflict in Uganda, Rauxloh gives a detailed account of the number of myths and public beliefs created and sustained by the video. She looks at three principal myths, namely the myths regarding the background and facts of the armed conflict and the current situation in Uganda, the myths regarding possible military and legal solutions and last, but not least, the myth surrounding the effectiveness of online activism itself. Rauxloh argues that the portrayal of a very long and complex conflict as simply a war of good versus evil and the presented solution of the 'mighty West' assisting the 'helpless Africa' perpetuates dangerous stereotypes, which are in direct contradiction to the aims of international criminal justice in general and the International Criminal Court in particular. At the same time, the online audience is given the impression that a few clicks is all that is needed to make the world a better place. Rauxloh also argues that one of the most damaging myths is the notion of the Internet as a freely accessible democratic forum that opens up the power of voice to everybody, wrongly implying that the Internet is freely accessible to all. While Rauxloh welcomes the wide publicity created by the video about child soldiers, Joseph Kony and the International Criminal Court, she warns that social media forms have an unprecedented potential for creating, spreading and perpetuating myths and public beliefs. Many of the oversimplified black-and-white claims are unhelpful and can even be damaging in the context of international criminal justice, whose role is to discover the truth about the multifaceted complexities of a conflict and support a reconciliation between the warring parties. The chapter makes a major contribution in showing the role of the new communicating forms of social media in the creation of myths and public beliefs about justice and law.

Matthew Smith, a practising barrister, examines in his chapter 'A comparative analysis of the criminal and civil justice systems in England and Wales', the current criminal and civil justice systems in England and Wales and compares their accessibility to the public, their value for money and their overall viability. The current international credit crisis has resulted in cuts by the government and the inevitable streamlining of legal services with the need to reduce the overall amount of criminal and civil litigation. In the criminal justice system, far fewer cases are prosecuted, whereas in the civil justice system, there is a desire to deter litigation by a number of technical and fiscal measures. Smith argues that this policy, of restricting access to the courts, is detrimental to both the English criminal and civil systems of law and has resulted in the reduction of *bona fide* litigation; moreover, that it has thereby rendered the accessibility of both systems difficult because of the built-in structural unfairness unrelated to notions of justice. Although the economic argument made by government concerning the cost of the legal system might initially appear to be reasonable, this chapter argues that overall the current restriction on access to the courts is not only to be questioned from an economic point of view, on its own terms, but it implies a far more fundamental change of mind in our contemporary understanding of justice and, beyond that, moral philosophy. What Smith brings to the table is little short of a full-on assault upon the commonly held beliefs, myths and perceptions that people hold about the operation of the criminal justice system. Smith explodes those beliefs, myths and perceptions from the perspective of a working barrister. His chapter not only sets out the engineered-in structural unfairness of the English legal system but, in doing so, he raises profound questions about the nature of justice itself. After demonstrating how recent changes to the operation of the court service were driven by economic considerations he asks us to ponder the price of justice in moral, not monetary, terms.

Paul Johnson's chapter, 'Beliefs about the European Court of Human Rights in the United Kingdom Parliament', looks at a very unconventional aspect of myth building around law, namely the role of Parliamentarians in shaping public beliefs about an international court. The chapter illustrates how parts of the current mistrust of the European Court of Human Rights in this country stem from the views hold and disseminated by politicians when debating controversial legislation proposals. Johnson examines the recent debate of the Marriage (Same Sex Couples) Act 2013 in both Houses of Parliament. He shows two different dimensions of these myths. The first myth is that the European Court of Human Rights, rather than protecting the human rights of UK citizens, poses a risk that the rights of one group will be eroded by the rights of another group, and that the legislator who tries to build in protective safeguards will be overruled in some way by this apparently omnipotent court. The second myth is that the European Court is biased against religious groups and their members. As both myths are used to underpin the specific political arguments during the legislative debate, the chapter thus demonstrates very clearly how ostensible legal arguments are used to give strength and credibility to political opinions. Furthermore, Johnson shows how some politicians create and sustain ideas about the European Court which are claimed to be based on the Court's jurisdiction although closer examination of the cited cases proves little substance for these beliefs. By citing specific cases, politicians in both the House of Commons and the House of Lords give their arguments the appearance of being based in jurisprudence. Johnson explains, however, how little these claims are sustained by the cited cases. The broad assertions that the European Court values the human rights of same-sex couples more than those of religious organisations or their members cannot be found in the referenced decisions. Although the alleged preference of the former group is seen as a threat to opponents of same-sex marriage because they fear the European Court of Human Rights will interfere in the national legislator's safeguards for the protection of religious freedom, it seems that on the contrary, the cited decisions actually are in favour of State discretion, allowing for a broad margin in which it is up to the State rather than the European Court to balance the different human rights of different groups and individuals. While Johnson leaves it open as to whether the authors of such claims suffered from a lack of knowledge or intentionally aimed to misinform, one has to ask whether the politicians have read the lengthy European Court decisions or whether they hoped that nobody else would, or even both. This chapter fearlessly examines the different origins of public beliefs in law and demonstrates how even at the heart of law, namely the places of law-making itself, myths are created and retained.

Ronnie Lippens has carved an international reputation through his use of both philosophical and artistic insights into the criminological canon. In his chapter, '*Forward!* Coding, decoding and recoding order in public art for urban regeneration', he explores how public artworks are themselves part of a system of coding and recoding that informs both our ethics and our aesthetics. His contribution explores the coded dimension of large public artworks (sculptures or installations in particular). Public space is dotted with such artworks, some of which are built on a monumental scale. He shows how one of the oldest forms of media, public art, helps in creating and perpetuating myths about authority in the shape of rules and laws in the broadest sense. The focus in Lippens's contribution is upon the normative codes that are supposed to be embedded in both the material structure and the aura of the works. Indeed, when authorities decide to commission public artworks the brief to artists will often include specifications that pertain not just to the desired visual and expressive effect of the work (the artwork is then supposed to express a particular idea or content), but also to a more normative intention (i.e. the artwork is then required either to tap into or mobilise an existing set of cultural, social or political codes, or indeed consolidate, propagate or even generate them). An element in the normative coding of public artworks, on which this contribution is focusing in particular, relates to notions or indeed visions of *public order* that the works are assumed to radiate and project. Public artworks are often meant to project the following message: 'This is us. Or at least: this is how we ought to be and what we ought to be like. And you, visitor, are now entering a particular space with a particular code. Beware and behave "accordingly".' By examining a number of selected cases, Lippens questions whether public artworks are at all able to realise any of their intended effects and whether it is not the case that the intended codes embedded in the artwork are bound to be subjected to continuous decoding and recoding. For Lippens, public art not only displays the conventions, censures and moralities of its own age but allows for reconceptions of those same conventions, censures and moralities. Moreover, public art is atypical of much of our built environment in that it resists eviction, by which he means it is typically in place longer, and more solidly, than much that passes for architecture.

Part III: Perception of those at the fringe of society

David Wilson is the leading UK authority on serial killers. His chapter, 'The legacies of Clarice Starling: myths, media and realities about the phenomenon of serial murder', explores the enduring popular myths about the phenomenon of serial murder generally and serial killers in particular, in Britain between 1960 and the present. In his chapter, he argues that many of these myths have been created and continue to be perpetuated by the print and broadcast media. It is suggested that this process was ignited by American popular culture about serial murder, to the extent that many British students engaged on criminology/psychology courses within higher education do so because they want to emulate the heroine of the popular novel *The Silence of the Lambs* by Thomas Harris and 'become' the fictional character Clarice Starling. This observation is used to explore other myths about offender profiling, the role of the profiler in police investigations and the idea that this involves 'entering the mind' of the serial killer by the profiler. Based on his own applied work on police investigations and with serial murderers after their conviction, the chapter reveals the realities of the phenomenon of serial murder, serial killers and the limits of offender profiling. Examining a number of situations encountered during police investigations and with serial killers the chapter concludes with a call to harness rather than dismiss student interests in this territory in more productive ways, such as adopting a structural/victim perspective about serial murder, as opposed to a relentless focus on what might motivate the serial killer to kill. Wilson ends by suggesting how this new approach could be encouraged both within the academy and, more broadly in public policy. Wilson asks why Clarice Starling has enduring appeal and locates it in her gender and her class. This working-class female can be easily understood and empathised with. Her struggle to get on in a male-dominated environment and her capacity to pass examinations are inspirational to students of crime. However, Wilson is certain it is not to new Clarice Starlings that we should look to reduce the incidence of serial killing, but rather to other, more social, factors such as the need to address homophobia, the regulation of sex work and the treatment of, often isolated, elderly citizens.

In her chapter, 'Writing to Casey Anthony: imagined relationships, personal identification and autobiography in letters to a woman accused of murder', Lizzie Seal painstakingly analyses letters sent by members of the public to Casey Anthony, while she was awaiting trial for the capital murder of her daughter, Caylee. The case of the alleged murder received very high profile and intense media coverage, including via social media. This chapter analyses letters sent to Casey by people who did not know her personally. It will explore how the writers negotiated what they already knew of Casey and her case from media sources in relation to their own experiences and biography, in order to relate to Casey. In doing so, it analyses how correspondents variously drew on, utilised, reshaped and rejected discourses of femininity that circulate in legal and media constructions of high-profile cases of women accused of murder. The chapter also examines how correspondents' identification with, or rejection of, Casey Anthony and elements of her story was part of the process of the writers' own identity construction. The chapter makes a sustained case for the interrogation of the celebratory rebellions of transgression and deviance in gendered terms. Moreover, Seal shows how such an interrogation of the cultural representations of real, or imagined, deviant and transgression females is not new and goes back way beyond Lizzie Borden or Bonnie Parker. What is new is the form of that deviance which breaches the established taboo around female murder generally and around child killing in particular. The author shows how the breaking of this taboo, by a woman, created a celebrity 'from below', as Casey Anthony, the person, became Casey Anthony, the mythic 'celebrity, somehow fusing her gender identity with the dynamics of contemporary culture, criminal life and representation.

Robert Jago has specialised in the law as it relates to gypsy and traveller lifestyles. In his chapter 'The gypsy's lot: myth and reality', Jago focuses upon one group that has been long-since subject to a plethora of myths – the travelling community (which he refers to as the gypsy community). He argues that the relationship between the legal system and the specific lifestyle of this group is itself causing many tensions which cannot be separated from the long-held *myths* about gypsies. Jago shows how the standing of modern travellers in the UK legal system has, in turn, become the object of various myths. He demonstrates how judgments by the European Court of Human Rights in favour of gypsy claims created in many an image of the law being always on the side of the gypsy, which he demonstrates is far from being true. After addressing the nature and role of myths in general, Jago illustrates the tension between positive, romanticised myths about the freedom of gypsy lifestyle and three derogatory myths, namely the gypsy as 'child snatchers', as thieves and as 'land grabbers'. He illustrates that these myths are linked to deep-rooted beliefs around the notion of property and ownership. The 'free travelling' gypsy is unrestricted from the duties, worries and responsibilities of property but also lacks what so often is perceived the core of identity in mainstream society, namely the bound the native soil,

to one's own piece of land. At the same time, the three most common negative myths not only share that each of them concern violations of law, but,
moreover, that they describe the gypsies as taking something precious close
to our heart, be it children, land or thieving in general. Both negative and
positive myths evoke the image of 'the other', but the negative myths create
the dangerous, treacherous, threatening 'other', whose values are outlandish.
When analysing the legal standing of the gypsy today, the chapter focuses
on the relationship between law and legal myths regarding the public's fear
of the gypsy as land grabber. Jago shows how both courts and the legislator
struggle to balance property rights (especially on the Green Belt) with the
gypsy nomadic lifestyle. Although the law was quite supportive of the gypsy
way of life in the 1960s, in obliging local councils to provide for land where
necessary, this trend was reversed in the 1990s, when the legislation became
very restrictive. Since the 1990s, there seems to have been a shift towards
putting pressure on gypsies to purchase land on which to build their own
sites, but at the same time a number of high-profile cases exemplify how difficult it is for gypsy families to get planning permission for their sites. The
chapter shows that although there is a public belief that gypsies are favoured
too much by law and courts, the reality is that they find themselves between
a rock and a hard place. The cited case studies illustrate very clearly not
only how the legislation and the implementation in the courts have become
increasingly intolerant of the gypsy lifestyle, but also how these cases have
cemented the myth of the gypsy as a land grabber and increased the distrust
of mainstream society of the gypsy community. The originality of Jago's
contribution lies in how he deals with very old concepts in folklore of the
'other' interlinked with modern myths about how the law deals with this
'other'.

Three conclusions

The aim of this volume is to tackle the broad question of how law is
understood and perceived by the public. Each chapter has explored the
ways in which members of the public come to their beliefs about the
law and how law is, in turn, related to how collective and individual
behaviours are created, shaped and perpetuated in terms of myths about
law. A number of contributions explore how these beliefs about the law
go on to influence the behaviour of the public in specific ways, such as
jury behaviour (Amatrudo), social media action (Rauxloh) and preferred
study choices (Wilson) and how the labelling of behaviour as deviant
can create the reality of 'us' (Seal) and 'the other' (Jago). After looking at
these contributions the editors of this volume have arrived at the following three conclusions.

1. *Law needs myths for its legitimacy*

The first point to note is that law is a form of media *itself* through which more is conveyed than simply a proclamation about what is permissible and what is not. Law is a vehicle of communication through which messages about belonging (Jago), identity (Seal), power relationships (Lippens) and balance of conflicting rights (Johnson) are communicated. Therefore, the myth that law is apolitical (Rauxloh), that it punishes those the most who cause the most social harm (Sumner), that forensic evidence is easily available and reliable (Amatrudo), that serial killers can be profiled (Wilson), and that citizens have access to justice when they need it (Smith), are all part of the broader, deeper, political message that 'Law can make the world a better place.' The idea that the law, in all its manifestations, can help to solve the problems of an increasing complex world is a reassuring and comforting one, but of course it is often a myth. Since law benefits from the creation, and conservation, of many of the myths, law itself becomes a form of media, a vehicle of communication of messages beyond the primary content of law, creating its own myths and sets of public beliefs.

2. *Law needs myths for its existence*

While law seeks to steer the behaviour of individuals and to shape public perception in a conformist way, law is itself moulded by the very same public it seeks to control. The bond between law and public perception, however, goes far beyond the need for positive myths about law and the co-dependent relationship between media, in the widest sense. The most important finding emerging from this volume is that the assumption that law can be created in a vacuum, or outside of the society, to which it is applied is a myth. It is the normative myth. Law should be understood as something more than the sum of the rules in statute books and case law. Unlike natural sciences the discipline of law is based on the person-made construction of rules which aim to influence human behaviour. Law is a mental construct that has reality only in the form in which it is understood by the person who is applying or subject to it: be it through compliance or deviance. It becomes clear that law is both created by lawmakers on the one hand and perceived by the public on the other: together they co-create the reality of law. Law is a living, changing, intangible organism and public myths and beliefs whether positive or negative are part of this organism. The aim of law is to construct the 'social', while at the same time being itself a social construct.

3. *Unveil the myth about law-making*

The findings in this volume lead us to the conclusion that there would be great value in reconsidering the current focus of public criminology. While law seeks to steer the behaviour of individuals and to shape public perception in a conforming way, law is itself moulded by the very same public it seeks to control. This close co-dependency of law and the public is not only fascinating as a phenomenon, but also an eminently important field of study. We, therefore, think it is insufficient to criticise the media, and other forms of communication which present the law, without taking into consideration the creation, or perpetuation, of myths about the law. Rather, our conclusion is that it is for the legal sphere, and thus also for socio-legal and criminological scholarship, to become much more aware of how law in its manifestation in the public sphere is created far away from courts and legislators. We hope that this volume will be a starting point for further research concerning the creation, and perpetuation, of myths about the law, and in such a way lead to a greater understanding of the nature of myth and reality, and their socio-legal operation.

Reference

Reiman, J. (1995) *Rich Get Richer and the Poor Get Prison*. Needham Heights, MA: Allyn & Bacon.

I

PERCEPTION SHAPED BY TRADITIONAL MEDIA

Criminology through the looking-glass

What is on the other side of criminology's mirror reflection? What is on the dark side of its moon? The answer for many would be 'nothing, there is no dark side' – because, they say, criminology is merely the mirror of the society it inhabits. Criminology simply documents and reflects the world that spawned it, or so the story of science goes. But is this an unrealistic understanding of science? It is a form of positivism, and that was always linked to a naive optimism about objective neutrality that few in 2015 would now defend.

Scholars study, observe, research and re-present crime; some independently within institutions aiming to deliver science, others tied to their paymasters' interests and limits. Lawyers, politicians, intellectuals, artists and journalists, our creative and talented graduates, then re-present that scholarship, or at least the sedimented 'Chinese whispers' of that scholarship, and turn it into talk, debate, moral indignation, legislation, films, magazines, novels and television programmes. These 'chattering classes' create a set of new products, some chillingly real, some abstract, others emotional, others ideologically spun, that are variable in levels of realism but maintain some relationship, however selective or tenuous, with the original scientific 'findings'.

Science, law and media – all the ducks in a row – give the impression that there cannot be anything behind the mirror of criminology's reflection of society. Yet, a media-massaged zeitgeist, together with the need for regular salaried work, drives people to study criminology in the first place, thanks to the pull of CSI imagery, the monstering of serial killers, and a systematic silence on corporate crime, state crime, the violence of hegemonic masculinity, and on explanatory theory, philosophy and politics in general. This structured symbolic distortion produces the mentality in criminology that shapes and colours the findings that are behind the television programmes and the criminal law. Such a circle of virtue! Or is it the circling of disaster vultures?

This circle breeds followers, and all the positions in the inner circle of the criminological establishment are thus taken, as part of what Ralph Miliband called *The State in Capitalist Society* (1969). This includes youthful radicals who question the circle, but who never manage to break the 'structure-in-dominance' (Althusser) of cultural reproduction within criminology. In the end, as Rock observed, 'the erratic history of criminology has been marked by the organised neglect of many, if not most, of the phenomena that constitute crime' (1977, p. 392).

Of course, there is room within a liberal democracy for the critics to chatter and complain, but the mirror reproduction of standard findings, such as 'violence is mostly the product of damaged and angry working-class males', 'crime is the product of strain in the social structure not its normal working', and 'prisons are where you find the criminals', continues unabated. The other side of this virtuous circle is rarely entered and decoded, and when it is sporadically exposed that revelation is denied, denounced, or simply, and more often, ignored. The master narrative is protected, relentlessly affirming that crime is a by-product of contingent and minor structural glitches and of eternal lower-class inadequacies – one that can be managed out or de-risked.

But who is actually holding the mirror up to criminology so that it can see itself in this circular and entirely comfortable way? And is it really impossible to see behind that mirror?

> One thing was certain, that the white kitten had nothing to do with it – it was the black kitten's fault entirely. (Carroll, 1950, p. 13)

The white kitten cannot be the source of the mischief, writes Lewis Carroll in his *Alice through the Looking-Glass* (1950), because it had been having its face washed by the older, and probably fat, cat. Old cats do tend to look after white cats and kittens, and do not like being disturbed by those troublesome black kittens. Unfortunately, the answer to our question is that only the black kitten can see behind the mirror! White kittens are enjoying themselves too much to go through the looking glass to the other side and, besides, they hate to upset the wealthy, older fat cats.

When black cats look through the looking glass, they see books whose words are in reverse order and upside down, and are in another world where things are completely different. These books, although superficially very strange, when held up to the looking-glass, can actually be read by anyone. They say, funnily enough, to be on the brief side of mischief and the mischievous side of brief, that it is actually white criminology that is upside down and in reverse order. The latter, like Alice, has lost its way. 'I don't know what you mean by *your* way' said the Red Queen (1950, p. 34, emphasis in original), 'all the ways about here belong to *me*'. 'When you say "hill"', the Queen interrupted, '*I* could show you hills, in comparison with which you'd call that a valley'. 'A hill *can't* be a valley', says Alice, 'that would be nonsense'.

Behind the veil of self-appointed respectability, of what I shall call conventional or canonical criminology, a scientific world exists of such comfortable circularity that its proponents rarely even try to be comprehensive and rarely read all the relevant work on the subject, especially that authored by the black cats. Well, why would they, asks the Red Queen, when they already know the script?

After all, there is no need to be pedantic – there is actually no other world. Some might say: the world of the obscene real. Others might call it the world that cannot speak its name, at least any other way than upside down in reverse order. Where hills are valleys, and valleys hills. Where nonsense is a dictionary of definitions, and dictionary definitions are nonsense. It is the world in which Western governments and UN peace-keepers promise to protect Bosnian Muslims, pen them in accordingly within 'protected sites', and then stand by when Mladic's troops march in and predictably slaughter 8,000 – a mass slaughter, a big crime, enabled by a Western strategic paralysis bordering on a desire for the removal of an awkward issue.

It is a world where 'To be First Nations in this country is to know that the very history outsiders are telling you to get over – if they know the history at all – isn't something of the past but what continues to rock communities every day. Many have come to label it intergenerational trauma ... The highest suicide rates in the world aren't the only by-product of generations of trauma.' and where 'Prime Minister Stephen Harper adamantly refuses to green light a national inquiry into MMIW [missing and murdered indigenous women], claiming it's simply a criminal issue and not a sociological one' (Boyden, 2015).

> For seven generations Canada attempted what a representative of the most powerful court in the land recently labelled cultural genocide, never a term to be thrown around lightly. Our nation attempted to completely destroy the very fabric of Indigenous life by literally tearing apart its most valuable and sacred cornerstone: the family. Untold scores of children were regularly physically and emotionally assaulted, so much so that this became the norm across the country, generation after generation. Most horrifically, a grotesquely high percentage of children, boys and girls alike, were repeatedly raped throughout their childhoods by those put in charge of their well-being. Have I even mentioned the most basic and public tenet of these schools was to exterminate the languages, traditions, and religions of these children? The last residential school in this country closed its doors in 1996 ... Child abuse is certainly a criminal issue. Institutional child abuse of the most heinous kind, not just allowed but encouraged by the state for more than 120 years, is far more than that. It's a festering sociological, psychological, and very human crisis residing in the heart of this nation. (Boyden, 2015)

This is the world into which criminology does not look: the obscene reality of normal life through the looking-glass where everything we cherish is upside down and in reverse. This is the normality that a prime minister says is not the correct object of sociology. This is the other side of the mirror. This black cat criminology that can see it has few if any textbooks, for fat cat publishers in the white world prefer saleable lowest common denominator safety; it has no established scripts and belongs to Others. Its monographs are published – as 'critical' or 'radical' criminology, as if not mainstream or ever establishable. Its proponents are smeared and their works ignored or talked about as if they are not science. It is ultimately sidelined from the mainstream and its contribution airbrushed from institutional histories. It is not really widely read or understood, or accepted as scientific, on the right side of the mirror. I know, for this is my world, the realm of criminology in reverse, of black cat criminology, of the criminology by and for Others.

When we go through the looking-glass and read this reversed, upside-down text, this below is the criminology we see that describes the world they do not want us to see. I will order it according to its own inner way.

Crime through the looking-glass

Crime is not a behaviour; it is a social censure. Anything could in principle be picked out and censured as a crime; anything could be criminalised: what is censured depends on the historical period and culture, the context, the level of outrage, the depth of interest and the perspective of the viewer. It is rather like beauty – very much in the eyes of the beholder. But only certain beholders seem to see certain things as crimes; and only some see crimes as offences against the State. Other beholders see things otherwise, and are able to see crimes by the State or that the State defines what is or is not crime. It is interesting to note that these different sets of beholders seem to be on different sides of the mirror, locked in different starting positions.

The real magic, the trick of the *camera obscura,* that powerful engine behind and within ideology, the flick of the wrist missed by labelling theory, is that the image of the one is the reverse of the image of the other and actually co-exists with it in a causal relationship. White cats do not just label black cats, they made them black in the first place. The social construction of crime is not mere words or naming and shaming, it is the creation and establishment of social facts worthy of a bad name. In other words, it is no accident that criminology appears in reverse through the looking glass.

On this other side, by reading the reversed, upside-down text, we can see, for example, that trivial mistakes are severely punished and major assaults are ignored or pardoned. Alice said 'I see nobody on the road' and the King commented that he wished he had the ability to see nobody, especially at that distance, and that it was hard enough seeing real people. This is not selective vision but the reproduction in culture of a structure of domination so well established that its concrete real practical birth has been long forgotten, as history.

In *Flowers at the Altar of Profit and Power* (2012), Frank Pearce and Steve Tombs document and examine the Bhopal disaster of 1984, the world's biggest industrial disaster, one resulting in thousands being killed through a chemical explosion that night and many later dying, becoming cancerous or remaining disfigured for decades afterwards. No one has been convicted in a criminal court for what Pearce and Tombs show to be systematic professional negligence. In this sort of case, where thousands are killed, no one, says Alice, goes to prison but they do pay $485 million in compensation and little shame is attached – to the point at which their successor company can even bid for sponsorship at the 2012 London Olympics. This is the bizarre, upside-down world that we call 'business as usual'.

In the world of the old cats and white kittens, the fundamental outrage is theft, taking someone else's property. Of course, that would be the case, we would expect, when one's livelihood is dependent on retaining one's private property and keeping others off it. In the world behind the mirror, the world of black cats, the fundamental outrage is the taking of people's land and calling it private property, sometimes even when the women and children are still on it, and then expelling the people from their former territory. Or perhaps more accurately we should say the fundamental outrage is the denial of others' humanity after the theft of their land and the destruction of their families. In this world, the landless black cats steal to survive and to feed their families, or they try to mitigate the pain of their loss with anaesthetic substances, or even campaign to get their land back and their dignity and human rights restored – for which 'offences' they are often charged with theft or breach of public order or removed from their families for treatment and even compulsory sterilisation to ensure they have no more families.

Curiously, in white cat criminology, the invasion and capture of other people's land is not described as theft but as evolution and development. This seems to be upside down and in reverse order, for surely it would be a genuine evolution and a true development if the people were to retake their land and charge those who had stolen it with grand theft or a reversal into prehistoric barbarism; or at least to recover their dignity through Truth and Reconciliation Commissions into the decades of violence against the victims of internal and external imperialism.

As E. P. Thompson observed in 1975, telling a story of the loss of use-rights in eighteenth-century England that we will return to later and of which many now understand the significance:

> If we see Britain within the perspective of the expansion of European capitalism, then the contest over interior rights and laws will be dwarfed when set beside the exterior record of slave-trading, of the East India Company, of commercial an military imperialism ... Did a few foresters get a rough handling from partisan laws? What is that beside the norms of the Third Reich? (1975, p. 259)

The point is well made. But, as Thompson shows throughout his story, whatever the level of seriousness, crime is deeply imbricated within the practico-social structures of development, within the social practices whereby use-rights are turned into crimes, whereby the thieves of land become the judges and their victims become the judged. Crime is not so much the mirror of society as the result of its inversion. In the Other world through the looking-glass, there is a veritable hierarchy of predictable disasters, extreme human venality, and a minimal justice that means the practices of the masters are rarely dealt with as crimes.

Manuel Lopez-Rey, once the voice of UN criminology, was one of few who noticed that establishment criminology is anything but naturalistic, and is on the delusional treadmill of its own virtuous circle, its own mirror image. He said that it 'persists in styling itself a natural or naturalistic science' but 'ignores the fact that natural science is unable to provide the sociopolitical approach required by the extent of crime' (1970: xii). It 'overlooks the fact' that even if conventional theories were successful they would 'never be valid for the whole of crime, the greater proportion of which is conveniently ignored not only by most' criminologists but also by most governments and agencies in both developed and developing countries.

Jock Young once said to me he viewed my work on crime, justice and underdevelopment as of profound importance for criminology (see Sumner, 1982). So did Sir Leon Radzinowicz. Few have picked it up since, preferring the bland view of modernisation and then globalisation, with its general view of initial violence settling into stable and localised working-class property crime patterns. This closes off the world behind the establishment mirror image: the history of conquest and exploitation where slaughter, rape and cultural destruction are not crimes; the world of robber barons, 'land-grabs', lethal diseases, ruined environments, holocausts, genocideal conflicts, oil wars and death by computerised drone. Opening that up would spawn another criminology – one currently written upside down and in reverse order behind the looking-glass. Of core importance to that yet-to-be-properly-written criminology is the discovery that this history of imperial slaughter and exploitation, its effects and deadly offspring, is the predicate – the founding condition of the virtuous circle of establishment criminology.

Yet, those founders, in the UK alone, included Grünhut, Radzinowicz and Mannheim, all men fleeing from fascist Germany. Indeed, Mannheim had already been stripped of his academic post but his judicial position and life itself were under threat. As for Sir Leon Radzinowicz, I know he had no inclination to shy away from the historical-structural transformations that, through ideology, a subject he wrote upon with distinction, turned worlds upside down. But none of these founding fathers of UK criminology ever travelled back academically through the worm-hole of time to study the historic and very painful subversions and holocausts that moved them forward to found a social-democratic criminology. Understandably, they wanted to build a new life abroad and a new discipline based on an idea of social justice. But if they had applied their scholarship to fascist Germany, and the general subject of social development, they would have demonstrated how convulsive societal transformations and authoritarian and exploitative social practices produce the serious crimes, the under-studied, under-prosecuted ones that they themselves were running away from; the ones that predicate and are precursors of the 'normal crimes' of their new 'normal' criminology.

Criminal law, land and social destruction

Comments on Lewis Carroll's books emphasise his notion that 'language has the capacity to anticipate and even cause things to happen' (*SparkNotes*). That is as may be. But it is certainly true that on one side of the criminological mirror language defines crime, whereas on the other crime enables its perpetrators to define language. Or is my camera too obscura? According to Dali (n.d.): 'Mistakes are almost of a sacred nature. Never try to correct them. On the contrary: rationalise them, understand them thoroughly. After that, it will be possible to sublimate them.'

The great crimes enable their perpetrators to rewrite legislation and history itself so that the damaged, victimised and landless rebels become the criminals. Crime in this way redefines the language of the law.

'Robber baron' is a term used for a powerful nineteenth-century American businessman. By the 1890s, the term was typically applied to businessmen who were viewed as having used questionable practices to amass their wealth. These 'questionable practices' usually included a perception that they offered their products at extremely low prices (and paid their workers very poorly in order to do so), buying out the competitors that could not keep up. Once there was no competition, they would hike prices far above the original level. It combines the sense of criminal ('robber') and illegitimate aristocracy ('baron') (Boundless, 2015).

Owing to the robber barons' unethical business practices, such as the exploitation of labour, the general public typically regards these aggressive capitalists with disdain. However, some historians argue that the late-nineteenth-century entrepreneurs usually referred to as 'robber barons' – including Andrew Carnegie and John D. Rockefeller – are responsible for building a large portion of the USA's current economic clout, because of their large investments in burgeoning American industries. Many also went on to become high-profile philanthropists (Investopedia, 2015).

With the level of power created, and after centuries of numerous atrocities and unregulated European diseases, the Native American population had been reduced on one calculation from over 10 million to less than 300,000 (Unite to end Genocide, 2015). This was not always unintended, for George II is said to have encouraged subjects to pursue every opportunity to kill 'Indians'. This genocide and its associated 'land-grab' turned Native Americans into a subjugated people, with a destroyed internal organisation, who became targets for 'assimilation' in 1949 (with the Hoover Commission). Thousands were relocated into the cities and many children forcibly removed from their families (Unite to end Genocide, 2015). Today, they are stigmatised as alcoholic, as ridden with social problems and criminal in intent, albeit with a growing recognition that the truth to this has been formed through and in a sustained Reservation poverty:

> At a time when there's a spotlight on America's richest 1%, a look at the country's 310 Indian reservations – where many of America's poorest 1% live – can be more enlightening. To explain the poverty of the reservations, people usually point to alcoholism, corruption or school-dropout rates, not to mention the long distances to jobs and the dusty undeveloped land that doesn't seem good for growing much. But those are just symptoms. Prosperity is built on property rights, and reservations often have neither. They're a demonstration of what happens when property rights are weak or non-existent. (Koppisch, 2011)

It does not have to end this way, of course. Of key importance is property rights. Without them, inherited social problems will arguably continue unabated:

> Canada faces the same issues with its 630 bands – as tribes there are called – but thanks to the effort of a dogged reformer, there's a push to allow reservation land to be privatised. Manny Jules, a former chief of the Kamloops Indian band in British Columbia, is lining up support for the First Nations Property Ownership Act, which would allow bands to opt out of the government ownership of their land and put it under tribal and private ownership. Reserves would become new entities that would have some of the powers of municipalities, provinces and the federal government to provide schools, hospitals and other services, and to enact zoning laws … What's forcing the issue is an acute

housing crisis on the reserves. Without private property rights, little housing is being built even as the Indian population grows, and the Assembly of First Nations estimates that the reserves need 85,000 new houses immediately; the government is building only 2,200 a year.

'Markets haven't been allowed to operate in reserve lands,' says Jules. 'We've been legislated out of the economy. When you don't have individual property rights, you can't build, you can't be bonded, you can't pass on wealth. A lot of small businesses never get started because people can't leverage property [to raise funds]. This act would free our entrepreneurial spirit, but it's going to take a freeing of our imagination. We have to become part of the national and global economies.'

But even if Jules succeeds, there is no reformer like him in the U.S. to lead the charge here. Any effort at land reform must go through the Bureau of Indian Affairs. But the bureau, originally part of the War Department and one of the federal government's oldest agencies, isn't about to pave the way for its own demise by signing off on an effort to privatise reservation land. (Koppisch, 2011)

Privatisation and insertion into the circuits of global capitalism may be returning the Native Americans to the Satan that destroyed their civilisation in the first place, and absence from it means they will be weak and vulnerable capitalists initially, but a communalist total exclusion is no protection against tribal disintegration and of course the value of the natural resources under the Reservation lands is probably what is ultimately holding the state authorities back.

Returning to *Alice through the Looking-Glass*, when the old cats took the land, they made the white cats, often their offspring, into the judges of all that was wrong, via arcane and incestuous rituals whereby they ended up dressed in long white wigs and black gowns and perched upon a high bench above the black cat rabble. These judges, drawn from a chattering class of lawyers, were able to speak and write incomprehensibly and in long parchments. They ate from the fat of the land taken by the old cats; their elevated benches rested upon the crimes of invasion, conquest and expropriation of land. They hate change, preferring their fat cat position, as it was, laden with land, power, cream and long words. Fat white cats and their lawyers wrote out their moral views in incomprehensible and long parchments, calling it criminal law. Not surprisingly that law condemned many of the activities and words of the black cats as crimes, and converted the crimes of the old and white cats, via a newly created Land Registry, into 'titles' to land. This was reiterated within the institutions of government, also using the word titles; a love of the word emerging perhaps out of a sense of entitlement. Renaming their own class of people as 'nobles', and as Nietzsche wrote, the noble man deals 'with others as means to his ends' (*Beyond Good and Evil*, sections 26, 212 and 273), they gave themselves other kinds of titles such as lord and lady, earl and baron, and they appeared to be above the black cats and other ordinary people at the 'other' side of the looking-glass. These latter people were often abusively censured as savages, degenerates or just peasants and plebs, but mostly were not mentioned much in the long parchments; largely they were invisible in what became known as 'history', otherwise known to the black cats as 'intergenerational trauma'. And, as Hitler said, who remembers the Armenians?

None of this process of 'detribalisation', as colonialists called it, has finished. The conversion of 'natives' into 'criminals' is relentless. For example, not long ago,

> The Oglala Sioux and Lakota Sioux of the reservation were told by the US Federal Government that the National Parks Service will be taking land that comprises the South Unit of the Badlands National Park as a new 'Tribal National Park', only the wording in the bill clearly indicates that it will be a federally managed national park under the Department of Interior, giving mere lip service to its *tribal* title. ...
>
> Thousands of tribe members will be affected by the land-grab. Some residents will be forced to relocate, and many more others will lose their income from grazing allotments on the land – a result which will ultimately force any remaining independent cattle ranchers out of business. In addition to all this, Tribal members will lose their share of income from entrance fees collected at the adjacent North Gate of the Badlands National Park – a punitive measure which will further compound the existing economic depression on a reservation where the average annual income is around $8,000 per year. (Henningsen, 2014)

But not only are misery and crimes created by these supposedly non-criminal 'land-grabs', sometimes the grabs exploit present poverty. With echoes of the US invasion of Iraq and oil-driven imperialism, some 'land-grabs' are shameless and immoral exploitation of others' pre-existing misery:

> In 2010, a former Wall Street trader flew into war-torn Sudan to negotiate a deal with a thuggish general. He had his eye on a 1 million acre tract of fertile land fed by a tributary of the Nile in the southern section of the country, a region that later claimed its independence as South Sudan. The investor, who planned to profit by developing and exporting agricultural commodities, boasted about how the region's instability was a principal variable in his financial model: 'This is Africa,' he told reporter McKenzie Funk, who shadowed him for a riveting piece in *Rolling Stone* [PDF]. 'The whole place is like one big mafia. I'm like a mafia head.'
>
> Over the last decade (and especially during the last four years) wealthy nations have increasingly brokered deals for huge swathes of agricultural land at bargain prices in developing countries, installed industrial-scale farms, and exported the resulting bounty for profit. According to the anti-hunger group Oxfam International, more than 60 percent of these 'land grabs' occur in

regions with serious hunger problems. Two-thirds of the investors plan to ship all the commodities they produce out of the country to the global market. And droughts, spikes in food and oil prices, and a growing global population have only made the quest for arable land more urgent, and the investments that much more alluring. (Jacobs, 2013)

Whigs and hunters

Thompson's wonderful book documents the story of the most draconian penal legislation in British history, the 1723 Waltham Black Act; a law noted in Radzinowicz's voluminous history but not understood in its historic and social fullness. Passed, like much 'emergency' legislation in the modern day, in a hurry with little debate, amid an atmosphere of political paranoia over a hypothetical Jacobite threat, it created fifty new capital offences (Thompson, 1975, pp. 21–24). These offences focused upon blacking up and appearing armed in a park or common with intent to hunt deer, poach hares or fish, or breaking the heads of fish ponds, cutting down trees, taking bark, maiming cattle and setting fire to barns. The Black Act was targeted at ancient forest communities who had ancient use-rights over their common lands and took the fruits of the forest when needed. These communities were outraged by the enclosure of common lands by the King and his cronies, aristocrats and nouveau riche merchants to create parks and estates for their weekend hunting parties.

As Thompson put it succinctly: 'offenders were subject to economic and social oppression, and were defending certain rights' (1975, p. 193, and see pp. 190–198 generally); 'if this were a "criminal subculture" then the whole of plebeian England falls within the category' (1975, p. 194).

> During the eighteenth century one legal decision after another signalled that the lawyers had been converted to the notions of absolute property ownership, and that … the law abhorred the messy complexities of coincident use-right … capitalist modes transmuted offices, rights and perquisites into round monetary sums, which could be bought and sold like any other property … The rights and claims of the poor, if inquired into at all, received mere perfunctory compensation, smeared over with condescension and poisoned with charity. Very often they were simply redefined as crimes: poaching, wood-theft, trespass. (1975, p. 241)

Such crimes were subject to the merciful interventions of the local squirearchy, clinging to their notions of a community under their direction, but often defendants received transportation or hanging.

Use-rights became crimes as the commoditisation of land in England gathered pace. Private property made rights in common an 'inconvenience'. These crimes did emerge from a psychology: the mind-set of the Hanoverian Whigs, 'the mind and sensibility of Walpole'. No one remembers the so-called emergency spewing them. If they emerged from a subculture, says Thompson, it was that of the Hanoverian Whigs.

> The Black Act could only have been drawn up and enacted by men who had formed habits of mental distance and moral levity towards human life ... men, for whom property and the privileged status of the propertied were assuming, every year, a greater weight in the scales of justice ... this elevation of property above all other values was a Whig state of mind. (1975, p. 197)

Maintaining class assets, Marx and resistance to the new order of private property

Marx wrote several articles in 1842 about the theft of wood in the Rhineland, and one historian has suggested that this interest in 'the problem' of theft even made the young man realise his ignorance of political economy (Linebaugh, 1993, p. 102). His early journalistic work impressed on him the contradictions between 'private self-interest and the public good' (1993, p. 103), but it was less than a clear analysis for Linebaugh. In his focus on struggle and conflict of interests, Marx occluded the fact that this was resistance to the onset of the capitalist mode of production and a struggle to protect the concrete values or assets of the non-proletarianised poor (1993, pp. 105, 118).

We are only just beginning to understand the multifaceted relationships between capitalism and crime, but this particular aspect, of protecting existing assets, social organisation and culture, is clear in Van Onselen's excellent book, *Chibaro* (forced labour), on the history of the gold-mining industry in Southern Rhodesia, today's Zimbabwe, from 1900 to 1933. Pre-capitalist cultures tend to resist the encroachment of capitalist property relations, and in this case that simple fact is exemplified by Van Onselen's account of the Rhodesian Native Labour Board (RNLB) having to seek, chase and capture labour – otherwise known as kidnapping – for subsistence farmers had little inclination to go down dangerous mines a long way from family, society, their land and food.

A hut tax, followed by a head or poll tax (later borrowed with equal class effects by Margaret Thatcher), forced people in a non-monetised economy to seek cash and their only cash machine was the mine. Conditions down the mines were poor, many died in loneliness from sexually transmitted diseases, and supervisors were brutal. Desertion was common, making it necessary to ship labour in from afar, and was criminalised in 1902 through the expediency of Pass Laws, a genre of coercion later to become famous for being much hated by black people in South Africa, making it an offence not to possess a pass, and of course deserters had no valid pass (Van Onselen, 1976, p. 80). We must note that the colonial mentality even tried to represent desertion as proof that labour was not forced, because it proved the workers could leave the mine whenever they wanted (1976, p. 281 n. 27). A camera most obscura …

Deserters were often rounded up by the RNLB, a working class of males was gradually brought into captivity, and gold mining developed for European profit. A working class had been made and divorced from its land and society. Worse came with the disruption and destruction of families as indigenous brewing was banned and taken over by mining capital, watering down the beer, so that drunkenness, from the strong local beer brewed historically by the women left at home, did not interfere with production. The village women in increasingly vulnerable and isolated family units had to survive by selling their assets: sex, food and drink 'in the service of industry and state' (Van Onselen, 1976, p. 174). Their illegal brewing was criminalised and prostitution eventually medically regulated. Males of all ages down the mines resulted in the new behaviours of sodomy, male rape and child abuse; there were many offences of drunkenness and fights or assaults about women and gambling. The most noble mine-owners indeed, as Nietzsche said, cared little for the destruction of others' society.

What Van Onselen's epic tale also shows us is that the radical transformation of economic relationships in Southern Rhodesia resulted in the emergence of new crime categories, not arbitrary labels but ones that were well suited to their task of regulating the offences generated in the new mode of production (see also Sumner, 1982). By the late 1930s, it would have seemed that the nature of 'crime' was as it appeared on the surface (thefts, gambling debts and fights between workers) and that the big crimes of invasion, conquest and appropriation of land and labour had been forgotten or airbrushed from a newly rewritten 'history'. The serious crimes of colonialism had produced a new normality, where 'crime control' was the sustainable self-justification of the established, but eternally criminal, colonial state.

Punishment again preceded crime, just as violence precedes hegemonic dogma, and, contrary to the stories told in the white world of empire, the history shows not a voluntary evolution but a coerced insertion, after much resistance, into the capitalist mode of production, into someone else's future. This then is rewritten in white criminology as the need for crime control to keep the blacks under control and prevent them damaging themselves, conveniently excluding the part of the story where the white cats steal the black cats' land, killing many and beating survivors into submission with superior power.

Behind the criminological mirror where things are upside down and in reverse

So began the long history of so-called working-class crime, so fundamental to the formation and daily operations of criminology for most of its life-course. Criminology rarely looked back, behind its mirror reflection, seeing only the daily, self-justifying, recurrence of what therefore must be true: that the poor commit crime and needed to be controlled and punished.

If only criminology had looked behind the mirror and seen, for example, like Thompson and Van Onselen, that the roots of modern crime categories lay not in some deep-rooted ontological moral disorder, or some psychological depravity of the landless poor, nor in some abstracted and anodyne legal logic freed from messy social class reality, but in the situated ideology of the newly rich mercantilists, the new white fat cats in wonderland, obsessed with property and the accumulation of wealth.

'Political life in England in the 1720's had something of the sick quality of a "banana republic". This is a recognised phase of commercial capitalism when predators fight for the spoils of power and have not yet agreed to submit to rational or bureaucratic rules and forms' (Van Onselen, 1976). If only criminology had focused upon the socio-historic contexts of criminalisation and seen that appearances were indeed upside down and in reverse, for in the 1720s, and in many cases later, it was clear that the punishment came first before the crime – the taking of the common lands preceded the smearing of forest community resistance as 'criminal' and as the sins of a 'subculture'. It was also clear that this was all upside down: the crime lay in the Whig subculture taking other people's shared land and it was the victims who were punished.

To rephrase Erving Goffman, crime has to fit its punishment, and, I would add, a public created that will have the correct opinion on the matter – which is that we should always punish 'crime' and ignore the major crimes of social transformation, or just not see the violence of historic change as crimes, the conditions that breed the new 'social problems', the normal crimes, the suicides and acts of self-destruction so familiar to victimised and vulnerable populations.

When these crimes of social transformation are committed by establishment folk devils such as Stalin, whose forced movement of labour killed hundreds of thousands if not millions, they are visible and of course are seen, as the work of the devil incarnate. You see, major crimes, which are so integral to the formation of our states and our reality, are actually visible but which ones you see depends on which side of the looking glass you are on. And Americans wonder why radical Islamists refer to their country as Satan? Alice might have said that the white rabbits understood historic blindness all along – but knew that it was best not to talk about it in case it disturbed Others to talk about Hitler and the likes of Cecil Rhodes.

References

Boundless (2015) 'Robber barons and the captains of industry', Boundless U.S. History. 1 July. www.boundless.com/u-s-history/textbooks/boundless-u-s-history-textbook/the-gilded-age-1870-1900-20/the-rise-of-big-business-146/robber-barons-and-the-captains-of-industry-771–2148/. Last accessed 4 July 2015.

Boyden, J. (2015) 'First came the truth. Now comes the hard part', *MacLean's*. 25 June. www.macleans.ca/news/canada/first-came-truth-now-comes-the-hard-part/. Last accessed July 2015.

Carroll, L. (1950) *Through the Looking-Glass: And What Alice Found There*. London: Max Parrish.

Dali, S. (n.d.) www.brainyquote.com/quotes/authors/s/salvador_dali.html. Last accessed 5 September 2016.

Henningsen, J. (2014) 'Are Feds threatening "third wounded knee" with eminent domain land-grab on Indian reservation?', 21st Century Wire. 25 June. http://21stcenturywire.com/2014/06/25/feds-threatening-third-Wounded-Knee-with-eminent-domain-land-grab-on-sioux-indian-reservation/. Last accessed July 2015.

Investopedia (2015) www.investopedia.com/terms/r/robberbarons.asp. Last accessed July 2015.

Jacobs, R. (2013) 'Charts: the top 5 land-grabbing countries', *Mother Jones*. 6 February. www.motherjones.com/blue-marble/2013/01/top-land-grabbing-countries. Last accessed July 2015.

Koppisch, J. (2011) 'Why are Indian reservations so poor? A look at the bottom 1%', *Forbes*. 13 December. www.forbes.com/sites/johnkoppisch/2011/12/13/why-are-indian-reservations-so-poor-a-look-at-the-bottom-1/. Last accessed July 2015.

Linebaugh, P. (1993) 'Karl Marx, the theft of wood and working-class composition' in D. F. Greenberg (ed.), *Crime and Capitalism* (pp. 100–121). Philadelphia, PA: Temple University Press.

Lopez-Rey, M. (1970) *Crime*. London: Routledge.

Miliband, R. (1969) *The State in Capitalist Society*. London: Quartet.

Nietzsche, F. (1973) *Beyond Good and Evil*. Harmondsworth: Penguin Books.

Pearce, F. and S. Tombs (2012) *Flowers at the Altar of Profit and Power*. North Somercotes: CrimeTalk Books. Available at: www.crimetalk.org.uk/index.php?option=com_content&view=article&id=767:bhopal-flowers-at-the-altar-of-profit-and-power&catid=947:crimetalk-books.

Rock, P. (1977) 'Review symposium', *British Journal of Criminology* 17(4), 390.

Sumner, C. S. (1982) *Crime, Justice and Underdevelopment*. London: Heinemann.

Thompson, E. P. (1975) *Whigs and Hunters: the Origin of the Black Act*. London: Allen Lane.

Unite to end Genocide (2015) 'Atrocities against native Americans', http://endgenocide.org/learn/past-genocides/native-americans/. Last accessed July 2015.

Van Onselen, C. (1976) *Chibaro*. London: Pluto.

What do they know of law who only cop shows know?

As a result of an increased consumption of the media, mainly through the medium of the Internet though not exclusively, the idea that the law is something understood only by experts has given way to what we might term a folk understanding of law; and here I mean a notion that law may be readily understood by the general public in a fairly extensive way without recourse to specialist training or the idea of doctrine. The ways in which the media represent law, and the processes involved in that endeavour, are now more interesting to researchers than the technical nature of the ways in which specialists go about law and law-making. Indeed, there has been a great deal of scholarship given over to this phenomenon centrally, but not exclusively, around the interplay of the law and the way in which it is consumed through the use of the Internet, films and television and also in terms of the performativity of law, notably in relation to post-modernity. However, the problem of legal language and the ways it is consumed, represented and reflected to the general public cannot break away from the core drawback of a simplification which can, at times, usher forth a host of difficulties in terms of the gap between the law, as it is, and the law as it has to be consumed, represented and reflected to non-specialists. This stated the our contemporary life exhibits a real fusion of law and culture in the ways in which we typically see the real and the represented blended on our television screens, but also in films, journalism and the Internet. We might also say that our traditional ideas about participation and spectatorship are also blended. Though we should expect this as it is merely the corollary of a form of media production that exhibits an unquenchable thirst for *stories* about the law which originate in the news consumption by the society it serves and which commercial imperative demands is acted upon.

As has been noted by Lawrence Friedman, it is crucially not the law, as such, that affects behaviour; rather it is representations of it (Friedman, 1989). In other words, people always act in terms of how they believe the law is and not in terms of how it truly is. A more general point has been made by Shuy, though more narrowly in terms of civil litigation. He argues that persons are typically unaware of how they are using language or indeed where that language and their understanding of it came from. According to Shuy, the public's notion of law is unconscious (Shuy, 2008, p. 3). This insight that people suppose they know the law though in truth their knowledge of it is entirely non-technical and usually consequential upon the consumption of media, notably the Internet. People typically consume what they understand to be law but largely ignore the fact that it is derived in a wholly unsystematic and ad hoc manner. This we might term a folk idea of law. People routinely discuss cases in the news and venture opinions about their outcome but they rarely acknowledge their own limitations as non-lawyers in this process. Yet this relationship between the law and how it is represented and discussed has in turn given rise to a change in legal practice (Robson, 2006). This is most readily noted in legal cases which involve celebrities where we witness an infinite demand for details and here the O. J. Simpson case stands out, though similar examples are legion. In such cases, themselves often untypical themselves, the demand for information feeds demand for yet more information. We should also note an explosion of law-related television drama, which is often supposed to have a real educational role in the understanding of law whether, or not, it actually has. Though these television dramas tend to immerse the audience in their plots and be accurately scripted this does not undermine the central issue at stake here; that of the possibility of a partial understanding of law being not just incomplete but erroneous. Moreover, as Mezey and Niles have argued it is far worse than the screening of a partial understanding of law rather the screening of legally related television drama has real ideological facets (Mezey and Niles, 2005). The intermingling of law with popular culture is readily detected, notably in those countries that regularly screen court cases, as in the USA. The discussion of legal cases by the general public has definite repercussions in terms of our typical understanding of what exactly are the legal principles that guide the judicial system and beyond that about our whole ethical landscape (Williams, 2001). We can safely say that both the law and its popular understanding are fused and confused by the consumption of popular media; indeed that there is no way around it. Lawyers themselves have not escaped this process (Friedman, 1989). So, as the law has become more complex, variegated and technical, members of the public have a greater confidence than ever before that they understand legal procedure and statute. The mismatch between law and its popular understanding is overwhelming (Sherwin, 2008). It can no longer be argued, and nobody any longer does, that in real-life legal situations the jurors and witnesses come to the court *tabula rasa*: rather they are immersed in a view of law garnered through a lifetime of consuming a whole host of popular media both of a fictional and factual nature. This really matters as Zedner has illustrated in *Criminal Justice*. The media do not generally use legal principles to explain cases but instead tend to oversimplify cases and elucidate generalities. Zedner has argued in relation to sentencing that: 'Newspapers, radio and television carry reports of sentences, of judges' comments upon passing sentence, of their implications, and of reactions to and criticisms of them. Media commentary amplifies (and in amplifying may also distort) the message of the sentence, maximising its impact and inviting public debate that amplifies it further still' (Zedner, 2004, p. 172). This view of things is akin to moral panic and we have witnessed the role of the media in it for many years in relation to such things as mugging and pickpocketing. It is something about which both academics and practitioners have long since been aware (Cohen, 1980). More worrying still it has been noted that: 'Social censures, as negative ideological formations, are thus highly targeted, despite the universality or indeterminateness of their form of language, especially legal language. Moral language is formed and developed in social practice; its expression of unified ideological formations in censures is enabled, primarily by that unity, which itself forged in the targeting process' (Sumner, 1990, pp. 30–31).

Generating social censures

A good example, within contemporary criminology, of how language can impact on the operation of the criminal justice system is afforded by Colin Sumner. In his work, Sumner emphasises the importance of history, ideology, social structure in determining social censures, as opposed to their normative character (Amatrudo, 2009, pp. 23–26). In other words, social censures are always problematic for they necessarily exhibit an ideological legacy. The social censure signifies the power relations that gave rise to it rather than saying anything essential about the jurisprudence in which it is located. Sumner's account should be located within a tradition of Marxist scholarship that prioritises the power and state as key concerns. In Sumner's collection of essays *Censure, Politics and Criminal Justice* (1990), the criminal law is set out in terms of the application of dominant social censures produced by a criminal justice system which is itself formed ideologically by the dominant capitalist forces of its age rather than in terms of a normative legal account of social censures. It represents both a critique of a traditional sociology of deviance account within the social sciences and of the criminal law itself. Sumner drew upon historical as well as sociological research. He argued as follows:

> Whether we take their abstract, discursive definitions or their practical definitions in the course of law enforcement or moral stigmatization, it is clear that the definitions of deviant behaviour, even within a single society, exclude what

should be included, include what should be excluded, and generally fail to attain unambiguous, consistent and settled social meanings. To this we add massive cross-cultural differences in the meaning, enforcement and even existence of categories of deviance, and endless instances of resistance to them involving alternative categories. Clearly, they are highly acculturated terms of moral and political judgement. (Sumner, 1990, p. 26)

Therefore the notion that one might use the categories of crime and deviance in a consistent, systematic or normative fashion is to be doubted and such categories themselves should be interrogated to determine the moral and political position from which they derive, with crime itself being merely what one might term an ideological category, albeit a negatively defined one. Sumner's view is that crime is best understood in terms of the institutional forms and practices that gave rise to it and in terms of how, and why, it tends to be focused upon certain groups at certain times and places; and how this is articulated in everyday language. We note here how crime is said to have the definite hegemonic functions of signifying, denouncing and regulating persons; it is an aspect, in Marxist terms, of capitalist control and regulation of society. Moreover, the criminal justice system in all its aspects reflects and seeks to perpetuate capitalist economic, political and social relationships. On this understanding the criminal justice system itself is little more than a system of regulation for the maintenance of capitalist class control. Social censures do not relate a commonly held truth concerning crime; instead they offer 'a world-view which had not come to terms with its repressed unconscious – the fear of women, blacks, radicals, the working class and the colonized' (Sumner, 1994, p. 310).

Taking his inspiration from Marxist ideas about class, Sumner set out how, in any social structure, the dominant class will always preserve its hold over subordinate groups through a 'capacity to assert its censures in the legal and moral discourses of the day' (Sumner, 1990, p. 27). Central to this endeavour, Sumner maintains, is not merely the criminal justice system operating through a system of police and judicial oversight and enforcement but also the operation of language itself, notably in terms of the popular media. This will ensure popular support for the discourses and practices of the capitalist state and limit the extent of any dissenting narrative. Social censures are far more than labels: they are 'categories of denunciation or abuse lodged within very complex, historically loaded practical conflicts and moral debates' (Sumner, 1990, p. 28).

The theory of social censures that Sumner developed was built upon earlier engagements with ideology and culture within academic sociology, especially Hall et al.'s *Policing the Crisis* (1978). One of the central ideas behind *Policing the Crisis* was the notion that the focus on black crime, notably, 'mugging', was the outcome of a censorious press in league with the public authorities; who in lieu of any substantial evidence for this focus perpetrated a moral panic about black crime because it suited the political situation, at the time, and cohered with the police's emphasis upon the inner cities and upon blacks. The authors of *Policing the Crisis* maintained that the censure of blacks should be understood as an ideological phenomenon and not as a problem with law-breaking, as such (Hall et al., 1978). It expressed the idea that the black 'mugger' was merely a scapegoat for much broader, and deeper, concerns relating to economic and political conditions. The treatment of black 'mugging' was no more than a distraction from a far more pressing crisis in hegemony, in other words, a crisis. Sumner understood that traditionally academics had largely taken the categories of crime and deviance as straightforward terms and had, more or less, overlooked the fact that these categories, and the public consensus around them, were arrived at largely as the result of ideological determination. He maintained that *deviance* was typically understood as a deviation from the pre-existing dominant moral code; that is, as a divergence from a social convention. On this reading, the categories of crime, deviance and difference are far from being objective terms; rather they are radically subjective terms and useless in the task of sociological analysis (Sumner, 1994, pp. 309–312). Crimes, and the management of it, are crucially issues that relate to social regulation. Moreover, that: 'crime and deviance cannot be disentangled from the social facts of collective life' (Sumner, 2004, p. 29). In other words, in order to understand crime one must first understand the ways in which the world works. Social censures are an important aspect of the hegemonic working of society since they 'combine with forms of power and economy to provide distinct and important features of practices of domination and regulation' (Sumner, 1990, p. 35). Sumner completely reorientates the debate around crime and affords us the motivation to enquire about commonly expressed social censures in terms of their origins and purposive role. In doing so, he redirects our attention away from the everyday treatment of crime towards a form of explanation of crime, and criminalisation, which asks questions about the purpose of social censures. As *Policing the Crisis* had maintained, social censures are generated through, and by, the media; and in such a way that they combine with news coverage of crime to illustrate a real crisis in the need for a more repressive state. Moreover, news coverage tends to play down the extent of white-collar crime and crimes undertaken by the State. Over time, a belief takes hold in the general population that crime is a matter, more or less, exclusively undertaken by the working classes. Crime is viewed as an urban phenomenon. Most of the knowledge people have about crime and the running of the criminal justice system is gathered in an ad hoc manner and it is done so largely through the consumption

of the media. The upshot of this is that typical social censures of the day
are rarely challenged and neither are the material conditions, and forms of
social organisation, which gave rise to them. It is interesting to note that
through his work in another area entirely, namely linguistics, Basil Bernstein
had earlier argued that, given the inherent power relations existing in society, the generally accepted relationship between the classification and frames
of symbolic order and the structuring of personal experience in seeing the
world can lead to the pathological structuring of experience: in other words
a disjunction between the real and the represented. Bernstein argued that the
corollary of there being high levels of social homogeneity, between persons,
the more likely also is it that their language will take a specific form. A nar-
rower set of social relations, in turn, narrows the likely range of meanings,
because language is always expressed against a background of commonly
held assumptions, histories and interests and that 'the unspoken assumptions underlying the relationship are not available to those outside the relationship' (Bernstein, 1970).

In looking at the work of Sumner, we note how the language we use
is itself socially and politically determined; always, of necessity, contami-
nated by a history of usage that reflects an earlier social settlement. Sumner
noted: 'Now if criming cases is a very active, creative, process involving
some social and legal skill, and much awareness of what magistrates and
judges will accept, then presumably the fact that cases are *crimed* in a highly
patterned and predictable way, leaving the world's prisons full of poor people, is hardly an accident' (Sumner, 1994, p. 219).

Victims in the criminal justice system

The ways in which individuals consume social norms and values through
engagement with the media is acutely focused on in the work Rentschler
concerning the ways in which victims are generally portrayed in the media
in terms of their being 'a class of citizens without rights' defended by an
emerging class of victim's rights 'champions' (Rentschler, 2007, p. 219). She
has shown how this new form of discourse, concerning victim's rights, has
rapidly taken hold of media production, including journalistic practice, and
how this, in turn, has given rise to the creation of new narratives about the
operation of the criminal justice system. She argues that these are more than
unbalanced; they are positively harmful to justice and usually shed no light
upon established legal principles. What she has in mind here is the right-
ful attribution of a defendant's guilt, or otherwise, and the marginalising
of hard-fought-for judicial safeguards for those accused in criminal cases.
She maintains that recent journalistic practice tends to encourage: 'the news
industry to further invest in the coverage of crime by framing crime news

as a form of narrative therapy for some victim's families' (Rentschler, 2007, p. 219). Worse still, how

> victim's rights to and in the media signifies that it seeks access to and participation in media-making on crime as part of the process of re-assessing a definition of crime as interpersonal battle between offenders and their vicarious victims, the families of killed victims. In this scenario, victim's rights advocates and journalists both function as reporters of socially constructed knowledge and editors of the documentary realities of crime from the perspective of victim's rights. While law enforcement and the court system have long been the preferred sources for crime news and other non-fiction media programming the victim's rights movement encourages reporters, and victim advocates, to direct victim's rights discourse into the news media. They teach journalists to direct victim's rights discourse into the news media. They teach journalists how to identify with the grief, anguish, and other painful feelings expressed by crime-victim families in order to give the typical law-and-order character of news a therapeutic sheen through a re-orientation of the news interview context itself. They teach advocates how to translate victim's rights into strategic calls for victim-oriented news. And they teach us that calls for a more therapeutic and hospitable news environment for news victims can mean many things, one of which signifies the links between the news media's need for crime news and the political struggles for victim's rights. (Rentschler, 2007, pp. 235–236)

It is easy to see how a regular diet of victim-oriented media coverage can come to influence individuals in terms of how they understand the criminal justice system. Moreover, that it tends to move society from one made up of rational consumers of news to one characterised by a more retributive mindset with much less regard for defendants (Dubber, 2002).

Television depiction

The public largely come to understand law, more especially criminal law, through media coverage of real-life cases and popular dramas that focus upon crime. This can be genuinely misleading (Harris, 1993). It tends to portray a world far more violent than it actually is and a host of other falsehoods, including fostering the idea that criminals tend to be successful, furnishing a wholly inaccurate account of crime statistics and clear-up rates, overstating the racial profile of offenders and completely failing to address technical matters of legal procedure or to set out how the criminal justice system operates.

Without a doubt American television has been enormously influential in terms of its impact on the popular understanding of law and the ways that it operates. The formats it produces tend to precede those of other countries. For example one of the first portrayals of a practising lawyer was first broadcast in 1957. Perry Mason an urbane and virtuous man, upright, humane and moral in every way (Kittei, 1999). He was shown as being on a never-ending quest for the truth. He was a man who saw in the everyday cases of his clients profound, often existential, issues of justice that needed to be addressed. In the courtroom, he was measured and impeccably well prepared and witnesses would confess before him as he lanced their stories with a perfectly aimed question. It has been said that: 'Mason doesn't get his client acquitted by showing the prosecutor failed to carry the burden of proof. Instead, he proves his client's innocence by exposing the real killer. Surprise witnesses appear at the last minute, just before it is too late. After Mason's cross-examination, prosecution witnesses break down on the stand. As far as we can tell, Mason has never represented a guilty client or engaged in plea bargaining' (Macauley, 1987, p. 198). Perry Mason was the personification of everything good about the American criminal justice system and all that was worthy in American life.

The television series, *The Fugitive*, aired in the 1960s tried to show another side to the US criminal justice system. Its plot involved a doctor called Richard Kimble who found his life turned upside down when he was falsely accused of murdering his wife. In the series he had luckily escaped execution and was on the run, living as an outlaw, and committed to clearing his good name. This was cutting-edge television, at the time, and though its plot could seem radical it actually rested on two key principles. First of all, the idea that the innocent man will always overcome whatever injustices befalls him. Secondly, the practical notion that the criminal justice system, more especially the legal system, should be guided by engaged citizens. The series aimed to immerse the viewer in Richard Kimble's pursuit of justice.

The series that, arguably, did most to show off the law and the lawyers working in it was *L.A. Law*, which began its first run in 1987. It was a series set amid the power, glitz and affluence found in a leading law firm during the 1980s in the USA. Its lawyers had all been to Ivy League Law Schools and spent their money on high-end cars, clothes and beautiful houses. These were America's brightest and, although they may have possessed individually some character flaws, as a whole their elite education and sheer capacity for hard work had ensured their material success (Friedman, 1989). Perhaps inevitably, the series tended to make their working lives far more interesting than they actually were, and there was scant coverage of letter drafting, consulting past cases and the like (Gillers, 1989). *L.A. Law* was novel in that it did raise questions about the capacity of lawyers to maintain an ethical professional life while working in a system which was, in part, tainted by the corruption of a legal system dependent upon the rich and the powerful (Simon, 2001). Although *L.A. Law* aired as a mainstream popular drama, it

nonetheless raised profound questions about the ability of the law to be neu-
tral and the ability of lawyers to act ethically. Gillers has argued that *L.A.
Law*, from his perspective as a practising lawyer and academic, is a wholly
inaccurate representation of the American legal system. He maintained that
the role played by lawyers is overemphasised, in *L.A. Law*, and in any case
it 'inaccurately represents the kinds of legal issues lawyers routinely address,
especially lawyers in private practice' (Gillers, 1989, pp. 1607–1608). This
deepens the disjunction between how the public come to understand the
law and the criminal justice system and how the legal profession themselves
think about law and the criminal justice system. However, in making *L.A.
Law* for US television, the producers ensured that entertainment, and not
public education, would win out; and that moot points, and legal complexity, would not be included. Gillers also argued that types of ethical considerations that lawyers deal with in the real world are *never fully discussed*
in *L.A. Law*. He argues that 'As with legal issues, the immediate ethical
problems are answered because they must be, but the larger conflicts they
signify are unresolved' (Gillers, 1989, p. 1618). Therefore, the simplification
that television demands is a distorting feature and allied to the fact that the
viewing public typically has no legal knowledge the programme should be
understood as merely drama and not indicative of the state of the law today.
However, the account of *L.A. Law* that Gillers furnishes of the law firm is
pretty typical of that particular genre of television where lawyers are often
used as stock characters rather than as vehicles for illuminating legal principles and the lives of real-world lawyers.

The shortcomings which Gillers and Kittei dealt with were taken up in
the television series *The Practice*. It aimed to show a corrupt legal system
and corrupt lawyers working within it and its central characters did not
always win in court: justice was not always done. However, *The Practice* was
more usually taken with the love of law, and its highest values, and its main
characters were illustrative of this. It has been argued that ' our discomfort
with the existence of the morally ambiguous criminal defence attorney was
assuaged by her important role in the criminal justice system, which was for
all its imperfections, is mostly effective, just, and superior to the imaginable
alternatives' (Mezey and Niles, 2005, p. 127). Certainly, the lawyers in *The
Practice* were aware that they had to make deals, negotiate and settle, after
all they were streetwise. However, they were not corrupt per se and the television format placed definite limitations on the ethical flexibility and ability
to stray too far from the straight and narrow (Kittei, 1999, p. 29). We may
conclude that though updated and more in tune with contemporary themes
the basic portrayal of the law and of lawyers on American television is little
more than an attenuated rendering of the *Perry Mason* narrative. What is
upheld is the principle of American justice as virtuous. An account of justice

that believes that truth always wins the day and that class, and race are no hindrance in the court of law. For almost sixty years, America has given the world a range of legal characters, all of whom have a steadfast commitment to the highest ideals of justice. The only dispensation being that the characters themselves tend to be more nuanced than previously and the matters they deal with tend to be more multifaceted than in the past.

The problem is that although American television does show aspects of the legal system, it rarely does so accurately and in failing to account for what happens typically and what happens rarely it distorts the range of cases presenting themselves to lawyers (Macaulay, 1987, p. 210). What these television series really wish to achieve is the presentation of a decent and beneficent American to their viewing audience and in so doing the narrative is, to critical eyes, positivistic on the one hand and naive on the other (Bergman et al., 1996). What is concerning in terms of thinking about substantive issues for the criminal justice system is that this diet of television production tends to heighten subjectivity in the general public around culpability and this is a real concern when this public is the same one from which jurors are selected (Finkel and Groscup, 1997). Moreover, it has long since been argued that the general public get a very bizarre idea of what constitutes crime, and what its scale is: and here the over-emphasis upon murder, a comparatively rare event, is a case in point (Stark, 1987). For the sake of drama too, the important safety mechanisms built in to any system of law for suspects are often portrayed as unnecessary barriers to justice, most recently in the form of Miranda warnings (Rogers et al., 2007). The general treatment of crime in American television drama is reactionary and is more about criminals getting their just deserts than educating the citizenry (Robson, 2006). What Doyle and Ericson have argued about the British television drama is pertinent to the American case: 'Even if the system changed its methods, in the public and media culture, criminal justice is still often understood as a spectacular, highly emotionally charged, drama of retribution' (Doyle and Ericson, 2004).

One issue that has animated discussion is the so-called *CSI*-effect, which posits that the value of forensic evidence is grossly exaggerated, by jurors, in large measure because of television drama coverage of it. Jurors now wish to see absurdly high standards of proof, notably in terms of forensic evidence, and this has raised to level of proof required to gain a conviction in court (Tyler, 2006). Initially, it was claimed that the so-called *CSI*-effect was somewhat of a scare story and that there was no evidential basis for it. Others claimed the so-called *CSI*-effect was reflective of profound insecurities within society about the shortcomings of the American criminal justice system and its failure to keep the public safe. It was claimed that there was no *CSI*-effect, but that talk of it was another way of stating that convictions rates in court system were unacceptably low (Podlas, 2006). However, more recent studies do seem to confirm that there is indeed some version of a *CSI*-effect at work within the American legal system. It has been demonstrated that jurors who had viewed *CSI* were far more reluctant, than those who had not, to believe the forensic evidence that was presented to them during the course of a trial (Schweitzer and Saks, 2007). Moreover, that the CSI-effect, Lawson argues, has had a real and very disturbing impact in the American court system in terms of the 'Realm of warping, skewing, and manipulating the realities of evidence in a way that threatens the accuracy of the verdict and the legitimacy of the criminal justice system' (Lawson, 2009, p. 169). His major point being as follows:

> That the danger that the CSI infection presents is not that jurors expect more forensic science, but rather that fictional entertainment will lead to misinformation about criminal investigations, prosecutions, and forensic science. The problem is not merely a television show. The greatest threat is the inappropriate application of fictional analysis in real life cases, which in some instances has induced erroneous conclusions of fact and faulty decisions. The criminal justice system relies on laypeople, ordinary citizens untrained in the law to consider the evidence presented to them in court as neutral outsiders ... The crime novels, television shows, and films depicting crimes, criminal investigations and criminal prosecutions are altered purposely for entertainment purposes, causing the line between reality and fiction to be intentionally blurred by artists to make film, novel, or television show seem real, yet still entertaining. The artists' motivation is not malicious; instead from such sources may trick viewers into believing they are trained to some degree to interpret the law and science. (Lawson, 2009, p. 171)

Furthermore, as Thomas has noted, in the real world the reasonableness and the sheer economic practicality of utilising advanced forensic science techniques is to be doubted. Although increasingly the use of forensic evidence is at the forefront of prosecutorial decision-making, as there is now a sense within the legal profession that jurors are not so much taken with legal processes and the routine of court practice as they are with forensic evidence (Thomas, 2006, pp. 70–72). At a deeper level, Cole and Dioso-Villa have shown how the *CSI*-effect is reflective of a struggle between two competing forms of explanation, or language, those of law and science and that

> The answer seems clear: rising authority and prestige of science in a modern society. Science is popularly associated with such positive values as truth, certainty, goodness, enlightenment, progress, and so on ... CSI-Effect would seem to resonate with anxieties about using law too little, and increasingly abrogating its truth-producing function to science ... the *CSI*-Effect would seem to give voice to fears of what we might call *hyperscientia* – too much science. (Cole and Dioso-Villa, 2009, p. 1373)

The *CSI*-effect is still a concern to both academics and lawyers and it denotes a straightforward link between consuming television crime drama, together with its language and world view, and effects upon the practical operation of justice.

A great deal of American programming migrates to British television and this has long been the case. There is also a home-grown genre of British, typically English, television drama tackling the law and the lives of lawyers, notwithstanding the vast number of crime drama series. In large measure, this home-grown genre shadows the American modus operandi while maintaining a local focus in its productions; often centred around the eccentric traits of its characters, such as the hard put-upon barrister, Horace Rumpole, or the maverick judge, Judge John Deed (Robson, 2006, p. 343). It is important to note that these two genres, American and English, are distinct forms of programming. In America, although legal processes are depicted, they are of less significance to the producers, and the audience, than specific signifiers of judicial authority, such as court architecture (Machura and Ulbrich, 2001). The debate here is not about the ability of the programmers to pass on important legal principles, or even the everyday realities of the criminal justice system; rather it is concerned with the development of what one might term a *legal consciousness* and the beginning of a more general discussion in terms of the public's perception of legal matters. Of course, there may not be effects we can measure only an immeasurable, and heightened, understanding. It is safe to say, at least in the English case, that workings of the legal system are usually shown focusing on a fight for justice and for truth. Though, as Robson has argued, this

> justice agenda dominates, TV lawyers challenge the malpractices of the system. A group of fighters for justice may legitimate the whole socio-economic system with their apparent demonstration that day in, day out, the individual has his or her day in court … The focus on the individual and the local hides what is happening at a structural level. The poor are not being enfranchised through court actions. Systemic institutional racism is not declining through the legal process. Solutions to the abuse of women are emerging from extra-legal organisation and actions like the refuge movement. Trusting in the legal system's remedies as shown on screen is comforting but involves a misplacing of trust. (Robson, 2006, pp. 355–356)

Practical matters: real-world policing and the law courts

The police communicate with the news media and to set their own news agenda; indeed this has become a mainstream part of contemporary policing. The problem here is that the police tend also to overstate their successes in relation to crime fighting as one might expect given their important role and the self-serving legitimation of it (Doyle and Ericson, 2004, p. 472). We may see the situation, in the same way as Hall et al., and note the police as the *primary definers* of news to a news media, in many ways itself, structurally *dependent*, if not entirely structurally subordinate, to the diet of news fed to it (Hall et al., 1978, p. 59, emphasis in original). There is a great deal of academic agreement about the role the police play in structuring the news coverage of crime. The tendency is always towards the more sensational end of the spectrum, notably in terms of violence, and what Robert Reiner has usefully termed high status victims and offenders (Reiner, 2010). Moreover, in doing this the police have systematically shown themselves to be far more effective than is typically the case. What we usually left with is a form of news media that overwhelmingly supports the status quo and often helpfully so around issues of class, gender and race, in its emphasis upon violence and on the efficiency and effectiveness of the police themselves. This sort of news coverage has in practice tended to 'reinforce one system of meaning about crime which is (already) prominent in public culture' (Doyle and Ericson, 2004, p. 474). Moreover, as Doyle and Ericson have shown, the quality and scope of this police-informed news coverage is likely to

> reinforce the punitive current in public media, and political discourse. The current feeds back into the system itself, fuelling alternative tendencies towards more expressive and punitive forms of criminal justice. It also justifies the elaboration of the surveillance-oriented risk-communication systems that characterize the everyday world of police work. (Doyle and Ericson, 2004, p. 482)

In an important study, not of crime news coverage but of police dramas, Regina Rauxloh detected a similar set of issues to those set by Doyle and Ericson in her historical study of democratic West Germany or communist East Germany and the crime dramas they produced. In short, she showed how rather than challenging the audience's notions about crime the producers actually feed back to the audience their own folk ideas about the nature of crime. The production process was necessarily conservative. Therefore, although the society was different, there is evidence of a general tendency to what might be termed 'conservative production values'. She showed how whether extolling the virtues of economic liberalism, or of Marxist-Leninism, the same tendency to show the police, and the criminal justice system in general, in terms of an ideal type was present. Beneath the flattering depiction of the police, there was always a profoundly positive understanding of the 'image of state and society' (Rauxloh, 2005, p. 1000). She demonstrates well how although the producers of television crime drama can be critical of the criminal justice system, notably in the form of the police, they hardly ever are. The production process usually restates the pre-existing set of ideas its audience has and certainly does not routinely address the deeper issues that relate to criminalisation itself (Rauxloh, 2005, p. 981). In relation to the police's routine work, 'arraignments, pre-trial hearings, jury selection and plea-bargaining are rarely shown' (Rauxloh, 2005, p. 990).

The depiction of historical trials, often through the vehicle of drama, is an established part of the BBC radio output. It has always been advanced as part of the educative function of the BBC and something alluded to in its charter. However, in a much cited article in the *Modern Law Review*, Suzanne Shale has counselled scepticism of the BBC's claim to further the public's understanding of legal principles and the legal process, more generally (Shale, 1996). To begin with, Shale underscores the fact that such radio portrayals are also informed by the values, and assumptions, of the medium that produced them, importantly in terms of such things as pre- and post-production and editorial decision-making. In selecting famous trials, the tendency is to exaggerate the heroic character of the criminal justice system in the typical case. Moreover, the demographic data on the BBC radio listening audience for such coverage tends to show a self-selecting middle-class audience. The radio programmes Shale looked at tended to be far less interested in setting out legal principles than it was in reproducing popularly held views about how the law operates. Shale maintained that

> The trial is a public ceremony and, in the contemporary world, the mass media determine the nature of the public for whom the ceremony is conducted. In conveying the message of the criminal trial, media do not passively represent an object to a public. On the contrary, if by legal process we mean all of the functions that law performs, the media are participants in the legal process in their role of reproducing the public ceremony ... Whether or not we want to call famous trials broadcasts a form of law ... they are indisputably part of something we should call popular legal culture: that constellation of attitudes, beliefs, knowledges, half-knowledges and flat misunderstandings about law that are by and large shared among members of a social group. The notion of a popular legal culture is perhaps undermined when we pose questions about the nature of the populus or social group which shares it. (Shale, 1996, pp. 843–844)

It is an interesting and often neglected point to bear in mind about all forms of media, especially radio, that although it is broadcast to everyone it is always, and unavoidably, always received as a narrowcast (Priestman, 2004). The audience for any programme is made up of self-selecting individuals, and in the case of BBC radio drama on famous trials a further subset of BBC radio listeners, which itself is made up of the aggregate number of listeners to a multiplicity of forms of programming in general.

Practical matters

The relationship between the public understanding of law and the criminal justice system is important not only for the proper functioning of a democracy but for the routine, day-to-day, operation of justice. It has major social policy consequences. The problem is simply that ordinarily the public has no involvement with the criminal justice system and little, or no, formal education in the matter through their schooling. However, the public generally consume media and it is this consumption which generally furnishes them with knowledge of the law and the broader criminal justice system. It is generally to the media that members of the public look to for their knowledge of the law and the broader criminal justice system both in a news format and through factual drama. The result is that the public understanding of law and the broader criminal justice system is problematic (Gies, 2008, pp. 5–7). While it is surely good that there is an increased awareness of legal services, and how to obtain them, and some heightening of awareness around issues such as child abuse, it is also true that this awareness, such as it is, is gathered piecemeal, is non-technical in nature and is, of necessity, stripped of much of its complexity. As Gies has also illustrated the types of material that members of the public are able to access online, for example, is generally so generic in nature and simplified in form as to be of little assistance to them in terms of a specific circumstance in which law might come into play (Gies, 2008, pp. 74–91). The understanding of law is very complex and one must determine whether it can be understood on a variety of different levels and from a variety of different perspectives. Although a given broadcast, or single piece of information gathered on the Internet may not be wrong per se, it is this acquisition of knowledge in a piecemeal and untutored fashion that will always make it fall some way short of an in-depth understanding. The lawyers will always have the last say. Gies's point being that there is a real, and ongoing, battle between the law, as it is, and the media's account of it. Her concern is that the dominance of the media's version is all too apparent and that this is an unhappy state of affairs (Gies, 2008, p. 130).

In many ways, the public's understanding of law through consuming media is best conceived of as Delanty expressed it: 'that contemporary society involves the proliferation of second order observations for direct observation … We are approaching a society that in perpetually experimenting with forms of communication is making the form of communication central to the experience of social content: content has become form' (Delanty, 2000, p. 83).We should note here that in looking to Delanty we are conceding, however, that content has become a subordinate variable in the equation. The huge chasm that has emerged between actual legal knowledge and the popularly consumed form of it has concerned Smith and Natalier in relation to the criminal law where they cite the public's unjustifiably high level of confidence in the police's ability to tackle crime, the public's unrealistic faith in forensic science to solve cases and the misrepresentation of ethnic minorities within the criminal justice system as but three examples of the problem. They conclude by following Friedman is noting that people necessarily understand law through the ways it is represented to them and which they consume: popular understanding of law has only a passing resemblance to law as it truly is (Smith and Natalier, 2005). The deeper point beneath all of all of this is surely that the entire system of production itself in terms of interests, values and politics, and the rather large matter of thinking about law sociologically, go largely unconsidered.

Conclusion

There has been a huge increase in the portrayal of law, notably criminal law, in the media both of a factual and dramatic nature; and all of this output has, one way or another, been consumed. Whether this has been positive, or not, and whether it has actually increased awareness is open to discussion. Though there is extensive coverage about the law and its processes it is difficult to sustain the proposition that the public are better informed and yet popular opinion seems to hold that they are. The public are certainly consuming something but it is generally, in Platonic terms, a simulacra or a partial account. They consume law as it is represented to them not as it generally is. If the public know anything of law in is in elemental form. The social awareness of law that holds in contemporary society is at a very basic level of engagement. Bernstein's notion of the relationship between the classification, and frames, of symbolic order and the subsequent 'pathological structuring of experience' is noteworthy. As people hold to a greater level of commonality of experience, for example, by way of consuming similar representations of the law through media then their language tends to converge in such a way that the range of possible meanings tends to diminish as do the assumptions we hold to about the world. In other words media has a real hegemonic capacity to pacify people. The public may even be proud of the legal knowledge they obtain from the media although it is a fairly modest knowledge in reality. Moreover, the real-world effects of such knowledge may be detrimental to justice, as we noted in terms of the so-called *CSI*-effect. Lawson noted how this has resulted in a ' realm of warping, skewing, and manipulating the realities of evidence in a way that threatens the accuracy of the verdict and the legitimacy of the criminal justice system' (Lawson, 2009, p. 169). Moreover, media production can itself be appropriated as has happened with victim's rights (Rentschler, 2007, pp. 235–236). After all it is only possible to consume the media available. The account provided by Sumner that details the generation of censures by the media; which themselves combine with news events to centre attention on calls for a more authoritarian state. A good example of this is provided in the miners' strike of the 1980s (Fine and Millar, 1985). The media are generally interested in sensation and this means that when crime is tackled it is usually at the blue-collar end of the spectrum around street crime or traditional cops and robbers narratives. The matter of white-collar crime is largely disregarded. When the media tackle crime it is generally as an urban phenomenon related to the lives of the working class. The media is not self-critical and never opens up for discussion the nature of its productive processes, nor the fundamental socio-economic arrangements that made it possible at all. What do they know of law who only cop shows watch?

References

Amatrudo, A. (2009) *Criminology and Political Theory.* London and Los Angeles: SAGE Publications.

Bergman, P., M. Asimow and M. Reel (1996) *Justice: the Courtroom Goes to the Movies.* Kansas City, MO: Andrews and McMeel.

Bernstein, B. (1970) *Class, Codes and Control.* London: Routledge.

Cole, S. and R. Dioso-Villa (2009) 'Investigating the "CSI Effect": media and litigation crisis in criminal law', *Stanford Law Review* 61, p. 1373.

Cohen, S. (1980) *Folks Devils and Moral Panics.* Oxford: Oxford University Press.

Delanty, G. (2000) *Modernity and Postmodernity: Knowledge, Power and the Self.* London: SAGE Publications.

Doyle, A. and R. Ericson (2004) 'Two realities of police communication' in C. Sumner (ed.), *The Blackwell Companion to Criminology* (pp. 471–485). Oxford: Blackwell.

Dubber, M. (2002) *Victims in the War on Crime: the Use and Abuse of Victim's Rights.* New York: New York University Press.

Finkel, N. and J. Groscup (1997) 'Crime prototypes: objective verses subjective culpability, and a common-sense balance', *Law and Human Behaviour* 21, 209–230.

Fine, B. and R. Millar (eds) (1985) *Policing the Miners' Strike.* London: Lawrence and Wishart.

Friedman, L. (1989) 'Popular legal culture: law, lawyers and popular culture', *Yale Law Journal* 98, 1579–1606.

Gies, L. (2008) *Law and the Media: the Future of an Uneasy Relationship.* London: Routledge-Cavendish.

Gillers, S. (1989) 'Taking *L.A. Law* more seriously', *Yale Law Journal* 98, 1607–1624.

Hall, S., C. Critcher, T. Jefferson, J. Clarke and B. Roberts (1978) *Policing the Crisis.* London: Macmillan.

Harris, D. (1993) 'The appearance of justice: court TV, conventional television, and public understanding of the criminal justice system', *Arizona Law Review* 35, 785–837.

Kitei, B. (1999) 'The mass appeal of *The Practice* and *Ally McBeal*: an in-depth analysis of the impact of these television shows on the public's perception of attorneys', *UCLA Entertainment Review* 7, 169–187.

Lawson, T. (2009) 'Before the verdict and beyond the verdict: the CSI infection within modern jury trials', *Loyola University Chicago Law Journal* 41, 169.

Macaulay, S. (1987) 'Images of law in everyday life', *Law and Society Review* 21, 198.

Machura, S. and S. Ulbrich (2001) 'Globalizing the Hollywood courtroom drama', *Journal of Law and Society* 28, 117–132.

Mezey, N. and M. Niles (2005) 'Screening the law: ideology and law in American Popular Culture', *Columbia Journal of Law and the Arts* 28, 92–186.

Podlas, K. (2006) 'The CSI effect: exposing the media myth', *Fordham Intellectual Property, Media & Entertainment Law Journal* 16, 465.

Priestman, C. (2004) 'Narrowcasting and the dream of radio's great global conversation', *Radio Journal* 2, 77–88.

Rauxloh, R. (2005) 'Goodies and baddies: the presentation of German police and criminals in East and West television drama', *German Law Journal* 6, 1000.

Reiner, R. (2010) *The Politics of the Police*. Oxford: Oxford University Press.

Rentschler, C. (2007) 'Victims' rights and the struggle over crime in the media', *Canadian Journal of Communication*, 31.

Robson, P. (2006) 'Lawyers and the legal system on TV: the British experience', *International Journal of Law in Context* 2(4), 333–362.

Rogers, R., K. Harrison., D. Shuman, K. Sewell and L. Hazelwood (2007) 'An analysis of Miranda warnings: comprehension and coverage', *Law and Human Behaviour* 31, 177–192.

Schweitzer, N. and M. Saks (2007) 'The CSI Effect: popular fiction about forensic science affects the public's expectations about real forensic science', *Jurimetrics Journal* 47, 357–364.

Shale, S. (1996) 'Listening to the law: famous trials on BBC Radio, 1934–1969', *Modern Law Review* 59, 813–844.

Sherwin, S. (2008) *When Law Goes Pop: the Vanishing Line between Law and Popular Culture*. Chicago, IL: Chicago University Press.

Shuy, R. W. (2008) *Fighting Over Words: Language and Civil Law Cases*. Oxford: Oxford University Press.

Simon, W. (2001) 'Moral luck: legal ethics in popular culture', *Columbia Law Review* 101, 428–432.

Smith, P. and K. Natalier (2005) *Understanding Criminal Justice: Sociological Perspectives* (pp. 159–163). London: SAGE Publications.

Stark, S. (1987) 'Perry Mason meets Sonny Crockett: the history of lawyers and the police as television heroes', *University of Miami Law Review* 42, 229–282.

Sumner, C. (1990) *Censure, Politics and Criminal Justice*. Milton Keynes: Open University Press.

Sumner, C. (1994) *The Sociology of Deviance: an Obituary*. Buckingham: Open University Press.

Sumner, C. (2004) 'The social nature of crime and deviance' in C. Sumner (ed), *The Blackwell Companion to Criminology* (pp. 3–31). Oxford: Blackwell.

Thomas, A. (2006) 'The CSI-Effect: fact or fiction', *Yale Law Journal* 115, 70–72.
Tyler, T. (2006) 'Viewing CSI and the threshold of guilt: managing truth and justice in teality and fiction', *The Yale Law Journal* 115, 1050–1085.
Williams, S. (2001) 'Moral pluck: legal ethics in popular culture', *Columbia Law Review*, 2, 421–448.
Zedner, L. (2004) *Criminal Justice*. Oxford: Oxford University Press.

Matthew R. Draper and David Polizzi

Regurgitating the media image: towards a phenomenology of the 'visible' in criminal justice

Introduction

In his attempt to conceptualise the phenomenology of the photographic image, Hubert Damisch (1980) described the photograph as a cultural object situated within a very specific historical frame of reference. He continued by observing:

> The photographic image does not belong to the natural world. It is a product of human labor, a cultural object whose being – in the phenomenological sense of the term – cannot be dissociated precisely from its historical meaning and the necessarily datable project in which it originates. (p. 288)

As such, the photograph emerges as an artefact of this historical semiotic grammar, which conditions both its syntax and its meaning.

As a cultural object the photograph carries with it a variety of social meanings or, as Damisch (1980) has argued, 'a certain number of theses', that are inseparable from the way in which the image becomes meaningful for the viewer. As a product of human labour, the photograph evokes a specific array of intentional relations with the viewer by way of the intended meaning the image seeks to convey. Such a distinction becomes particularly salient when the photographic image is employed to configure the social meaning of crime. Within this context, the photograph emerges as a 'discursive' process related to the imagining of crime, which in turn, attempts to offer a specific thesis that seeks to figure the criminal image with that of the cultural meanings these images seek to reify.

As a cultural object, the photograph configures a specific set of social meanings that refer to both the image framed and the thesis which this 'framing' seeks to construct. Images of the criminally accused, for example, help to embody the subject of criminality, while at the same time reinforcing a set of socially constructed attitudes and beliefs that become 'recognisable' within the image of the perpetrator (Polizzi, 2013). In this sense, the photographic image, employed to construct the 'presencing' and ideological focus of criminality, also attempts to situate the 'subject' of the photograph within a specific behavioural frame of reference.

It is important, however, to recognise that the photograph does not itself create a cultural object; rather, it merely reflects a specific perspectival stance relative to an existing set of social meanings that are configured in the image depicted. Though these meanings are often contested, they always emerge or are informed by a specific perspective that is grounded in a very specific socially constructed reality. Stated more simply, it is clear that the photographic image is an image of something that is already in some way socially meaningful to someone. How then should we theorise the relationship between the photographic image and the cultural object configured in this process?

In describing the social visibility of the human body, Merleau-Ponty (1945/2012) states that, 'The very first cultural object, and the one by which they all exist, is the other's body as a bearer of behavior' (p. 364). From this perspective, the cultural object of the body is always perceived from a specific point of view, which also imposes a specific set of anticipated behavioural possibilities. The more 'variable' these points of view are, the more variable the human body's range of anticipated expression. If this presencing of the human body is viewed as more or less benign, the anticipated behavioural potentiality will likely be constructed in a similar way. However, if this same embodied presencing is viewed from a perspective of fear or potential danger, then even the most benign behavioural act will probably resonate with this anticipated threat.

The photograph, particularly those images employed to configure the meaning of crime, is often used to portray a static structure of meaning that conflates the subject into a vehicle of behaviour that is ontologically criminal in nature and more or less culturally 'specific'. From this perspective, the image seeks to evoke a very specific semiotic process that in turn structures this trajectory to its intended target. Once the image is employed in this way, the actual context of the photograph is lost and rendered irrelevant, insofar as it is now intended to serve the project of this socially constructed narrative.

In discussing the role of the photographic image Flusser (2012) makes the following observation:

> Images are mediations between the world and human beings. Human beings 'ex-ist', i.e. the world is not immediately accessible to them and therefore images are needed to make it comprehensible. However, as soon as this happens, images come between the world and the human beings. They are

supposed to be maps but they turn into screens: Instead of representing the world, they obscure it until human beings' lives finally becomes a function of the images they create. Human beings cease to decode the images, and instead project them, still encoded, into the world 'out there'. (p. 10)

Flusser's distinction between the decoded and encoded image reflects competing strategies of interpretation and meaning. The photograph as map reflects a directional strategy that allows the viewer to enter into the larger social world by the bridge that the image provides. However, when constructed as a screen, the image becomes self-contained and absent of any antecedent context from which to make sense of what is visibly present to the viewer. Though both of these strategies that are used to 'make sense' of the image reflect the phenomenology of visual semiotics as constructed between viewer, photograph and social world, the meaning of this encounter remains predicated upon the specific perspective of the viewer – both subjective and contextual – and the specific intentionality the image is intending to evoke and privilege.

How a cultural image or object impacts on individual or group behaviour reveals not a dialectal set of relations; but rather a dialogical configuration, which at every moment includes both individual points of view as well as specific competing points of cultural reference. When we view the image of the tattooed gang member or the mug shot of an individual being held over for trial, who is it that we see, and whose world have we entered?

If we configure these images as a self-contained *in itself*, then, as Flusser (2012) observes, we become transfixed by a very specific visual narrative, which intends a very specific socially constructed meaning and rhetoric. The image or visual sign of the tattooed gang member or arrested individual within this context comes to represent an encoded presencing of an *in itself* fabrication of the image of criminality. However, this fabricated image does not provide a point of reference or bridge by which to enter the social world; such a meaning-generating process constructs an alternative social reality that seeks to capture the image within a very specific defining point of view. Flusser warns that such an image no longer reflects a point of entry into the world with its various overlapping social contexts and competing social perspectives; rather, these images replace the world, which in turn results in the transformation of human experience into a function of the images we create. Said more simply, it is the image which becomes the world.

The decoded image, on the other hand, is the image of personal analysis and reflection. As such, it rejects the notion of the image as self-contained, and seeks to recognise 'The swarm of positions surrounding the phenomena, thereby overcoming the limits of objectivity and of limited vantage points, that is, the limits of ideological valuation' (Finger et al., 2011, p. 70). Within this context, the bridge which Flusser attributes to the decoded image represents the 'swarm of positions' that each individual brings to this hermeneutic. However, this swarm of positions is really no less vulnerable to the more overt difficulties identified with the conceptualisation of the image as self-contained and apparently self-defining.

The decoded image does provide access to the world, but whose world do we enter? Would this bridge lead us to the world that the image evokes or to a world situated within the consciousness of the perceiver? The process of personal reflection or politically charged analysis is still vulnerable to the construction of the image into an objectified and ideological artefact of subjective perception; but can it ever truly be otherwise? The decoded image is encountered from a very specific socially constructed reality; yet the bridge that it invites us to cross may still lead us to all too familiar ground. However, the meaning of the decoded image is never reducible to a singular point of view and therefore evokes a variety of meanings or interpretations based upon the perspective of the viewer, even when these potentialities remain present but unrecognised.

Implied in Flusser's distinction between these two conceptualisations of the image is the way in which the decoded image retains a fluid, yet unfinished configuration of social meaning. When viewed as a bridge to the social world, the decoded image becomes that vantage point from which the world unfolds, and reveals to the viewer a multiplicity of potential meaning. For example, the photographs of gang members either displaying their tattoos for the camera or the images of detained individuals having their tattoos photographed and catalogued by law enforcement authorities, reflect a meaning-generating process that is still contingent upon the eye of the beholder. Each image seeks to evoke a particular set of interpretations, yet remains fluid, and, therefore, cannot guarantee that this same meaning will be recognised by all viewers. Flusser (2012; 2013) expands his examination of the image by including what he calls the technical image.

'Technical images are difficult to decode. To all appearances, they do not have to be decoded since their significance is automatically reflected on their surface' (Flusser, 2012, p. 14). Flusser continues by observing 'What one sees on them therefore do not appear to be symbols that one has to decode but symptoms of the world through which, even if indirectly, it is to be perceived' (2012, p. 15). The photographs of Trayvon Martin used in the Zimmerman trial represent such a dynamic.

Martin's image is intended to remind the jury automatically of the symptom of black criminality which is used to overwrite any another possible interpretation of its meaning (Flusser, 2013). The image of defiant gang members, scenes of impoverished crime-infested areas or the seemingly unrepentant defendant, all reflect this idea of image as symptom. In all such instances, the image is attempting to disburden the viewer of its more complex symbolic implications and reality through its request for the viewer to focus only on its surface. The photographic images used in the George Zimmerman murder trial reflect this struggle.

Although a variety of photographic evidence was introduced during the Zimmerman murder trial, it will perhaps be recalled that two 'competing' photographic images of Trayvon Martin played a significant role during courtroom testimony. The first photograph depicted Martin approximately three to four months prior to his death. In that photo, Martin is dressed in a hoodie as he leans into the shot and stares into the camera, looking somewhat ominous. His 'dark' features are framed by a pale coloured hoodie and the white background of industrial light frames, walls and ceiling. That image of Martin would be used by Zimmerman's defence counsel to depict the individual his client confronted in that Florida neighbourhood the night Martin lost his life.

The second important photographic image introduced during Zimmerman's trial reflects a much different visual narrative; in that image, we see Martin's lifeless body as it lay on the autopsy table. Martin's image as depicted in the autopsy photograph no longer reflected the possibility of danger, thereby allowing the jury to see Martin in a more 'sympathetic' light. The cold image of Martin's lifeless and sutured body was much more likely to evoke a sense of empathy in the jury, who would in turn perhaps come to view Martin as the victim in this case. In his attempt to dispel such notions, the defence counsel cautioned the jury not be to 'fooled' by the harmless demeanour of the deceased on the autopsy table; rather, he suggested, they should recognise that the image in the autopsy photo was not the Trayvon Martin his client confronted that night (Hart, 2013; Polizzi, 2013). The lesson here is obvious: the fact of Martin's death is attributable to the fact of his dangerousness as a black male and as such, 'disqualified' him from ever being viewed as a victim (Vargas and James, 2013). The image of Martin three months before his death becomes the screen upon which the narrative of anti-black racism may be projected; and the autopsy photo the conclusion of that story.

The technical images represented by the two photographs described above evoke the very problem observed by Flusser: How are these images decoded and what are we to glean from these surfaces? What we witness in the presentation of the Martin photographs is a set of competing meaning-generating processes or 'surfaces' concerning how these images should be read by the jury. One the one hand, these images are intended to portray Martin as dangerous black male, whose fate, which is depicted by the autopsy photo, becomes the 'legitimate' consequence of such predatory social behaviour. The prosecution, on the other hand, seeking to disrupt this encoded narrative, presents the image of the autopsy photo as the vehicle by which Martin's humanity and victimisation are exemplified to the jury. The fact that the defence counsel feels compelled to remind the jury that the autopsy photo does not depict the person who confronted Zimmerman on the night of Martin's death, seems to confirm that perhaps this battle of 'surfaces' is being lost.

With each photographic image, we can witness the manifestation of two competing social narratives, as these relate to the meaning of Martin's death. The selfie of the hooded Martin is intended to presence the onto-logical 'fact' of black criminality and the recognisable threat it invites; whereas, the autopsy photo is intended as a bridge, which invites the jury to decode that image and make possible the fact of Martin's humanity and victimisation. How this process was ultimately resolved probably deter-mined the final verdict in this case. What seemed to hang in the balance of this process focused solely upon what the 'surface' of these images actually defined.

Perhaps the most challenging aspect for a visual criminology, then, is the way in which the object of this process is conceptualised. If we focus solely on the surface of the technical image, the object of the photo and its implied meaning remains static and is easily manipulated by ideological concerns. However, if we view the photographic object as incomplete and not reduc-ible to a specific set of privileged interpretations, it retains a degree of free-dom from the perspective of the viewer and retains a degree of potentiality that is never completely exhausted. Such a configuration of the visible object can be witnessed in the semiotics of Charles Peirce.

Peirce's triadic semiotic theory includes object, correlate and interpretant (Liszka, 1996). Peirce argues 'that the sign can only represent the object and not furnish acquaintance with it'. The sign, he writes, 'stands for the object not in all respects but in reference to a sort of idea' (Pettigrew, 2000, p. 124). As we witnessed with the images of Trayvon Martin, the reference of the 'object' eludes to the 'idea' of blackness being synonymous to criminality.

In describing the quality of the semiotic object further, Hausman states that for Peirce, 'semeiotic objects have two sides or aspects: as immediate objects and as dynamic objects. Immediate objects are the immediately interpreted effects of dynamic objects' (Hausman, 2007, p. 277). Dynamic objects or real objects are seen by Peirce as the referent that prompts inter-pretation that prompts the signing of that object and provides it its meaning or idea (Atkins, 2008; Hausman, 2007; Jappy, 2013; Peirce, 1931). Peirce continues by stating, 'I define a sign as anything which is so determined by something else, called its Object, and so determines an effect upon a person, which effect I call its interpretant that the latter is thereby mediately deter-mined by the former' (Atkins, 2008, p. 65). Here, the sign is 'determined' by the perspective the perceiver brings to the object. Though a variety of signs or signifiers may be present in one's relationship to the object, these do not create the object, and in fact require something to be present for this process to begin.

In attempting to further clarify his configuration of the sign, Peirce observed that a sign must be either what he defined as an *Icon*, an *index* or a *symbol* (Jappy, 2013). 'An *Icon* is a sign which refers to the Object that it denotes merely by virtue of characters of its own, and which it possesses, just the same, whether any such Object actually exists or not' (Peirce as quoted in Jappy, 2013, p. 83). An index is best exemplified by a photograph and tends to reflect a completed event. Symbols are viewed by Peirce as general signs which have become associated with their meaning (Jappy, 2013). In the case of the Trayvon Martin photographs, we can see all three aspects of the Peircean sign present in the process of signification that was in play during the Zimmerman trial.

Beginning with the Peircean notion of the *Icon*, we see how the various images of Martin are used to reflect the character of blackness and by so doing the character of Martin as well. Within this context, the image of Martin is used to reflect the Object of an African-American male as a pervasive ontological threat. As an *index*, these photographs reflect the narrative of a singular event, beginning with the image of Martin three months prior to his death and ending with his image on the autopsy table. However, within this context, the *Iconic* signing of Martin as ontological threat is now conflated with the autopsy table signing the end of this 'singular' event. As symbol, these images seem to confirm both the *Iconic* and *index* aspects of the Object as signed and culminate within the perverse 'legitimation' of the racist narrative seemingly proposed by this visual narrative.

As was witnessed above, the object of the semiotic process involved in the presentation of the photographs of Trayvon Martin at trial, invited a reference to anti-black racism and the dangerousness such a configuration seeks to evoke. However, for the possibility of Martin's dangerousness to be 'recognised' by the jury, it was first necessary for the defence to dispel any thoughts concerning the possibility that it was actually Martin who was the victim in this case. Given that each of these photographs brought with them a very specific and intended semiotic process, it was essential that this narrative not be 'derailed' by the empathic construction of Martin by the jury.

What this process of social construction reveals is its underlying phenomenology as this relates to the perpetuation of the narrative of anti-black racism. Zimmerman's defence counsel was ultimately successful in his strategy for the simple reason that the phenomenology of anti-black racism was able to overwrite the possibility of any alternative narrative that could perhaps challenge this signing of black presence.

Teaching the reduction

The perpetuation of racism, or of any problematic value perpetuating through the media image is not inevitable. Through Merleau-Ponty, we learn that the body is a social object. Through Flusser, we learn that this social object is the one encoded and decoded in the media. Through the work of Peirce, we learn that certain images become *Iconic*. In essence, the encoding of the object in media is an inherently socially constructed and historically situated process. Through these socially constructed encodings and decodings of the social body, the body itself, the person himself (or herself) can be lost in this process.

In criminology, the socially constructed media image of the criminal body often conceals a more nuanced, complex, and at times relatable person than this image intends to portray. As instructors and students of criminology, we can take the person himself back up to learn about the nature of who he is and why he does what he does. The problem remains that when we have the media image we often study the image (that shared by various media) rather than the person himself, who is the intended object of study. By using language like 'the person himself', we do not intend to imply that treating a human being as a non-human object ready for objectified and empirical study, quite the contrary. We seek to uncover that which is covered over by the media image, the humanity of the person rendered into mere media image.

If our goal as criminologists is to study the phenomenon of crime rather than specific or groups of embodied criminals, the object itself becomes the crime. Like the criminal body, media images of crime often reveal as much as they conceal. Therefore, the goal becomes to uncover what the image conceals and to help students of criminology to learn to do likewise.

Some argue that statistical methods and positivist approaches serve the purpose of this revelation, and to a degree it seems they are correct. However useful and important these methods for gathering nomothetic data, they often cover over vital idiographic information. Whereas nomothetic approaches summarise data over larger samples within a population (the larger the better) they do so by comparing a given case to a statistical mean, or by summarising a phenomenon into a mean. Although this seems helpful when first considered, a more careful examination reveals some deep flaws. For example, in the prison system clinicians in certain jurisdictions are required to offer group therapies that are 'empirically proven' to work on prison populations and this proof the researchers render in the form of statistical significance due to average amount of behavioural change owing to the effect of the group (see Ho and Ross, 2012 for a methodological critique of this particular type of group study). The average effect of the group, however, may cover over the actual effect of the group on one particular group member, which can range from a life-changing one to a tiny one to real harm. It could be that one person greatly helped by the group brought the mean up to a level of significance worth publishing, when the other group members were helped very little, if at all. Granted, researchers attempt to control for such skew, but the principle remains that a few group members receiving more beneficial effect than the others may make the group appear, on average, very effective, which *on average*, it is. The particularities may prove very different, however. Take any one *particular* case and you may find that the group intervention proved very ineffective. Unfortunately, the statistical methods employed by many criminologists unintentionally cover over the particular in favour of the average. This average creates another encoded image, one that both reveals and conceals.

As scholars our concern should not just be for the average, but for all particulars as well, in order to reveal what the average conceals. This moral argument may seem odd in a realm where scientists tout their methods as objective or amoral. Granted, their methods may be amoral (even then, that is debatable, see Richardson et al., 1999 for an example), but the criminologists are not themselves amoral. Rather, these scholars often feel either an abiding concern for the welfare of society or a deep investment in understanding the nature of crime or criminal behaviour because they are ethically aberrant (by definition). As morally situated beings as researchers of crime and the criminal, it ethically behoves them to study the average and the particular.

Although a comprehensive presentation of an epistemology that unifies statistical and qualitative methods is beyond the limitations of this text, teaching students of criminology idiographic methods helps them understand crime and criminals to the depths they should, as people concerned for society or the nature of crime itself. To that end, their professors can teach them that the image, regardless of media-created or research-created, both reveals and conceals and that certain methods help with the reveal more.

Amedeo Giorgi (2010) asserted that phenomenology is a human science – one that helps the researcher understand the object itself, and the person himself. Phenomenology (to oversimplify) is the study of human experience – the study of *phenomena*. Although some critics who misunderstand phenomenology argue that phenomenologists subjectively experience to the point of solipsism, this is simply not the case. Given that subjective experiences vary across individuals when experiencing the same thing, there is an unfortunate tendency to believe that because phenomenologists study the experience of these individuals, and because the experience varies, phenomenologists study these relative subjectivities which fail to inform our understanding of the object itself. A phenomenologist would disagree, and say that is not necessarily the case. Our experience of phenomena is our experience of the *thing itself*, and the thing itself becomes the shared object of understanding. The object of understanding, from this perspective, exists in relation to the experience of that object, and phenomenologists freely grant that perspectives on the object will probably vary. This relativity, rather than detracting from understanding the object, may actually inform our shared understanding of the object. For example, imagine students watching a news video of a clip depicting a Caucasian sheriff's deputy bodily slamming an African-American suspect so hard onto the hood of his service vehicle that the suspect's feet fly off the ground. Some bystanders show varying reactions, from anger, to shock and dismay, to indifference. Likewise, the students watching the video may each have somewhat different experiences of this video. Some may presume that the officer must be justified in the action of slamming the suspect, while others may presume that the officer's actions demonstrated an unjustifiable use of force. By studying each person's reactions (those depicted in the media image and those watching the media), it may seem that we are studying their reactions and not the scenario depicted in the images. That study can prove informative regarding the individual's reactions, but is not necessarily the focus of a phenomenological study. Instead, by studying the object itself, the officer slamming the suspect onto the hood of his car, we can learn more about the object itself by studying each person's experience of the object itself.

We may do so by learning from each individual the nature and context of their experience. In the case above, a student of criminology might interview both the officer and the suspect in question, as well as the bystanders. They may learn that the suspect assaulted the officer repeatedly until the officer subdued him, and that the video clip depicted the suspect's third attempt to flee. The bystanders may have experienced this in the context of a community that fears members of law enforcement, and may vary from agreeing that the suspect should try to fight back and flee or believing that the suspect needed to be violently subdued. Nevertheless, the student of criminology has learned more about the suspect's actions – in this case, the object of the crime itself. The student who believed that this constituted an act of police brutality has learned more about the act by undertaking a phenomenological investigation, as did the student who presumed the act was justified.

In a similar way to the cases of O. J. Simpson and Trayvon Martin, the media image covers over important potential understandings. In the case of Simpson, *Time* magazine famously darkened his skin as the trial progressed, even though he was a light-skinned African-American (abcnews.com). With Martin, the initial images were of a fresh-faced young boy, but later images were of a brooding teenager in a hooded jacket, then as a sutured body in a morgue (as discussed above). With the change in imagery comes a change in encoding and consequently a change in decoding of these socially constructed images. There were other informative perspectives on Simpson and Martin that were covered over by these images.

Given that our students are passive and active consumers of media, it behoves members of faculty to teach them to regurgitate the image and their assumptions and to look more critically and more deeply at these issues, and looking at the media images phenomenologically is one way to do so. 'Phenomenology is concerned throughout with phenomena in this sense, not with things and objects simply, but with things and objects as they appear through acts of consciousness' (Gurwitsch, 1964, p. 167). Encouraging our students to engage in acts of consciousness will assist their critical thinking and their regurgitation of the media image so many take for granted.

The first step is to teach students of criminology that much of what they see from the media, if they take it for granted, will remain merely manifest. 'Manifest' indicates objects that are seen but not critically engaged with or explored more deeply (Marion, 2002, pp. 8–9). If the students watch CNN or the local news, for example, and do not wonder about or explore more deeply the reports of crime they see, then those images of crime remain merely manifest, at the 'rank of image' (Marion, 2004, p. 19). Consciousness does not really act at this point, but merely receives the media image. Because observers of the image often fail to engage with it critically, we see certain problematic issues grow out of it. One is the 'CSI-effect', wherein jurors expect categorical evidence quickly, such as the evidence provided on television shows depicting crime scene investigations (Schweitzer and Saks, 2007; *The Economist*, 2010). In addition, with the success of these shows universities have seen a great growth in enrolment in criminology programmes (Nagin, 2007).

As nascent scholars of crime, these students have an opportunity to engage in an 'act of consciousness' and by doing so will learn that actual crime and law enforcement is not like what they see on television or read in magazines. One such act of consciousness is a *reduction*. The reduction, phenomenologically speaking, is not a material or temporal reducing-down as from some practices, but rather an opening up of awareness of what is given (Marion, 2004). How reduction takes place is by teaching students to peel away the layers of social construction to get to the experience of the thing itself. Once the students peel away the layers, they grow in awareness of what is actually given – in this sense, given to consciousness. 'Givenness' refers to the way in which the object avails itself to consciousness, *as itself*. In order to approach the givenness of the object, the student would need to eliminate the taken-for-granted social constructions and even their own memories by realising that they have these, then marking them and trying to filter them from their understanding. Once they have done so, they are experiencing more of the object itself, which is more fully given to consciousness. As Marion described, the process involved 'as much reduction, as much givenness' (Marion 2002, p. 17). The more the students carefully reduce the crime or accused, the more the object of inquiry avails itself to them. In addition, as they mark and filter out anything that the media intentionally or unintentionally added to the image they learn even more about what clouds our perception of the object itself.

By bracketing and filtering their individual as well as our cultural con-structions of popular media, politics, race, violence, police and power, stu-dents of criminology may uncover what may be covered over by the media image. By doing so, they gain an awareness of the encoding of the media image that commonly informs the decoding. Once those are bracketed and filtered from the popular media image, they may experience the image of a *person* – one who may be relatable in some ways. Once the image reveals the personhood behind the image, the student can begin to ask more insightful questions about what happened in the image and why, rather than merely accepting the manifest image at face value. Regardless of what this per-son stands accused of or what crimes they actually committed, or the law enforcement or investigative techniques they used, the student can under-stand a person and therefore learn more about the nature and purpose of the crime or of the law enforcement practice. The person depicted in the image becomes more than merely the depicted image of 'black' or 'white' or 'monster' or 'terrorist' or 'good cop' or 'bad cop', but instead a person whose motives they can potentially uncover, trace, discern and understand. By so doing, they may learn more about the nature and purpose of the crime or of the law enforcement practice.

Gadamer's phenomenological hermeneutics can help students as they engage in the reduction. Gadamer argues for two different forms of under-standing (Gadamer, 1998). One form of understanding (for our purposes, the media image of crime and law enforcement) entails the understanding of truth content (Warnke, 1987). Truth content entails the sort of substantive knowledge we can argue like the ethical principle that murder is morally aberrant. It involves 'insight into the subject matter' abstractly and ration-ally (p. 8). In the case of homicide, we can understand why homicide is generally problematic, by relying upon reason and insight into the nature of the act. The second form of understanding entails the knowledge of the conditions of an action, the purpose and motivation of the actor. In essence, it entails 'an understanding of the psychological, biographical or historical conditions behind a claim or action itself' (p. 8). The second form of under-standing helps us uncover the general principles of the first. Understanding why someone committed a particular crime helps the student understand why the behaviour is deemed criminal. By understanding why the law is written as it is, they begin to understand the nature of law.

A test or method for them to check their own understanding is their interpretation of the image once they filtered and bracketed the layers. Interpretation, in the case of regurgitating the media image, entails not just their experience of the object behind the image itself, but the students' part in the interpretation of the image. No matter how well the student engages in the reduction, their situatedness, their unique position of interpretation at their particular point from their particular perspective relates them to the image. According to Marion, to interpret an object is to engage in a reduction of our experience of the object. This reduction, however, is undertaken 'from our unique and particular perspective during a specific point in time and from within a particular context' (Marion, 2002, p. 17).

It is this form of interpretation that results in understanding as they discern the layers they may still need to bracket and filter as they seek to understand. For example, a student who believes that homosexual behaviour is disgusting or disturbing may have a very different interpretation of the image of a serial killer who preyed only on gay men than another student who does not hold such reservations. He or she may experience the media image of the killer as a logical consequence to those living the gay lifestyle. The other may experience the killer as a monster predator. Both are interpreting from their frame, but their interpretations both reveal and conceal the person behind the image of killer as they seek to understand. By bracketing and filtering, however, they can seek to understand the motivation of this particular person in this particular time (the second type of understanding). By doing so, they will learn a little more about the phenomenon of murder itself (the first kind of understanding). But they will do so more accurately by reducing the media image to the object of crime or the person accused, bracketing and filtering the social constructions involved.

Some may observe that this phenomenological method teaches critical thinking skills, the tendency towards scepticism in the face of the media. We would argue that is certainly the cause, and that criminology journals are another source of media, not to be treated as sacred, but to be reduced as well, to encourage students to look beyond the obvious, to return to the thing itself (a crime, law enforcement, jurisprudence) to inform their understanding, an opportunity to return to it for ongoing verification and refinement.

Reconsidering media ethics

During the Summer Olympics of 1996, Richard Jewell worked in security at the Centennial Park. Noting a suspicious backpack, Jewell evacuated hundreds of people before the pipe bombs inside detonated killing one person and injuring approximately 100 more. Shortly thereafter, Jewell found himself in the eye of the media, and was at first hailed as a hero. The hero label quickly eroded, however, after an 'anonymous' source within the FBI reportedly slipped information to a local newspaper that Jewell had become the focus of the investigation. The anonymous informant (according to the newspaper) stated that Jewell's character matched that of the lone-bomber archetype, as a frustrated Caucasian male craving the heroism obtained by members of the military or law enforcement, but barred from serving (Williams, 1997).

Despite the fact that the FBI never formally identified Jewell as a suspect or even shared any evidence against him, the media at large began depicting Jewell as *the* bomber (Ostorow, 2000). In order to build their case, the reporters presented the personality profile of a man whom they believed met the archetype of the lone bomber. By selectively presenting quotes from Jewell's previous employers, and broadcasting at the front of his home as though a hostage crisis were unfolding, they constructed the image of a guilty man. The media image of a hero transformed extremely quickly into that of villain, with Tom Brokaw of NBC news announcing on the same day as the anonymous source's leak to a local paper that Jewell's arrest was imminent (Williams, 1997). The flash of the media's cameras faded over the course of several months, and he found himself as quietly exonerated as he had been publicly vilified, with the media quietly acknowledging that the FBI never found him a suspect. Two reporters for *USA Today* later described how the media sucked Jewell into a 'media vortex that made his guilt or innocence almost irrelevant' (Johnson and Mauro, 1996).

Students who have been taught the reduction, upon hearing of both the initial heroism of Jewell as well as his later vilification, would ask themselves such questions as 'What aren't we being told?' 'What are my biases that inform my interpretation of this event?' 'How can I learn more about what's going on from a less biased source?' 'What does this most recent statement by the media mean?' 'What are the media sources, and are they adequate?' This would aid them in their understanding of the crime itself and the social construction of this particular media image.

Clearly, the claim that students should engage in the reduction in order to facilitate understanding of crime is an ethical one. Werner Marx (1992) and James Mensch (2003; 2009) critique the Western philosophical study of ethics and argue for a new approach – one that the media could take up to alleviate the problems of their current approach, which (as the example above indicates) ranges from exaggeration to outright misrepresentation.

Media ethics, based largely on logic and rationality, prove worthy of admiration. Like many fields, the ethic of theory demonstrably differs from the ethic of practice. The ethical practice of the construction of the media image increasingly concerns capitalism, or the ethical valuing of a story for the sake of profit and increased income, with the loudest or most dramatic story capturing the most attention (Stevenson, 1999). Although human cost matters, as in the example above where the accusations against Jewell were quietly retracted, it does not matter as much as the profit.

The reason we respond to the media images, the reason for their power, is the same source of ethical understanding, that of the shared world and shared embodiment. From Marx's understanding, we share a sphere of concern, regardless of our background and regardless of the differences in our worlds (1992). The media pundits do not need to define every word they use because we share a common understanding. Even when the reporter translates her words into another language, she does not need to define every word, because even people across cultures share sufficient understanding of the world and of human relationships. Most everyone cares about their Being and the Being of those who matter to them, so even if two people know no one in common, the very experience of their care for others demonstrates this shared sphere. The well-being of self and others often weighs centrally, many other life concerns orbiting this weighty issue. The reason why well-being sits centrally for so many is our deep-realisation that existence terminates, all life proceeds until it does not. Phenomenologically speaking, an ethic and moral concern grows from this realisation. The authors, when working in supermaximum security settings, both noted that the men behind bars felt grave concern for their people, and some had a stark knowledge that well-being could deteriorate into death quite quickly. For Marx, this sometimes all-too-acute awareness of mortality united them with those for whom they cared. They felt this attunement to *their* people. Such attunement need not be directed toward only a narrow set of others (fellow media professionals, fellow criminals, members of *our* group versus outsiders), but to *all* others. The attunement to our personal foibles, limitations, and mortality can very well attune us to the same in others, starting with the visceral experience of embodiment, an awareness of our emotional feeling of ourselves and our awareness of the other, when we will but really look at them (Mensch, 2003). Our experience of embodiment unites us, as an experience we all share, the experience of disappointment, desire, suffering and joy. If we re-think ethics as arising not *just* from rationality (the logical solutions to problems), but from this experience of embodiment, then compassion becomes the source of this ethical decision-making.

By relating to those depicted, members of the media risk finding someone relatable behind the images they seek to convey (even if actually guilty of crimes). Owing to the nature of this relatability, the reporters and writers would temper more carefully their presentation of information, seeing foibles not just in themselves but in others as well. Just as their well-being may end, so too may the well-being of others, and just as they would prefer their own well-being not to end, so too could they prefer not to end it for others unnecessarily. Rationality becomes not 'What can I do to get the biggest story to get ahead?' or 'If I present what is known I might lose my status', but 'How can I present only what is known?' The compassionate ethic entails not just the shared concern with the identified or suspected criminal, but to all of the constituents concerned (like the consumers – participants – of their image).

Even if those creating and propagating media images choose to take up this compassionate ethic, criminologists will still find themselves well served by examining any of these issues through the critical perspective of the reduction. Crime, law enforcement and jurisprudence will remain fluid and uncertain topics of understanding, but with a compassionate ethic for those investigating these topics (whether as members of the media or as researchers) an ongoing approximate and ethical understanding could unfold. This unfolding would entail somewhat less of the deliberate manipulation for self-serving ends, and understanding of crime would develop in a more complex, deeper and thorough manner.

References

abcnews.com. Retrieved 19 April 2015, from http://abcnews.go.com/International/photos/pharrell-cover-controversial-magazine-covers-16328228/image-16328306.

Atkins, A. (2008) 'Peirce's final account of signs and the philosophy of language', *Transactions of the Charles S. Peirce Society* 44(1), 63.

Damisch, H. (1980) 'Notes for a phenomenology of the photographic image' in A. Trachtenberg (ed.), *Classic Essays on Photography* (pp. 287–290). New Haven, CT: Leete's Island Books.

Finger, A., R. Guldin and G. Bernardo (2011) *Vilém Flusser: an Introduction*. Dulith, MN: University of Minnesota Press.

Flusser, V. (2012). *Towards a Philosophy of Photography*. London: Reaktion Books.

Flusser, V. (2013) *Post-History* (trans. R. Maltez Novales). Minneapolis, MN: Univocal.

Gadamer, H. G. (1998) *Truth and Method* (2nd edn). New York: Continuum

Giorgi, A. (2010) 'Phenomenological psychology: a brief history and its challenges', *Journal of Phenomenological Psychology* 41(2), 145–179. doi:10.1163/156916210X532108.

Gurswitsch, A. (1964) *The Field of Consciousness*. Pittsburgh, PA: Duquesne University Press.

Hart, W. D. (2013) 'Dead black man just walking', in G. Yancy and J. Jones (eds), *Pursuing Trayvon Martin: Historical contexts and contemporary manifestations of racial dynamics* (pp. 91–102). Lanham, MD: Lexington Books.

Hausman, C. R. (2007) 'Metaphorical semeiotic referents: dyadic objects', *Transactions of the Charles Peirce Society* 43, 276.

Ho, D. K. and C. C. Ross (2012) 'Cognitive behaviour therapy for sex offenders. Too good to be true?', *Criminal Behaviour and Mental Health* 22(1), 1.

Jappy, T. (2013) *Introduction to Peircean Visual Semiotics*. London: Bloomsbury.

Johnson, K. and T. Mauro (1996) 'Jewell goes public to try to regain reputation', *USA TODAY*, A1 29 October.

Liszka, J. J. (1996) *A General Introduction to the Semeiotic of Charles Sanders Peirce*. Bloomington and Indianapolis, IN: Indiana University Press.

Marion, J.-L. (2002) *Being Given: Toward a Phenomenology of Givenness* (trans. J. L. Kosky). Stanford, CA: Stanford University Press.

Marion, J.-L. (2004) *In Excess: Studies in Saturated Phenomena* (trans. R. Horner and V. Berraud). New York: Fordham University Press.

Marx, W. (1992) *Towards a Phenomenological Ethics: Ethos and the Life-world*. Albany, NY: State University of New York Press.

Mensch, J. (2003) *Ethics and Selfhood Alterity and the Phenomenology of Obligation*. Albany, NY: State University of New York Press.

Mensch, J. (2009) *From the Body to the Body Politic*. Evanston, IL: Northwestern University Press.

Merleau-Ponty, M. (1945/2012) *Phenomenology of Perception* (trans. D. A. Landers). London and New York: Routledge.

Nagin, D. S. (2007) 'Moving choice to center stage in criminological research and theory: the American Society of Criminology 2006 Sutherland Address' *Criminology* 45(2), 259–272.

Ostorow, R. (2000) 'Richard Jewell Case Study, 13 June 2000'. Retrieved 31 March 2015, from www.columbia.edu/itc/journalism/j6075/edit/readings/jewell.html.

Peirce, C. S. (1931). *Collected Papers of Charles Sanders Peirce*, Vol. I: *Principles of Philosophy* (ed. A. W. Burks). Cambridge, MA: Harvard University Press.

Pettigrew, D. (2000) 'Peirce and Derrida: from sign to sign' in J. Muller and J. Brent (eds), *Peirce, Semiotics, and Psychoanalysis* (pp. 122–135). Baltimore, MD: Johns Hopkins University Press.

Polizzi, D. (2013) 'Social presence, visibility, and the eye of the beholder: a phenomenology of social embodiment' in G. Yancy and J. Jones (eds), *Pursuing Trayvon Martin: Historical Contexts and Contemporary Manifestations of Racial Dynamics* (pp. 173–181). Lanham, MD: Lexington Books.

Richardson, F., B. Fowers and C. Guignon (1999). *Re-envisioning Psychology: Moral Dimensions of Theory and Practice*. San Francisco, CA: Jossey-Bass.

Schweitzer, N. J. and M. J. Saks (2007) 'Popular fiction about forensic science affects the public's expectations about real forensics science', *Jurimetrics*, 47(3), 357.

Stevenson, N. (1999). *The Transformation of the Media: Globalisation, Morality, and Ethics*. London: Longman.

The Economist (2010, April 24). Retrieved April 19, 2015, from www.economist.com/node/15949089.

Vargas, J. C. and J. A. James (2013) 'Refusing blackness-as-victimization: Trayvon Martin and the black cyborgs' in G. Yancy and J. James (eds), *Pursuing Trayvon*

Martin: Historical Contexts and Contemporary Manifestations of Racial Dynamics (pp. 193–204). Lanham, MD: Lexington Books.

Warnke, G. (1987) *Gadamer: Heremenutics, Tradition, and Reason.* Stanford, CA: Stanford University Press.

Williams, B. (1997) 'Defamation as a remedy for criminal suspects tried only in the media', *Communications and the Law* 19(3), 61.

II

PERCEPTION SHAPED BY OTHER MEANS

'Kony is so last month' – lessons from social media stunt 'Kony 2012'

Introduction

The role of the International Criminal Court (ICC) is to bring those responsible for committing the most serious crimes to justice when no domestic court is willing or able to do so. Although as of 2015, the Court has as many as 123 member states, one of its most crippling weaknesses is its lack of enforcement power.[1] The ICC is entirely dependent on the co-operation of national states, whether it is for enabling investigation by permitting entry into a country, granting access to evidence and witnesses, executing arrest warrants, or carrying out the Court's sentences. Even though the member states are under a legal obligation to co-operate with the Court (Article 86 Rome Statute), there are numerous cases where both member and non-member states have refused to co-operate with the Court (Cole, 2013; Fairlie, 2011). This opposition is hardly surprising considering the high political sensitivity of ICC cases, especially when they involve sitting heads of state.[2] At the same time, those states that are not directly affected by the atrocities have little interest in jeopardising diplomatic relations over a problem far removed from their electorate, who are rarely aware of the crimes and even less aware of the ICC. While there are more and more people in the West who have heard about the ICC, their awareness is still rather hazy. The trials of Charles Taylor (Special Court of Sierra Leone), Slobodan Milosevic (International Criminal Tribunal for former Yugoslavia) and Uhuru Kenyatta (ICC) seem to be reduced to the proceedings of a single court in The Hague, quite often also confused with the International Court of Justice. The Special Court of Sierra Leone is more known for the appearance of Naomi Campbell in the witness stand than for the historical trial of the Liberian President. The result is that some of the most important criminal trials in history are held with very little knowledge or interest from the international public. An outreach programme is placed at the Court, which aims to increase information and communication but it is targeted only at the population affected by the crimes rather than the public in general.[3] A more interested and active public in non-affected states on the other hand could encourage governments to co-operate better with the Court. But the question is how to inform and engage the wider public in the work of the ICC?

This chapter examines to what extent both new communications technology and the subsequent interdependence and interconnectedness among citizens around the world can increase the engagement of the global public in the work of the ICC. Already there have been examples of when social media was the primary tool for facilitating political engagement, such as the 2008 Obama campaign or the Occupy Wall Street movement in 2011 (Karlin and Matthew, 2012). The most cited example of where social media are claimed to have been essential in shaping historical events are the protests in the Middle East, which were also called the 'Twitter Revolution' or 'Facebook Revolution' (Tufekci and Wilson, 2012, p. 365). The prominent role of internet communications in these movements led to claims that social media could dramatically change political participation at the grassroots level and revolutionise civic engagement (Hill, 2010).

In 2012, the non-governmental organisation Invisible Children released the video 'Kony 2012'[4] to raise the awareness of one of the oldest ICC cases, namely the case against Joseph Kony, leader of the African paramilitary rebel group 'Lord's Resistance Army' (LRA). The video became almost instantly the most watched video on YouTube, attracting 100 million views in the first six days (Haris, 2013, 265). This success was especially surprising considering that the film was comparatively long (30 minutes) and comparatively serious for a popular YouTube clip. One reason for the instant 'virality' of the film undoubtedly lay in the various forms of modern social media that enabled easy sharing of the video, such as Twitter, Facebook, and MySpace pages (Bal et al., 2013, p. 204). The quick and widespread dissemination of the video begs the question of whether social media can be used to benefit the ICC by promoting its public profile and thereby encourage state co-operation. As one commentator expressed enthusiastically: 'I think "Kony 2012" has the potential to blow wide open the hidden power of public opinion in this country and the media that can now harness it as never before' (cited in Curtis, 2012).

Looking at the potential of social media for public awareness and grass root activism this chapter asks what lessons can be learned for the ICC from 'Kony 2012'. It will argue that the danger of social media campaigns is that rather than informing and engaging the public, they easily create myths and beliefs far remote from the aims of international criminal justice. It will also be shown that the potential of social media for popular activism is in itself but a popular myth. The chapter will briefly set out the background of the organisation, and examine the video and the situation in Uganda before analysing the three main myths created or perpetuated by 'Kony 2012'.

'Kony 2012'

Background: Invisible Children

Invisible Children, the non-profit organisation based in San Diego which produced and released 'Kony 2012', was founded in 2004 by Jason Russell, Laren Poole and Bobby Bailey, to raise public awareness about the violent LRA and their victims in the Acholi region, northern Uganda. From the very beginning, Invisible Children organised biannual tours across the USA, where they showed short films and raised funds (usually on the autumn tour) and promoted action days (usually in the spring tour) (Finnegan, 2013, p. 138). In total, Invisible Children ran fourteen campaigns and produced and screened twelve films. The most successful campaign before 'Kony 2012' was 'The Rescue' in 2009, which achieved the mobilisation of 85,000 participants in the spring action day. The organisation also participated in projects in northern Uganda, such as building radio networks, providing services to displaced children and their families, helping to rebuild schools and offering scholarships. Their main focus, however, has been to increase awareness of the LRA outside Uganda and to influence US policy. By 2012, two-thirds of the organisation's funds were used for film production, travelling and lobbying rather than for Ugandan projects (Finnström, 2012, p. 129). Although the organisation Invisible Children has been criticised for not using more of its funds in Uganda on the ground, one must keep in mind that the organisers have not portrayed themselves as an aid organisation but rather as an 'advocacy and awareness organisation' (Jefferson, 2012). Invisible Children's greatest success was in 2010 when, together with Resolve and John Prendergast from the Enough Project, they allegedly managed to prompt US policy and to be instrumental in the passing of the LRA Disarmament and northern Uganda Recovery Act (Audette, 2013: 54). Invisible Children also claimed that they were influential in that in 2011 President Obama committed 100 military advisers to the Ugandan military to help arrest Kony (Finegan, 2013, p. 139). While Invisible Children questioned neither the motives nor the consequences of the military involvement of the US military in Uganda, militarisation of the area by AFRICOM has been criticised for having domestic objectives such as counterbalancing China's growing influence on the continent, advancing the global war on terror, and securing access to oil and other natural resources (Finnegan, 2013, p. 142). Thus rather than influencing US policy, it seems Invisible

Children supplied additional justification and legitimacy to a number of already established policy priorities of the Obama administration.

Invisible Children's fourteenth campaign was launched on 5 March 2012 with the organisation's twelfth film, 'Kony 2012', in order to prepare the new action event 'Cover the Night' on 20 April 2012. The goal of the video was to make Joseph Kony (in)famous and thereby raise international support for his capture. The film was released on YouTube, vimeo and the Invisible Children website with the target of reaching 500,000 viewings by the end of the year (Gregory, 2012, p. 464). Within only six days, the video had over 100 million viewings and was celebrated as 'the most viral video campaign in history' (Audette, 2013, p. 53). According to a telephone poll by the Pew Research Centre, 58 per cent of Americans aged between eighteen and twenty-nine had heard about 'Kony 2012' within a week of its release (Pew Research Centre, 2012). After only three days, the video was covered on three American national network newscasts and on 9 March it became the *New York Times*'s headline.

'Kony 2012' was the last campaign of Invisible Children which, in December 2014, announced that it would close all US-based activities and focus on Ugandan projects alone. In 2015, Invisible Children decided to close down completely. Sadly, the rebel group that Invisible Children set out to stop, has outlived the NGO.

Background: Uganda
Joseph Kony, a former army commander, became the leader of the LRA in the 1980s, opposing Yoweri Museveni who took control of Uganda in 1986 after leading rebellions against the northern-dominated government. After his coup, Museveni's army committed atrocities against the northern population, which in turn led to opposition and counter-rebellions. The twenty-year-long conflict between the armed rebel groups and the government led to over 100,000 killings, 2,000,000 displaced people and 60,000 abducted children (many of them turned into sex slaves and child soldiers). In 2003, Betty Bigombe, former Minister of State for Pacification of the North, started meeting senior LRA members for peace negotiations. In spite of the peace talks and subsequent ceasefires, in December 2003 President Museveni referred the situation to the ICC. In 2005, the ICC issued arrest warrants against five members of the LRA including Joseph Kony,[5] which clearly disrupted the ongoing peace negotiations between the LRA and Bigombe. In 2006, the LRA withdrew from Uganda and moved into the border region of the Democratic Republic of the Congo, the Central African Republic and what would become the Republic of South Sudan. Since then, thousands of LRA members have left the group which is now believed to consist of less than 200 fighters. Nevertheless, the LRA continues to terrorise local

populations and according to a report released by the UN in 2014, the number of attacks has been increasing every year.[6]

Three key myths

Soon after the release of the video, Invisible Children was attacked for a lack of transparency regarding the use of their funds, and the organisation's reputation suffered further when a video of co-founder Jason Russell emerged, exposing himself on the street after a nervous breakdown. This chapter focuses, however, on the role played by the video in creating and perpetuating myths about the conflict in Uganda, possible solutions and the impact of social media campaigns.

1. The myths about the depicted problem

The northern Uganda perspective

The first of the film's problems is the presentation of the factual background. Even though compared with other YouTube videos, thirty minutes is quite long, the film's information about Joseph Kony and Uganda is surprisingly inaccurate and simplified. The video gives the impression that Kony still has an army of tens of thousands of child soldiers and that he is still acting in Uganda. There are three points of misunderstanding here. First, while the LRA was operating in Uganda when Invisible Children was founded in 2004, the rebel group retreated from Uganda in 2006, six years before 'Kony 2012' was released. On the other hand, the Central African Republic, a country where brutal LRA attacks on villages occur on a regular basis, is completely absent from the video (Edmonson, 2012). Secondly, while throughout the duration of the war, the total number of recruited child soldiers is estimated to count over 30,000, today the LRA is believed to have less than 200 fighters. Thirdly, the film shows an outdated portrayal of Uganda, omitting the enormous recovery of post-conflict north Uganda in recent years. Thus, although not saying this explicitly, the film gives the impression that the Acholi region is still in the situation it was in 2004 when Invisible Children started its work.

Furthermore, the armed conflict itself has been misrepresented. The long war in Uganda, which now continues in neighbouring countries, has been reduced to a single individual attacking Ugandan civilian victims, mainly children. Co-founder Laren Poole sets out this simplistic narrative as follows:

> It's one man: it's Joseph Kony. He's a monster. You're going to hear about him today. We are going to be talking about ways this can become a reality. But I want you guys to know that this one man is preventing millions of people

from going home ... He is the world's first and arguably the worst criminal near here. Not because of him, but because of the victims, because of the mothers, the children, the people in the IDP camps, they stand with us to hope-fully end Africa's longest-running conflict. (Finnegan, 2013, pp. 153–154)

The film fails to explain the political background of the conflict, namely the causes of the conflict in the colonial period and Uganda's current complex dynamics of politics, economy and ethnicity (Maasilta and Haavisto, 2014, 457). It also remains completely silent on the many criticisms of the Ugandan government regarding its own poor human rights record (Curtis et al., 2012). Wolfgang Zeller from the Centre of African Studies, Edinburgh University, explains that

While the extreme atrocities committed by the LRA cannot be justified by any 'political cause', the LRA did originally emerge as a direct reaction to extreme atrocities committed since the late 1980s by the government and armed forces of Uganda against the Acholi people in northern Uganda. (Cited by Curtis and McCarthy, 2012)

Museveni is blamed for prolonging the conflict as a pretext for weakening resistance by the Acholi as well as obtaining high amounts of foreign financial aid for the search for Kony (Maasilta and Haavisto, 2014, p. 466). The depiction of the conflict between rebels and government as good against evil is also problematic when fighters change sides. For example, the LRA commander who carried out the 'Christmas Day massacre' in the DRC in 2008, has meanwhile joined the Ugandan government and is now working alongside the Ugandan and American forces to help find Joseph Kony (Finnström, 2012, p. 131). Neither Uganda nor the ICC is investigating against him for his crimes in 2008.

In sum, the depiction of the conflict lacks any historical, political, or cultural contextualisation. Indeed, Invisible Children created 'a magical master narrative; the lobby reduces, depoliticizes and dehistoricizes a murky reality of globalized war into an essentialized black-and-white story that pits the modern Ugandan government and its international partners against the barbarian LRA' (Finnström, 2012, p. 127).

While it is welcome that the plight of the Ugandan victims were brought to a global audience, the fact that the video is giving a false portrayal of both the conflict as well as the current situation demeans current efforts of the local communities. It also undermines the video's credibility and thus the legitimacy of its message.

The American perspective

Besides the simplification of the Ugandan conflict and the distortion of the current situation, another problem with the video is the transmutation of a

Ugandan issue into an American one (Budish, 2012, p. 756). While Invisible Children brusquely claims: 'We're just trying to do a little part to help change the world' (Jefferson, 2012), the film surprises by the 'near absence of African voices in a video about an African conflict' (Von Engelhardt and Jansz, 2014, p. 467). Clarke points out that the core of the film is a story 'about how American political participation and stopping a single leader will rectify Uganda's plight' (2012, p. 309). A story which is nearly completely silent on any Ugandan involvement in both finding Kony and rebuilding the victims' lives. The film focuses on the empowerment of its audience rather than the empowerment of the victimised community itself. Indeed, it is riddled with a narcissism which 'emphasises US youth's agency above all else' (Gregory, 2012, p. 465).

Victor Ochen, founder and director of AYINET (African Youth Initiative Network), an organisation which helps to rehabilitate victims of the LRA, not only expresses his disagreement with the offered solution but also the offensiveness of it: 'This Invisible Children campaign hurts. It's offensive ... The people who have suffered at the hands of Kony don't want to promote him or make him famous. They want to rebuild their lives ... We get the feeling that Invisible Children care more about their videos than about victims' (Jones, 2012).

Indeed, one public screening of 'Kony 2012' in Lira, a Ugandan town directly affected by the LRA, had to close after the audience got so angry that some started throwing stones at the screen (Edmondson, 2012). The video was condemned as 'a foreign, inaccurate account that belittled and commercialised their suffering, as the film promotes Kony bracelets and other fundraising merchandise'.[7] One former LRA abductee exclaimed that 'It celebrates our suffering' (Edmondson, 2012).

Insensitivity or at least ignorance of the Ugandan perspective is also shown by the choice of the action date for the action campaign stunt 'Cover the Night':

> Why 20 April? Don't they know or care that this is the anniversary of one of the worst LRA massacres, when over 300 people were killed at Atiak in 1995? ... This is a day when communities are trying to heal broken hearts, but Invisible Children want to plaster Kony's face everywhere ... People in the affected areas find it very difficult when an organisation encourages people to wear T-shirts bearing Kony's face. How do you think Americans would have reacted if people in another country wore Osama Bin Laden T-shirts? All of this just confirms to us that they do not care about the victims and ignore their suffering. (Jones, 2012)

Ochen also noticed that the 20 April is celebrated by many neo-Nazis as Hitler's birthday and that the stunt was planned to take 'place on his birthday is just another insult, and it makes the campaign feel more like a celebration than a condemnation of these individuals' (Jones, 2012).

2. *The myth of the depicted solution*

Criminal justice and military intervention

Not only is the presentation of the problem questionable, but also the proposed solution. Jedidiah Jenkins, Invisible Children's 'Director for Ideology', was confident of their role in international criminal justice, declaring that 'The ICC chose Kony, and *we've kind of partnered with them* in an unofficial way' (Jefferson, 2012, emphasis added). Like the depicted problem, the solution presented by Invisible Children too, is oversimplified. It seems to take for granted that a criminal prosecution is in the best interest of the affected region. In spite of the many criticisms of the ICC's decision not to withdraw the arrest warrants against the leadership of the LRA, Invisible Children did not doubt that an arrest was a blessing not only for Uganda but international criminal justice in general: 'If Kony is arrested, we'd like to see Kony tried at The Hague, and then it sets a precedent. It tells future warlords that if you want to commit genocide, if you want to commit war crimes, you cannot get away with it anymore' (Jefferson, 2012).

The way to achieve this, in the view of Invisible Children, is to raise public awareness of the LRA leader with the ultimate goal of influencing US policy makers to maintain US American military intervention (and raise support from other governments). Thus, the envisioned end result is to increase US military intervention in Africa and have Joseph Kony arrested and tried before the ICC. It is true that there were Ugandan voices who welcomed the increased international interest in Uganda with the possibility of help in capturing Kony (Maasilta and Haavisto, 2014, 463). Many of the affected Acholi people, however, seem to be mainly interested in securing peace and rebuilding their region and are afraid of further military action. Finnegan explains that 'numerous indigenous activists have … expressed thunderous anxiety about the plausible use of military in the LRA bill' (2013, p. 156), not least because there are still a number of children and women with the LRA today who would be put at serious risk by a military assault. Furthermore, rather than an abstract notion of justice for a handful of rebels, many victims would prefer the resources being spent on their current needs such as education, employment and health, especially regarding the nodding syndrome,[8] which is suspected to be linked to the war (Nothias, 2013, p. 124). Another concern is that offering military aid to the Ugandan military forces with their poor human rights record might be dangerous. Once again, the message in the film is clear-cut and rather simplified: only US intelligence and military intervention can halt the unstoppable LRA and only with the help of the mighty US armed forces can the LRA leadership be brought to justice. Another myth implied is that sufficiently sophisticated military equipment will succeed where the Ugandan army has failed for so long. The LRA operates in a vast area of dense jungle which is located on the territory of Central African Republic, Democratic Republic of Congo and Southern Sudan, none of whose governments have de facto control of the terrain. A group consisting of only a few hundred people cannot be located easily in such a vast terrain, even with the help of advanced technology such as satellite imagery or drones.

African stereotypes

The simplification of the armed conflict, together with the misrepresentation of the current situation in Uganda, and in particular the underrepresentation of the Ugandan peace building and reconstruction efforts and successes, causes more problems than just misinformation. It also feeds into the stereotype of a destitute Africa which needs salvation from an advanced USA. It conveys the image of a helpless, developing African country which needs the military strength, skills and technology of the developed West to save it from a monstrous individual hiding in the jungle. Nothias points out that the film 'epitomises three recurrent stereotypes that have pervaded Western representations of Africa: the good, willing Westerner, the helpless African and the cruel warlord' (2013, p. 125). The conflict between the LRA and the government is reduced 'to a colonist "Heart of Darkness" stereotype of primitiveness' (Finnström, 2012, p. 128). Even President Musevini, benefiting from such non-political evaluation of the conflict, takes advantage of the image of a conflict driven by animalistic enemy rather than its political causes. However, his description of his enemies as 'hyenas and a bunch of criminals driven by primitiveness and backwardness, witchcraft and mysticism, even obscurantism' effectively plays into the 'most essentialist colonial stereotypes about primitive savages in darkest Africa' (Finnström, 2012, p. 131). Of course, there is a highly political sub-context of African stereotypes in that the presentation of an inferior, helpless Africa and a superior West helps to rephrase any outside intervention as a humanitarian and non-political act (Finnegan, 2013, p. 145).

The film therefore uses a very simple narrative; as soon as the United States decides to arrest Kony, then this can and should be done. Russell proclaims '99% of the planet doesn't know who Kony is. If they did, he would have been stopped years ago' ('Kony 2012' video). Thus, the film depicts a vision in which the important question of how to deal with post-conflict justice in the region and how to reconstruct the affected areas has been taken out of Uganda and placed in the hands of the USA. It is the USA which has the power and thus, so it seems, also the right to decide what happens in Africa. Edmondson even speaks of the 'infantilisation' of Africa (2012) and not surprisingly nearly all Ugandans shown in 'Kony 2012' are children (Von Engelhardt and Jansz, 2014, p. 467).

Furthermore, the image of the Western saviour is extended to the donor audience by the video's promise that Africa's problems can be transformed by Western philanthropy: 'Russell's savior complex is catapulted with the message that by donating money through a simple click of your mouse, and buying a kit that will help find Joseph Kony's arrest, every American can also be part of the solution to help poor Ugandan victims' (Clarke, 2012, p. 309).

Nothias even claims that 'it could be argued that the video was so successful precisely because it tapped into a narcissistic, simplistic and reassuring Western narrative about Africa' (Nothias, 2013, p. 127).

3. The myth of the depicted means – clicktivism

Besides the depicted problem and solution offered by the film, the third principal myth relates to the depicted means to achieve the suggested solution.

Tangible actions

The storyline in 'Kony 2012' is that Jason Russell, a young American, makes a pledge to an African child to bring the villain to justice. It is a very simple archetypal illustration of the young, good-looking, American hero promising to help the innocent helpless African child to revenge his brother (and save tens of thousands of other children on the way). A large part of the film focuses on proposing five tangible, simple steps the audience can take in order to help make Russell's promise come true. The video asks the audience to do the following:

1. share the video link on social media;
2. contact celebrities and politicians to increase the visibility of the LRA;
3. make a donation to Invisible Children;
4. buy merchandise of the organisation (the 'Kony 2012 Action Kit' includes t-shirts, posters, stickers, pins and bracelets and costs $30) (Thomas et al., 2015); and
5. take part in one-day action 'Cover the Night' on 20 April 2012.

Indeed, the majority of viewers did not only watch the video[9] but also participated in at least one of these tasks. Thus, the narrative of the film with the accompanying technical infrastructure allows the audience to be transformed from passive viewers to active citizens (Harsin, 2013, p. 266).

Probably the most effective step for spreading the video was step 2, contacting a specific famous person. The 'Invisible Children Kony 2012' website provided a list of twenty so-called culture makers and twelve policy makers on whom viewers could choose to click, creating an auto-tweet which asked the chosen celebrity to support the cause. In this way, tens of thousands of mentions, targeting celebrity accounts, were created (Lotan, 2012). Celebrities who tweeted the 'Kony 2012' link included Oprah Winfrey,

Justin Bieber, Rihanna, Kim Kardashian, Nicki Minaj, Ryan Seacrest, Bill Gates, Puff Daddy, Taylor Swift and White House Press Secretary Jay Carney. When Oprah Winfrey tweeted to her followers about the film, 'Kony 2012', viewings jumped from 66,000 to 9 million (Audette, 2013, p. 55).

Not-so-active activism

Initially, the principal aim of the video was to mobilise the audience for the next one-day action stunt for Invisible Children, 'Cover the Night'. The idea of this campaign was to plaster every block in every city around the world with posters, stickers and graffiti of Joseph Kony, in order to raise awareness and put pressure on governments to make the necessary arrest. The online success did not, however, translate into any noteworthy offline action and the turnout for the 'Cover the Night' stunt rarely exceeded a handful of participants (Carroll, 2012).

Except for the flopped 'Cover the Night' campaign, the other four steps could be completed by simply clicking links. This easy participation has been described by the term 'clicktivism' or 'slacktivism' as it is as a form of activism without need for personal sacrifice (Budish, 2012, p. 750). It does not require any significant contribution of time or money and does not pose any physical danger, such as the risk of violent demonstrations or clashes with the police. Such 'armchair activism' is claimed to jeopardise traditional result-orientated activism, because it creates the impression that 'liking', re-posting, and 'PayPalling' is all that is needed to help capture the villain (Harsin, 2013, p. 266). Indeed, 'Kony 2012' conveyed the message that just by sharing the video, people could save countless children from the LRA. As Gladwell explains, social networks are not effective in increasing motivation but instead in increasing participation, by lowering the degree of motivation that would be required for any meaningful participation (2010).[10] Audette suspects that the same is true for the celebrities who got involved in the campaign, but who might have been reluctant to use their influence, if more than a few clicks had been necessary (2013, p. 57).

The convenience of the 'Kony 2012' campaign goes however beyond the effortlessness of clicktivism and is related to the message of the film. The reason why the video spread so widely so quickly is explained not only by the importance of the message regarding the plight of Kony's child victims but also, and maybe even more so, because of the message relating to the audience itself. Sharing the video contributed to the feel-good factor of the audience that is unprecedented in activist appeal films: 'The earnestness of "real" portrayals of suffering is being matched with – or even supplanted by – more lighthearted, postmodern pastiche and youth culture aesthetics, and glamorized or playful representations of the humanitarian donor-as-consumer' (Brough, 2012, p. 176).

Rather than focusing, as most activist video clips do, on the suffering of the victims, this clip concentrates on how easily the audience might take part in solving the problem. This message promises an immense empowerment to an audience who, often children themselves, are given the impression they can be part of ending the conflict by the end of the year. By offering the audience a big reward (the feeling of being an active part of saving children) for little effort (a few clicks), 'Kony 2012' appeals to an active young generation who wants to make the world a better place. The video also conveys the image of solidarity for a broader course in which every little action counts. The film is a 'celebration of a caring and acting "us"' (Von Engelhardt and Jansz, 2014, p. 480). An example of the self-congratulating attitude of the organisation is their evaluation of Obama's decision in 2011 to send 100 military advisers to Uganda. In the clip, Russell declares that for 'first time in history the U.S. took that kind of action *because* the people demanded it' (emphasis added).

Another concern when analysing the role that large-scale online campaigns such as 'Kony 2012' can play, is the potential of diverting attention from social issues nearer to home. Finnegan shows how many young Invisible Children activists get involved because they have an underlying feeling of guilt at having a prosperous life that African children lack (2013, p. 148). Comparing the safe life of Russell's son with the victims of the LRA, '"Kony 2012" aims to build up a sense of moral responsibility and pressure to act among its viewers' who are 'carrying a personal moral obligation to act' (Von Engelhardt and Jansz, 2014, p. 469). While the Invisible Children campaign offers a way to transform this feeling of guilt into action, it falls short of requiring the audience to address the reasons why they do have such a prosperous secure life when there is so much suffering elsewhere; it allows them to focus on scarcity in a different continent rather than face child poverty in their neighbourhood.

> If these privileged young people had chosen to reach out to others in their own communities, perhaps immigrants or poor people of color, for example, the related issues would he much more intimately intertwined with their own politics and that of their families. In such a scenario, exposing underlying causes may even implicate themselves as beneficiaries of racism or a predatory economic system. (Finnegan, 2013, p. 149)

Signing up for such an uncontroversial cause as saving children in Africa on the other hand, does not require the participants to confront socially imbedded norms and practices. Von Engelhardt and Jansz point out that

According to Chouliaraki, post-humanitarianism also marks a shift away from challenging political and economic structures that reproduce injustice and suffering, towards largely apolitical and issue-specific appeals, which 'privilege a self-oriented form of solidarity of short-term and low-intensity engagements with a cause, over an other-oriented solidarity of deeply felt, ideological commitments'. (Von Engelhardt and Jansz, 2014, p. 471)

As saving children from a monster in a distant part of the world does not address any remotely controversial beliefs, there is no threat of any social criticism by friends, family and later potential employers. Since the cause is so worthwhile and uncontested, unlike contentious issues such as abortion or gay rights, participation can only create praise and acknowledgement.

Furthermore, not only is participation quick, easy and effortless but, even more importantly, it is very visible on social networks. Indeed, part of the attraction of participation is the anticipated praise of one's peers. Schau and Gilly explain that online behaviour is often motivated by the wish to present a positive image of oneself (2003). Clicktivism is a way of labelling oneself not only as being on the good side but more importantly publicising that one is actively involved in doing good. Thus the use of social media does not only make the sharing of the video technologically very easy, more importantly the dynamics of social media makes it also very desirable. As a result, activism is reduced to an act of self-portrayal and self-empowerment rather than genuine critical engagement.

Conclusions

This chapter examined to what extent social media campaigns such as 'Kony 2012' create and sustain myths and public beliefs. In spite of the extraordinary virality of 'Kony 2012' which made the campaign an immediate internet sensation, when discussing whether social media campaigns are desirable in order to raise awareness of the ICC, the example of 'Kony 2012' is rather discouraging.

The myth of simple stories
One has to admit that in spite of all the problems of 'Kony 2012', one of the main objects of the film, namely making Joseph Kony infamous before the year was out, was achieved. The video managed to spread awareness of the plight of child soldiers in Africa on an unprecedented scale in modern international criminal justice. Many share the following comment by *Guardian* reader Raphael Hetherington: 'I didn't know who Kony was, or anything about child soldiers in Uganda, until I saw the video. Whatever you think about the charity, a lot of people now know, and want to do something about, the LRA and central-African conflict' (Curtis, 2012).

An Acholi priest declared 'It is a good thing, people from other parts of the world getting concerned' (Finnegan, 2013, p. 158) and the former ICC prosecutor Luis Moreno-Ocampo praised the campaign for having 'mobilised the world' (Holligan, 2012). Yet, the way in which the video shaped popular beliefs is rather worrying. It is not in the interest of justice in general, and of the ICC in particular, to circulate a story that oversimplifies both background and possible solutions of a longstanding, horrific, armed conflict. International criminal justice deals with highly complex political, historical and sociological situations which cannot be reduced to a question of good versus evil. Jenkins from Invisible Children counters any criticism of simplification with the explanation that the target audience were high school children and that the film was not 'made to be scrutinised by the Guardian' (Jefferson, 2012). One reader's comment in the *Guardian* agrees:

> My experience in Advocacy has shown that a message must be extremely simple for people to adopt. [Invisible Children] may be simplifying the issue through their film but they have to. If they tried to explain the complexities they would lose their audience within the first few seconds. From a pure campaigning point of view, their film is genius. (Curtis, 2012)

In addition, the film was only one part of a multifaceted campaign to be complemented by information on the Invisible Children website (which crashed owing to the volume of hits) and discussions at the screenings (Audette, 2013, p. 57). Nevertheless, the relationship between the necessities of the campaign, namely the need to summarise a complex context into a comprehensive story, needs to be balanced with the basic requirements for truth and information. Indeed, when the trailer to 'Kony 2012' states 'Don't study history, make history', it shows an approach irreconcilable with the aims of the ICC. It is the historical complexity of each situation which makes the work of the ICC so difficult but also why it is necessary. There is a reason why the judgments in international criminal law are often several hundred pages long. The reduction of the cause to one evil man is not sustainable, even if the facts have to be reduced for highschool children. The *Guardian* correspondent Hack Shenkar expressed his concerns regarding simplification of the message:

> ['Kony 2012'] defenders argue that this is largely an appeal to children and the young – which to me is all the more reason to avoid transmitting a dangerous message that the world's problems a) come down to individual evil, and b) can be solved by buying bracelets and tweeting ... I especially don't like the way the solution is couched as an exercise in celebrity-orientated clicktivism and consumerism, without any attempt to encourage viewers to think beyond existing structures and challenge the status quo. (Curtis, 2012)

Belief in online activism

Today's use of the internet, the so-called Web 2.0, has revolutionised communication within and between communities:

> the internet has moved into peoples' everyday lives introducing unmediated 'many-to-many' communication on a large scale and at relatively low cost. Through newsgroups, chat rooms and other media, internet communication allows the boundaries established by traditional broadcast media (newspapers, television, radio) and one-to-one media (telephone, letters etc) to simply be ignored. (Hill, 2010)

The same is true for video-sharing sites like YouTube and vimeo. Following the role the internet played, at least to some extent, in the Arab Spring movements, social media have proven that Web 2.0 has the potential for catalysing social change. Social media offer a platform which makes it easy to disseminate information about the cause as well as co-ordinating protests. Tufekci and Wilson point out that the internet played an important role in the protests in Egypt because 'social media and satellite TV were the main public spaces where politically sensitive subjects were openly discussed and dissent could be expressed' (2012, p. 364). However, research suggests that although the internet facilitated conventional networking, it has not replaced it and scholars keep emphasising the importance of face-to-face personal relationships (Lim, 2012; Tufekci and Wilson, 2012). Often months or even years of groundwork building face-to-face networks, preceded the protests. Invisible Children, too, built up a supporter network during the years before the viral success of 'Kony 2012' (Budish, 2012, p. 758). Research has shown that the tweeting about 'Kony 2012' started when Invisible Children held public screenings of the film and asked the audience to tweet the online link (Audette, 2013, p. 54) and where Invisible Children had strong networks of young supporters (Lotan, 2012). Thus releasing a video on social media alone is not sufficient, unless it is backed up by a strong, supporting community.

A related weakness demonstrated by 'Kony 2012' is the short lifespan of its popularity. 'Kony 2012' has been acclaimed for 'by far the most publicised online humanitarian campaign ever produced' (Von Engelhardt and Jansz, 2014, p. 465), but the hype was over as quick as it started. After the initial 100 million in the first week not many new views followed. As one tweet simply stated, 'Kony is so last month'. Not surprisingly, by the time the offline campaign was due six weeks later, very few people were still interested or willing to participate in offline activities. Thus, it is questionable what interest and support for the ICC a social media campaign could sustain, as the use of social media encourages short-lived superficial clicktivism rather than a genuine, thoughtful engagement.

On the other hand, while previous Invisible Children films went more or less unnoticed, when 'Kony 2012' suddenly became viral, it was exposed to criticism from all sides, including journalists, researchers, Web commentators, activists and NGOs (Maasilta and Haavisto, 2014, p. 457). Indirectly, the video initiated a global debate of not only the video and Invisible Children but also the situation in Uganda. For example, the Tmblr blog 'Visible Children', which set out manifold criticisms of the Invisible Campaign, attracted itself over a million views.[11] In this way, the discussion about 'Kony 2012', itself resulted in an indirect dissemination of information about the conflict and the current situation in northern Uganda. However, this informational side-effect of the internet success of the video is just that: a side-effect based on the novelty of the campaign, which will be difficult to replicate.

The power of voice
The wider issue when considering the role that internet campaigns, especially social media campaigns, can and should play in public beliefs surrounding international criminal justice is the power of voice. Alterman reminds us of the important role of social media not only in receiving but also creating content (2011, p. 104). The example of 'Kony 2012' reveals, however, the inequality of the power of voice of the internet.

An example is the involvement of Ugandans in the global debate. A positive effect of the publicity of 'Kony 2012' was that in reaction to the criticism of the exclusively American perspective, suddenly also Ugandan voices were sought, both in mainstream media and blogs. The increased involvement of Ugandans in the debate did however not mean that finally voices of the affected areas were heard. The discussion about 'Kony 2012' was again led mainly online and, in many parts of the world, including northern Uganda, there is limited access to the internet. In Uganda, the internet is mainly used in the urban centres and only 12.5 per cent of the population are estimated to have access to the internet via computers. For example, according to Maasilta and Haavisto (2014), in the northern town of Kitgum, which was central to the former conflict and has a population of about 46,000, there is only one internet cafe (with only four computers). Some people use the internet via their phones but downloading videos is expensive and usually very slow (Chalk, 2012). Thus, it does not surprise that many of the Ugandans who contributed to the debate were from the educated South, especially from the capital Kampala rather than from the affected Acholi region (Maasilta and Haavisto, 2014).

The seemingly anarchic, open-to-all internet, is not that at all. In order to create or access content on the internet one must be literate, English speaking,[12] have access to electricity and to the internet (with a fast enough connection to download or upload videos) or a mobile phone, and live in a country that does not censor the internet. Of course, the areas most affected by violent conflicts usually have the least opportunities. The power of voice follows the power of development. Thus, not only in its content but also in its choice of medium did 'Kony 2012' 'perpetuate the global inequalities of the status quo, rather than challenge them' (Von Engelhardt and Jansz, 2014, p. 469).

Concluding remarks

Even though 'Kony 2012' helped to publicise the atrocities of the LRA, awareness is not the same as knowledge and being informed is not the same as being engaged. Disseminating information about the ICC and encouraging the public to engage with its work needs much more than releasing a flashy video, even if it goes around the globe within a week. It seems that the social media campaign created and perpetrated a number of myths and public beliefs without at the same time triggering critical or active engagement. The misleading depiction of both the conflict and the current situation in Uganda went beyond misinformation and reinforced the myth of war as a good versus evil conflict and the image of a helpless Africa. The video also perpetuated a belief in both the feasibility and the desirability of foreign military intervention and reiterated African stereotypes about the mighty West helping inferior Africa. Thus, the main problem in the eyes of this author is that the video used its power of voice to perpetuate the inequalities between the powerful and the powerless. With the potential of a quick global reach the risk of creating misleading public beliefs and myths is multiplied to previous unreached levels.

The ICC should however learn from the experience that there is 'a hungry, millennial, global-minded youth' (Jefferson, 2012). It should use the internet's potential to connect better with those communities which are not directly involved in one of the situations before the ICC and enhance the Court's publicity, legitimacy and credibility. While it is not the role of the ICC to encourage more activism, this author believes that the ICC need to extend its outreach programme to the general public, beyond victimised regions. The Court could start by improving its website with faster and more detailed updates and releasing short videos which deal in detail with smaller but concise issues and thereby presenting a balanced picture which allows the audience to form their own views. While being aware of the potential problems of social media campaigns explored in this chapter, the ICC can utilise the fact that the internet and especially social media, can facilitate interconnectedness between citizens around the world, which corresponds to the idea that the crimes tried before the ICC are of concern of the whole of humanity.

Notes

1 At the moment nine arrest warrants are outstanding, some of which are now ten years old.
2 Omar Al Bashir, President of Sudan, Uhuru Kenyatta, President of Kenya and Laurent Gbagbo, former President of Côte d'Ivoire.
3 ICC Assembly of State Parties 'Strategic Plan for Outreach of the International criminal Court ASP-06-0241, ICC-ASP/5/12, 29 September 2006.
4 www.youtube.com/watch?v=Y4MnpzG5Sqc (last accessed October 2015).
5 Of the initial five arrest warrants, the only suspect currently in custody of the ICC is Ongwen, the alleged Brigade Commander of the LRA, who was surrendered to the ICC in January 2015. Lukwiya is now believed to be dead while Odhiambo, Otti and Kony remain at large.
6 UN Office for the Coordination of Humanitarian Affairs (OCHA) released on 10 November 2014.
7 Malcolm Webb, Ugandans React with Anger to Kony Video, Al Jazeera (14 March 2012, 7.55 a.m.), http://blogs.aljazeera.com/blog/africa/ugandans-react-anger-kony-video (last accessed October 2015).
8 The Center for Disease Control and Prevention explains: 'Nodding syndrome is an unexplained neurologic condition characterised by episodes of repetitive dropping forward of the head, often accompanied by other seizure-like activity, such as convulsions or staring spells. The condition predominantly affects children aged 5–15 years and has been reported in South Sudan from the states of Western and Central Equatoria and in Northern Uganda and southern Tanzania.' www.cdc.gov/globalhealth/noddingsyndrome/ (last accessed 12 October 2015).
9 Of course, it is not known how many of those who clicked on the video watched it, either in part or to the end.
10 As an example, Gladwell points out that the Save Darfur Facebook page has 1,282,339 member but that the average donation is only 9 cents per member.
11 A seven-minute-long YouTube clip 'Visible Uganda' by the Ugandan government on 14 April 2012 attracted until today less than 50,000 viewers (Maasilta and Haabisto, 2014, p. 466).
12 For example, Facebook in Arabic was introduced as late as 2009 (Tufekci and Wilson, 2012, p. 364).

References

Alterman, J. B. (2011) 'The revolution will not be tweeted', *The Washington Quarterly* 34(4), 103.
Audette, N. (2013) 'KONY2012: the new face of citizen engagement', *Exchange: The Journal of Public Diplomacy*: 4(1), Article 5. Available at: http://surface.syr.edu/exchange/vol4/iss1/5. Last accessed October 2015.
Bal, A. S., C. Archer-Brown, K. Robson and D. E. Hall (2013) 'Do good, goes bad, gets ugly: Kony 2012', *Journal of Public Affairs* 13(2), 202.
Brough, M. (2012) '"Fair Vanity": The visual culture of humanitarianism in the age of commodity activism', in R Mukherjee and S Banet-Wieser (eds),

Commodity Activism: Cultural Resistance in Neoliberal Times (pp. 174–194) New York: University Press.

Budish, R. H. (2012) 'Click to change: optimism despite online activism's unmet expectations', *Emory International Law Review* 26, 745.

Carroll, R. (2012) 'Kony 2012 Cover the Night fails to move from the internet to the streets', *Guardian*, 21 April. Available at: www.theguardian.com/world/2012/apr/21/kony-2012-campaign-uganda-warlord. Last accessed October 2015.

Chalk, S. (2012) 'Kony 2012: success or failure?', International Broadcasting Trust. Available at: www.ibt.org.uk/documents/reports/Kony-full.pdf Last accessed October 2015.

Clarke, K. M. (2012) 'Kony 2012, The ICC, and the problem with the peace-and-justice divide', *American Society of International Law Proceedings* 106, 309.

Cole, R. (2013), 'Africa's relationship with the International Criminal Court: more political than legal', *Melbourne Journal of International Law* 14, 670.

Curtis, P. (2012) 'Kony 2012: the reaction', *Guardian* 13 March 2012 (updated 20 May 2014). Available at: www.theguardian.com/politics/reality-check-with-polly-curtis/2012/mar/13/reality-check-kony-2012-reaction. Last accessed October 2015.

Curtis, P. and T. McCarthy (2012) 'Kony 2012: what's the real story?', *Guardian*, 8 March. Available at www.theguardian.com/politics/reality-check-with-polly-curtis/2012/mar/08/kony-2012-what-s-the-story. Last accessed October 2015.

Edmondson, L. (2012) 'Uganda is too sexy – reflections on Kony 2012', *The Drama Review* 56(3), 10.

Fairlie, M. (2011) 'The United States and the International Criminal Court Post-Bush: a beautiful courtship but an unlikely marriage', *Berkeley Journal of International Law* 29, 528.

Finnegan, A. C. (2013) 'Beneath Kony 2012: Americans aligning with arms and aiding others', *Africa Today* 59(3), 138.

Finnström, S. (2012) 'Kony 2012, military humanitarianism, and the magic of occult Economies', *Africa Spectrum* 2(3), 127.

Gladwell, M. (2010) 'Small change – why the revolution will not be tweeted',*Annals of Revolution* 4 (October). Available at: www.newyorker.com/magazine/2010/10/04/small-change-3. Last accessed October 2015.

Gregory, S. (2012) 'Kony 2012 through a prism of video advocacy practices and trends', *Journal of Human Rights Practice* 4(3), 463.

Harsin, H. (2013) 'WTF was Kony 2012? Consideration for Communication and Critical/Cultural Studies (CCCS)', *Communication and Critical/Cultural Studies* 10(2–3), 265.

Hill, S. (2010) 'Models of online activism and their implications for democracy and climate change', 18 April. Available at: www.fdsd.org/wordpress/wp-content/uploads/Online-activism-democracy-and-climate-change.pdf.   Last   accessed October 2015.

Holligan, A. (2012) 'Invisible Children's Kony campaign gets support of ICC prosecutor', BBC News, 8 March. Accessible at: www.bbc.co.uk/news/world-africa-17303179. Last accessed October 2015.

Jefferson, C. (2012) '"There's a rabid hunger to criticize": a "Kony 2012" creator defends the film', 10 March, *GOOD – A magazine for the global citizen*,

Available at: http://magazine.good.is/articles/a-kony-2012-creator-defends-the-film. Last accessed October 2015.

Jones, P. (2012) 'Kony 2012: Invisible Children prepares Cover the Night stunt amid criticism' *Guardian* 20 April. Available at: www.theguardian.com/world/2012/apr/20/kony-2012-cover-night-campaign. Last accessed October 2015.

Karlin, B. and R. A. Matthew (2012) 'Kony 2012 and the mediatization of child soldiers', *Peace Review: A Journal of Social Justice* 24(3), 255.

Lim, M. (2012) 'Clicks, cabs, and coffee houses: social media and oppositional movements in Egypt, 2004–2011', *Journal of Communication* 62, 231.

Maasilta, M. and C. Haavisto (2014) 'Listening to distant sufferers: the Kony 2012 campaign in Uganda and the International Media', *Forum for Development Studies* 14(3), 355.

McCarthy, T. (2012) 'Kony 2012 gets 70m hits in a week', *Guardian,* 9 March Available at: www.theguardian.com/world/2012/mar/09/kony2012-video-70m-hits. Last accessed October 2015.

Nothias, T. (2013) '"It's struck a chord we have never managed to strike": frames, perspectives and remediation strategies in the international news coverage of Kony2012', *Equid Novi African Journalism Studies* 34(1), 123.

Pew Research Centre (2012) 'The viral Kony 2012 video', 15 March. Available at: www.pewinternet.org/2012/03/15/the-viral-kony-2012-video/. Last accessed October 2015.

Schau, H. J. and M. C. Gilly (2003) 'We are what we post? Self-presentation in personal web space', *Journal of Consumer Research* 30(3) 30.

Thomas, E. F, C. McGarty, G. Lala, A. Stuart, L. J. Hall and A. Goodard (2015) 'Whatever happened to Kony2012? Understanding a global Internet phenomenon as an emergent social identity', *European Journal of Social Psychology* 45(3), 356.

Tufekci, Z. and C. Wilson (2012) 'Social media and the decision to participate in political protest: observations from Tahrir Square', *Journal of Communication,* 62, 363.

Von Engelhardt, J. and J. Jansz (2014) 'Challenging humanitarian communication: An empirical exploration of Kony 2012', *The International Communication Gazette* 76(6), 464.

5   *Matthew R. Smith*

A comparative analysis of the criminal and civil justice systems in England and Wales

Introduction

'Have you set off for the RCJ yet, Sir?' As I step off the East Coast 7 o'clock from Leeds, brief in one hand and Circuit Bag in the other, onto the sultry Platform 0 at London King's Cross, I promptly reply 'Yes' in anticipation of the next line of communication from my anxious clerk: 'Listing has just pulled your trial, Sir. No judges, apparently.'

And therein belies the great anomaly subsumed within both the civil and criminal justice systems in England and Wales: the ostensible and omnipresent immunity of Her Majesty's Court Service to the rule of law with a lip-service cover-up labelled 'access to justice' all in the purported attempt to save costs when, in reality, it is only serving to inflame them. For on countless occasions in my practice and those of many others, 'listing' will suddenly vacate a trial on the day or, if you are lucky, the afternoon before. Crown Court trials 'float on' and 'float off'. Access to justice is thereby suspended into an unknown vacuum without any proper judicial intervention, just a court official deciding there were too many balls to juggle on that particular day. The parties and their witnesses, who had opened all the doors asked of them to see justice in the flesh, having taken time off work, spent time and money getting to Court and spent months and years agonising over coming to Court and giving their evidence are simply told to come back on another day. The costs of this 'administrative decision' become ignored and glossed over. Counsel on a civil 'fast track' trial cannot recover his fees as Civil Procedure Rule (CPR) 45.37 only entitles Counsel to one fee. Counsel in the Crown Court trial recovers a miserly £100 – less than the minimum wage when preparation and waiting time are factored in. Like the parties, the lawyers simply have to swallow it.

The other great anomaly here is the fact that if the parties had sought to vacate this trial (for good or bad reasons), a formal application would need to have been made, attracting yet another Court fee, and the test employed by the Court would have been a very stringent one under CPR 3.1(2)(b) with the Court treating such a vacation as an 'order of last resort'.

As I contemplate what to do with my day now, another member of the Bar, whom I recognise from my days at the Criminal Bar, alights the same diesel-chugging carriage for which I had just paid £265 for the pleasure. But he alights a little further down the platform than I do. We exchange pleasantries and, anticipating his answer, I ask a series of 'tagged' questions:

> 'Going to the Court of Appeal, I bet?' 'CPS still paying First Class, I bet?' 'Appeal Sentence – just a bit more than the train fare on the Brief, I bet?' He answers all 3 questions in the affirmative and I remind myself why I ditched crime all those years ago, but dismay over the fact that the Government will still pay First Class train fares for trips to the Court of Appeal, yet not a proper fee for the actual work and anguish involved. As our paths depart, he mutters 'one of the only perks of the job left'. Alas, he is correct. I then recall the anecdote of a well known criminal hack of the Bar and of NEC about the fearsome Court of Appeal:
> 'Lad, if you can stomach a full English on the way down, you'll be right.'

But, as is the case for Her Majesty's Courts and Tribunals Service (HMCTS), there is no such service any more. In a purported effort to improve service and cost, the restaurant car and the full English breakfast is no more. Instead, a plastic cup of blistering coffee and a soggy microwaved bacon bap is the best that can be expected. The Great Hall of the Royal Courts of Justice (RCJ) is disappointed. It too serves the same for the same.

This chapter will demonstrate the unfortunate and harsh reality of the Government's strategy of budget reduction that seems to have escalated since the credit crunch of 2007. In its efforts to try to reduce the budget, justice is sacrificed over misguided and ill-thought-out policies. From small claims to rape trials and employment tribunals, the Government and HMCTS has become obsessed with saving costs. There is almost a perversion in this end. The hypocrisy is stark. The denial of justice is stark.

During my eighteen years at the independent Bar I have undertaken cases in most jurisdictions, ranging from ancillary relief and care proceedings in the Family Courts to burglaries and assaults in the Crown Court to neighbour disputes and fraud cases in the County and High Courts. One piece of legislation stands out to me as being of fundamental importance and significance. It has developed into a scapegoat and produced the state of our civil and criminal justice systems we have today. It was enacted at the start of my career and is something I have seen develop in all of those jurisdictions throughout my career. It is *The Civil Procedure Rules* 1998.

The Civil Procedure Rules 1998

This procedural code for civil litigation replaced the old County Court Rules that were seen as archaic and inefficient.

The new philosophy behind the rules was to save costs and make the Court system more efficient.

The buzz words were 'overriding objective' and 'proportionality'. This was the brainchild of Lord Wolf who had been appointed by the Lord Chancellor to reform and merge the RSC and the CCR. His report was entitled 'Access to Justice' and followed a two-and-a-half-year review of the system.

The original Part 1 of the CPR 1998 read as follows:

The overriding objective

1.1 (1) These Rules are a new procedural code with the overriding objective of enabling the court to deal with cases justly.

    (2) Dealing with a case justly includes, so far as is reasonably practicable –

      (a) ensuring that the parties are on an equal footing;

      (b) saving expense;

      (c) dealing with the case in ways which are proportionate –

        (i) to the amount of money involved;

        (ii) to the importance of the case;

        (iii) to the complexity of the issues; and

        (iv) the financial position of each party;

      (d) ensuring that it is dealt with expeditiously and fairly; and

      (e) allotting to it an appropriate share of the court's resources, while taking into account the need to allot resources to other cases.

This new philosophy and approach carried with it case management powers under Part 3. The Court was now empowered to actively manage cases without necessarily any involvement of the parties.

The new rules were welcomed and worked well initially. However, the advent of CFAs (no win, no fee) for personal injury litigation resulted in a tidal wave of claims (some genuine and some not) such that the Court system began to crack under the volume of work with which it was suddenly faced.

To make matters worse, the rules initially gave the trial judge a discretion with respect to the uplift on the CFA. That is to say a successful claimant's solicitor and counsel could have an increase in their fees to reflect the risk they were taking and the fact that if they lost they would receive nothing. Originally, the trial judge would assess the amount of the uplift in accordance with the risk undertaken. This worked well. However, somebody thought it appropriate to make the uplift a mandatory 100 per cent in all road traffic cases regardless of risks. This meant that in a case in which liability was admitted, for example, there would still be a 100 per cent uplift. This resulted in a further escalation of claims and the birth of 'accident management companies' all realising the cash cow that the Government had just rubber stamped.

After a good decade of this, the Government finally put an end to it with *The Jackson Reforms* in 2013. As well as abolishing the 100 per cent uplift and the recoverability of CFAs from the losing party, the CPR was tinkered with in mainly two respects. First of all, the overriding objective was amended to give 'proportionate cost' a firm front-row seat and, secondly, the concept of the Court controlling costs via 'costs budgeting' was made mandatory in most cases. While controlling costs inter partes is welcomed, the anomaly is the lack of any control on the Court's costs and its administration.

The current 'overriding objective' thus reads as follows:

The overriding objective

1.1 (1) These Rules are a new procedural code with the overriding objective of enabling the court to deal with cases justly *and at proportionate cost.*

   (2) Dealing with a case justly *and at proportionate cost* includes, so far as is practicable –
   (a) ensuring that the parties are on an equal footing;
   (b) saving expense;
   (c) dealing with the case in ways which are proportionate –
       (i) to the amount of money involved;
       (ii) to the importance of the case;
       (iii) to the complexity of the issues; and
       (iv) the financial position of each party;
   (d) ensuring that it is dealt with expeditiously and fairly; and
   (e) allotting to it an appropriate share of the court's resources, while taking into account the need to allot resources to other cases.
   (f) *enforcing compliance with rules, practice directions and orders.* (emphasis added)

This latter addition, compliance, was also echoed in a rewording of CPR 3.9 'Relief from Sanctions'. It was rightly felt that parties were being allowed to ignore court orders and simply apply for relief to rectify their errors which would therefore have a 'knock-on' effect on the administration of justice. This was a good idea. Unfortunately, the Court of Appeal has made a complete mess of it in two decisions that can only be described as being at complete odds with each other and a classic example of 'judicial gymnastics' in the extreme.

The first was *Mitchell v News Group Newspapers Ltd* [2013] EWCA Civ 1537. This was the 'plebgate' case concerning Andrew Mitchell MP, who sued News Group Newspapers for defamation. Under *The Jackson Reforms* CPR 3.13 was added that required parties to file and exchange costs budgets seven days before the Costs and Case Management Conference. The sanction for failing to comply with this rule is found in CPR 3.14, which provides that the party defaulting can only recover Court fees; that is, solicitor's and counsel's fees cannot be recovered.

Mr Mitchell's solicitors were late with their budget. The Court of Appeal approved the approach of the Judge at first instance and refused to grant Mr Mitchell's solicitors any relief from this sanction under CPR 3.9. This was the first time the Court of Appeal had before it a post-Jackson case so it took the opportunity to give some guidance to practitioners. This can be found at paragraphs 40–41 wherein it stated the following:

> 40. We hope that it may be useful to give some guidance as to how the new approach should be applied in practice. It will usually be appropriate to start by considering the nature of the non-compliance with the relevant rule, practice direction or court order. If this can properly be regarded as *trivial*, the court will usually grant relief provided that an application is made promptly. The principle 'de minimis non curat lex' (the law is not concerned with trivial things) applies here as it applies in most areas of the law. Thus, the court will usually grant relief if there has been no more than an insignificant failure to comply with an order: for example, where there has been a failure of form rather than substance; or where the party has narrowly missed the deadline imposed by the order, but has otherwise fully complied with its terms. We acknowledge that even the question of whether a default is insignificant may give rise to dispute and therefore to contested applications. But that possibility cannot be entirely excluded from any regime which does not impose rigid rules from which no departure, however minor, is permitted.

> 41. If the non-compliance cannot be characterised as trivial, then the burden is on the defaulting party to persuade the court to grant relief. The court will want to consider why the default occurred. If there is a *good reason* for it, the court will be likely to decide that relief should be granted.

The interpretation and effect of this guidance was one of opportunism and complete mayhem in the civil justice system for it resulted in all sorts of applications to strike out for non-compliance. For example, I attended a three-day trial at Central London County Court to be met with an application to strike out my defence because we had been two days late in filing our supplementary bundle. Thankfully, the Court took a pragmatic approach and the trial continued. However, some Courts embraced this guidance. For example, Bow County Court would vacate a trial if the trial bundle was not received on time and list it for a case management conference (CMC) instead. I had a case with an independent witness who was displeased about attending Court, but willing. The trial bundle was one day late. Neither party wished to take the point, but the Court vacated the trial and the independent witness, who had taken a day off work, refused to come back on the return date.

This mess was eventually resolved by the Court of Appeal in a conjoined appeal of *Denton & Ors v White Ltd & Ors, Decadent Vapours Ltd v Bevan & Ors and Utilise TDS Ltd v Davies & Ors* [2014] EWCA Civ 906. The Court of Appeal refused to acknowledge the problems of *Mitchell*, but instead stated it had been 'misunderstood' and that it 'remains substantially sound'. However, the new test they laid out is almost at a polar opposite to the test emanating from *Mitchell*. This is eminently obvious from a reading of paragraph 24 of *Denton* for the following 'restatement' is set out:

> We consider that the guidance given at paras 40 and 41 of Mitchell remains substantially sound. However, in view of the way in which it has been interpreted, we propose to restate the approach that should be applied in a little more detail. A judge should address an application for relief from sanctions in three stages. The first stage is to identify and assess the seriousness and significance of the 'failure to comply with any rule, practice direction of court order' which engages rule 3.9(1). If the breach is neither serious nor significant, the court is unlikely to need to spend much time on the second and third stages. The second stage is to consider why the default occurred. The third stage is to evaluate 'all the circumstances of the case, so as to enable [the court] to deal justly with the application including [factors (a) and (b)]'.

While this new test prevents the opportunistic and frivolous applications arising from *Mitchell*, its effect in practice is really to return things to pre-Jackson days i.e. most applications for relief are now being allowed on the basis it would be unfair not to rather than looking at the original zero-tolerance ethos of Jackson. Don't fix it if it isn't broken is the lesson here.

The concept of cost budgeting under *The Jackson Reforms* was available under 'costs-capping' orders under the original CPR 1998. However, it was never used, so the Government decided to make it more mandatory. The alleged reason: to control costs so that parties knew in advance their exposure. The real reason: to deter litigation in the courts and thereby reduce access to justice. This is because *The Jackson Reforms* brought with them another important change – the increase in the Small Claims Track limit to £10,000 from £5,000.

That is to say, any non-personal injury claim worth less than £10,000 must be commenced in the Small Claims Court, where, unlike the other civil courts, neither party has any costs exposure meaning that the winning party does not get its legal costs paid for by the losing party. The upshot is, therefore, that parties do not have legal representation unless they can afford it as even if they win they still have to pay their lawyer. Therefore, is that access to justice is severely curtailed. A debt of up to £10,000 is not 'small' in anyone's imagination and could be the difference between sink or swim for many small businesses.

To add further fuel to this raging fire, a further anomalous reform has just bitten. While *The Jackson Reforms* seek to control and lower the parties' costs (a good thing on the face of it), the Government seems to think it is immune from such philosophy as it has just enacted a fees reform such that for all claims over £10,000 the issue fee (i.e. the amount one pays the court to log one's case into their system and send out one's forms to the other side) is a crushing 5 per cent of the value of the claim. This is insurmountable for some people and small businesses. Access to justice is therefore denied and seems to be a concept only for the wealthy.

A further example is seen in the on-and-off push for mediation. This seems to be the flavour of the month every now and again. The purpose is obvious – if parties mediate (i.e. have their dispute 'mediated' by an independent mediator), the parties are not in Court, thus, in theory costs are saved. The problem with mediation, however, is that it is not right for the vast majority of cases. Parties who have spent a great deal of money on solicitors' letters to try to resolve their differences are unlikely to turn their minds to a mediator's unbinding views of their dispute. Unless the parties agree to be bound by the decision, then this course just wastes more of the parties' money.

The employment tribunals are another recent victim of the Government's strategy of deterrence. Originally brought in to redress the imbalance between employer and employee, the employment tribunal signalled an important vehicle for an employee who may have been summarily dismissed unfairly, without pay and any means in which to seek justice, by not charging, the employee was able to bring his grievance without expense. However, as from 29 July 2013, all claimants bringing an Employment Tribunal claim or lodging an appeal with the Employment Appeal Tribunal have been required to pay the applicable tribunal fees or make an application for a remission. This is the first time that fees have been applied for tribunal cases. The stated aim for introducing the tribunal fees is twofold:

1. To reduce the number of speculative or spurious claims from reaching tribunals. In previous years bringing (or threatening to bring) a case has

been used as a tactic to force employers to settle cases early. The introduction of fees is expected to greatly reduce the number of claims reaching tribunals. However, it is argued that fees will prevent many cases proceeding as claimants will be able to afford the fees.

2. To make the tribunal service pay for itself or at least reduce the cost of running the service.

Issue fees range around £400, whereas the actual hearing fees can be over £1,200.

The Government white paper entitled 'Employment Tribunal set to encourage mediation and arbitration' (first published in July 2012) was at least honest in this regard. To quote a passage:

> By introducing fees, people using employment tribunals will start to contribute a significant proportion of the £84m cost or running the system. The aim is to reduce the taxpayer subsidy of these tribunals by transferring some of the cost to those who use the service, while *protecting access to justice for all.* (Emphasis added)

And there we have the punchline again – 'access to justice': a phrase that seems to be rolled out every time the Government is preventing justice, as if we are all stupid and accept that just because we are told that access to justice is protected for all, somehow that is the truth and we should accept it.

The trade union Unison unsuccessfully challenged these fees in the case of *R (on application of Unison (No. 2) v Lord Chancellor & Equality & Human Rights Commission* [2014] EWHC 4198 (Admin). The High Court dismissed the case. Lord Justice Elias said that the imposition of fees to help pay for the service was 'plainly in principle' a legitimate aim designed to ensure users make a contribution to costs.

Lord Justice Foskett added that it was 'speculative' to suggest that a reduction in applications was due directly to the imposition of fees.

However, according to statics published in the Law Society Gazette on 17th December 2014, the number of claims dropped by 81 per cent to 6019 between January and March 2014, compared with the same quarter in 2013. In the last quarter of 2013 claims fell by 79 per cent, compared with the last quarter of 2012.

From my experience, I have seen how waiting rooms at employment tribunals that were jam packed a year ago with barely a seat or table to use are now deserted. The proof, here, is in the pudding.

The Family Procedure Rules 2010

The Family Courts were the second in line for the 'overriding objective' some ten years on from the the Woolf Reforms. As is seen below, The Family

Procedure Rules 2010 largely emanate The Civil Procedure Rules 1998 with the important proviso of 'welfare issues' being added – the cornerstone of The Children Act 1989.

The overriding objective

1.1 (1) These Rules are a new procedural code with the overriding objective of enabling the court to deal with cases justly, having regard to the welfare issues involved.

    (2) Dealing with a case justly includes, so far as is reasonably practicable –
       (a) ensuring that it is dealt with expeditiously and fairly;
       (b) dealing with the case in ways which are proportionate to the nature, importance and complexity of the issues;
       (c) ensuring that the parties are on an equal footing;
       (d) saving expense; and
       (e) allotting to it an appropriate share of the court's resources, while taking into account the need to allot resources to other cases.

The Family Law Bar Association has recently prepared a briefing paper on issues surrounding access to justice in the Family Court to explain how changes to civil legal aid under the Legal Aid, Sentencing and Punishment of Offenders Act 2012 (LASPO) are causing injustice to many children and their families.

The paper reads that the removal of legal aid for most private law family disputes and the lowering of the financial eligibility criteria have caused injustice to many families in the last two years. As a result of LASPO, 160,000 fewer family cases were funded in 2013–14 compared with the previous year. One of the consequences is that the number of cases in which neither party is represented has increased by 30 per cent across all Family Court cases.

Litigants in person who have no choice but to represent themselves inevitably struggle to present their cases. The treatment of vulnerable people in the Family Court is so poor that it has been described as 'shameful' by the President of the Family Division, Sir James Munby.

The efficient delivery of family justice intended by the creation of the single Family Court is under threat. Judges, magistrates and barristers have all provided evidence that delays in the Family Court have increased as a result of LASPO. The assertion of the Ministry of Justice that there is no evidence of delays is based on experimental and unreliable statistics.

As a result of these delays, children across the country are suffering damage to relationships with non-resident parents and some are losing contact altogether as parents give up on pursuing contact through court proceedings. Being denied access to legal help means many women are effectively trapped in abusive relationships thereby exposing themselves and their children to further harm.

Something I have observed from robing room conversations is how the overstretched local authority will try (or have no choice) and put costs before welfare. For example, a few years ago HMCTS increased the issue fee for care proceedings to the huge sum of £3,000. However, for a grandparent to make an application for residence, for example, the issue fee would amount to a small fraction of this. So rather than make the right application for a care order, the LA would support a grandparent in making an application for a residence order in order to save on the issue fee. The effect of this, of course, is that there would not automatically be a children's guardian as there would be in care proceedings. Accordingly, the rights of the child and all those involved and 'justice' are once again curtailed for the sake of saving money.

This raises another cost issue – the instruction and separate representation of a guardian in the first place. Guardians are expert witnesses. In private law proceedings (e.g. applications for contact) they are called CAFCASS (Children and Family Court Advisory Support Service) officers. They produce a report and are called by the Court to give evidence and are cross-examined by the parties. They are not legally represented. However, in care proceedings it is seen as necessary that they have legal representation in every case. Where there might be complicated cases or matters of conflict between a LA and a guardian, perhaps this can be justified, but in the average care case it is difficult to see such a justification: they can be called by the Court, they are professional people and experts. Thus, if costs are really at the forefront of our justice system then there is a simple reform that could shave thousands of pounds off the legal aid bill per annum.

If legal representation for Guardians was the exception rather than the norm this might also assist in the Government's strategy of 'the twenty-six-week rule'. That is to say that there is an expectation in every care case that the case will be concluded in twenty-six weeks. The alleged reason: it is in the child's best interests. The real reason: to save costs. While it is appreciated time is an important factor in care cases, the problem is, like the civil and criminal justice systems, that it becomes the main factor with the result that important factual, expert and procedural issues are ignored or glossed over in order that the twenty-six weeks are met.

The spanner in the works for the twenty-six-week rule, however, is the increasing number of litigants in person. While parents in care proceedings are automatically granted legal aid, grandparents, for example, are only granted legal aid if they pass a means and merits test. Very often grandparents do not pass this test with the result they do not get legal aid and therefore represent themselves. This, of course, means a care case takes longer with the result that the ill-thought-out twenty-six-week rule is unachievable.

The Criminal Procedure Rules

Last in line of the three jurisdictions of Civil, Family and Crime – The Criminal Procedure Rules 2014. Emulating The Civil Procedure Rules and The Family Procedure Rules, there is the scapegoat again – 'the overriding objective':

1.1 (1) The overriding objective of this new code is that criminal cases be dealt with justly.
    (2) Dealing with a criminal case justly includes –
        (a) acquitting the innocent and convicting the guilty;
        (b) dealing with the prosecution and the defence fairly;
        (c) recognising the rights of a defendant, particularly those under Article 6 of the European Convention on Human Rights;
        (d) respecting the interests of witnesses, victims and jurors and keeping them informed of the progress of the case;
        (e) dealing with the case efficiently and expeditiously;
        (f) ensuring that appropriate information is available to the court when bail and sentence are considered; and
        (g) dealing with the case in way that takes into account –
            (i) the gravity of the offence alleged;
            (ii) the complexity of what is in issue;
            (iii) the severity of the consequences for the defendant and others affected, and
            (iv) the needs of other cases.

Four further parts need to be quoted at this stage:

1.2   The court must further the overriding objective in particular when –
        (a) exercising any power given to it by legislation (including these Rules);
        (b) applying any practice direction; or
        (c) interpreting any rule or practice direction.
3.2 (1) The court must further the overriding objective by actively managing the case.
    (2) Active case management includes ...
        (e) ensuring that evidence, whether disputed or not, is presented in the shortest and clearest way;
3.5 (1) In fulfilling its duty under rule 3.2 the court may give any direction and take any step actively to manage a case unless that direction or step would be inconsistent with legislation, including these Rules.
    (2) In particular, the court may ...
        (b) give a direction on its own initiative or on application by a party;

3.11   In order to manage a trial or an appeal, the court ...

   (d) may limit –
        (i)   the examination, cross-examination or re-examination of a witness, and
        (ii) the duration of any stage of the hearing.

While mention is made of justice and human rights in this procedural code for criminal cases, it is CPR 3.2(2)(e) and 3.11 that are the mischief, for they give the Court the power to 'limit' the evidence. When somebody's liberty is at stake the fact that a Court can prevent a defendant from fully putting their case strikes at the heart of injustice and potentially renders their trial unfair.

This is also echoed, to an extent, by the introduction of section 28 of The Youth Justice and Criminal Evidence Act 1999. This allows a vulnerable witness or intimidated witness to pre-record their evidence before the trial. It was originally piloted in 2013 and was seen as a good thing for such witnesses. The devil, however, is in the detail and the pragmatic problems that have developed. For example, *The Guidance Note for section 28 ground rules hearings at the Crown Court in Kingston, Leeds and Liverpool* reads as follows:

Page 2, para. 4:
The hearing enables the court to ensure its process is adapted to enable the witness to give his or her best evidence whilst ensuring the defendant's right to a fair trial is not diminished.

Para. 11:
Topics of discussion at the hearing will include the length of cross examination and any restrictions on the advocate's usual duty to 'put the defence case'. As was made plain by the Vice President of the Court of Appeal Criminal Division in Regina v Lubemba and Pooley, advocates cannot insist upon any supposed right 'to put one's case' or previous inconsistent statements to a vulnerable witness. If there is a right to 'put one's case' it must be modified for young and vulnerable witnesses.

Page 3:
In a series of decisions the Court of Appeal has made it clear that there has to be a different and fresh approach to the cross examination of, in particular, children of tender years, and witnesses who are vulnerable as a result of mental incapacity. The following propositions have support in decisions on appeal:

'The reality of questioning children of tender years is that direct challenge that he or she is wrong or lying could lead to confusion and, worse, to capitulation which the child does not, in reality, accept.

... It is common, in the trial of an adult, to hear, once the nursery slopes of cross-examination have been skied, the assertion 'you were never punched or kicked, as you have suggested, were you?

It was precisely that approach which the Court is anxious to avoid. Such an approach risks confusion in the minds of the witness whose evidence was bound to take centre stage, and it is difficult to see how it can be helpful. We struggle to understand how the defendant's right to a fair trial was in any way compromised simply because Mr X was not allowed to ask the question 'Simon did not punch you in the way you suggest?'

... It is particularly important in the case of a child witness to keep a question short and simple, and even more important than it is with an adult witness to avoid questions which are rolled up and contain, inadvertently two or three questions at once. It is generally recognised that, particularly with child witnesses, short and untagged questions are best at eliciting the evidence. By untagged we mean questions that do not contain a statement of the answer which is sought. That said, when it comes to directly contradicting a particular statement and inviting the witness to face a directly contradictory suggestion, it may often be difficult to examine otherwise.

Page 7: contradictory –
... Tag questions must be avoided...eg 'John didn't touch you did he?' The question should be 'Did John touch you?'
... Suggestions that the child is confused or lying are likely to impact on concentration and accuracy

Page 8:
The directions that I have given to Mr X in this case are that he can and should ask any question to which he actually wants answers, but he should not involve himself in any cross-examination of the witness by challenging her in a difficult way. In this case the defendant has already set out in some detail what his defence is. It is not a question of putting it to a witness and challenging her about it, so you won't hear the traditional form of cross-examination. I thought you should all know that from the outset.

The upshot of the above is that in a rape trial, for example, the vulnerable witness complainant will have given their evidence via a video-recording weeks before the actual Crown Court trial. They will have been asked only a few questions that will have been approved by the Court beforehand. The defence counsel, in closing, can make great play of this. The jury will not have seen the complainant in the flesh. The defendant might be acquitted when otherwise they might not.

Even in cases that do not involve such witnesses, the Crown Court is curtailing questions and thereby preventing a party from fully putting its case.

However, there is a rumour that 'the section 28 pilot' may be shelved – not on merits, but on costs.

Another problem for 'access to justice' in the Criminal Courts is the availability of quality advocates. Over ten years ago saw the introduction of higher rights of audience for solicitors and the birth of 'solicitor advocates' or 'HCAs' (higher court advocates) as they have become known. They were supposed to open the courtroom doors to the forces of the marketplace with competition and consumer choice. Instead, however, solicitors continue to have virtually uncontested access to individuals who have been arrested and detained at the police station. Thus, a client can journey through the system from arrest to charge, to trial, to conviction and to sentence without a barrister even being made aware of the existence of their case. This is not competition, it is a cartel.

Access to justice is thereby denied, yet again.

In an attempt to give some parity, 'Direct Access' was invented in order to allow clients to go direct to a barrister without the usual intermediary of a solicitor. The problem with this, however, is that a barrister is a sole trader and can only be in one place at one time. Thus, in order to be effective in the criminal justice system, a barrister would have to employ a large number of staff to attend on police stations and general administration. Effectively, becoming more of a solicitor's firm rather than an independent barrister specialising in advocacy of the highest level.

Some say a single merged profession is therefore the answer. There would be little more damaging to the administration of justice. The independent Bar is an outstanding legal asset, a dynamic knowledge of excellence that will fall by the wayside should professionals be forced into 'jack-of-all-trade' roles.

The American legal system provides for 'advocates' working a case from cradle to grave. It is no accident that their courtrooms are as polarised as their politics, the standard of advocacy and case preparation ranges from the sublime to the punishingly absurd. Take the South African system as well and the recent Pistorius trial – it might be said that the advocates and the judge were pedestrian to say the least.

Solicitors are very necessary intermediaries and their profession should be held in great esteem. They carry out work that a Crown Court advocate could not do – attending police stations at 2 a.m. to represent a client, interviewing witnesses and organising exhibits. Advocacy is greater than the words you say, and good-quality advocacy requires time and dedication.

There are many eminently qualified solicitor advocates, but if advocacy is their calling they should join the Bar. Many solicitors have crossed the divide and many Barristers have taken the reverse leap.

According to a recent report on criminal advocacy by Sir Bill Jeffrey, there has been 'a marked shift' in the distribution of advocacy work in the Crown Court away from the Bar. Between 2005/06 (the time of Lord Carter of Cole's review of publicly funded legal services) and 2012/13, the percentage of publicly funded cases in which the defence was conducted by a solicitor advocate rose from 4 per cent to 24 per cent of contested trials, and from 6 per cent to 40 per cent of guilty pleas.

The most recent Solicitors Regulatory Authority (SRA) statistics show 6,426 of the 129,552 practising solicitors in England and Wales are solicitor advocates. By comparison, there are more than 15,000 practising barristers.

Another problem for the criminal justice system is the charge rate. Ask any criminal lawyer worth their salt, and they will agree – the CPS are not prosecuting as much as they did and they should, as a result of cuts in spending. The two-stage test of (1) reasonable prospects of a conviction and (2) Public interest seems to have been interpreted to mean guaranteed conviction. It all seems to be about conviction rates and costs. A 'no comment' interview is apparently a decisive factor in some decisions to prosecute on the misguided basis that the CPS take the view there is less evidence in which to secure the conviction. Justice is therefore denied ab initio.

Magna Carta

Magna Carta, agreed to by King John on 15 June 1215, was the triumphant achievement of rebellious barons. It has become a foundation stone not just for the criminal and civil justice systems in England and Wales, but for many other countries too. That profound influence is particularly expressed in clauses 39 and 40 of Magna Carta which set out two fundamental principles: the rule of law and access to justice:

> No free man shall be taken or imprisoned or disseised or outlawed or exiled or in any way ruined, nor will we go or send against him, except by lawful judgment of his peers or by the law of the land.

> To no one will we sell, to no one will we deny or delay right or justice.

My original conclusion here was going to be the fact that although court fees are applicable in civil and family, they are not in crime. Magna Carta is at least preserved for criminal cases where somebody's liberty is at stake. However, following some guidelines that were slipped into legislation in the final days of the last Parliament, the new criminal court charges were laid as a statutory instrument enabled by a clause of The Criminal Justice and Courts Act 2015. From 13 April 2015, any defendant in the magistrates, Crown Court and Court of Appeal has been liable for this new charge. Justice is plainly being sold, therefore, and Magna Carta has plainly been breached.

The new charge applies to any defendant who pleads guilty or is convicted of a criminal offence. They will be ordered to pay 'the criminal courts charge'. The amount of the charge varies depending whether there is a plea or a trial. The seriousness of the offence and the means of the defendant are irrelevant. The philosophy behind this is the purported belief that adult offenders who 'use' the criminal courts should pay towards the cost of running them. This, of course, is a nonsense – defendants have no choice, unlike litigants in civil and family cases.

The actual charges are set out in The Prosecution of Offences Act 1985 (Criminal Courts Charge) Regulations 2015. Some examples are as follows:

- Conviction in after Crown Court Trial: £1200
- Guilty plea in Crown Court: £900
- Dismissal in appeal to Crown Court: £150
- Dismissal of appeal to the Court of Appeal: £200
- Conviction in the Magistrates Court: £1,000

The charges are collected in the same way as a fine.

These changes have incurred much criticism including the encouragement of innocent people to plead guilty and the fact that they were originally supposed to be capped at £600, but instead have doubled via a back-door statutory instrument, thereby avoiding any proper scrutiny, debate or challenge.

This latest money-making vehicle of the 'Justice System' in England and Wales is just that and represents, yet again, a willingness to sacrifice 'access to justice' over the desire to reduce the deficit.

Reforms

A recent report by a working group of the independent Civil Justice Council (CJC) calls for a dedicated state-run 'Online Court' to operate alongside the traditional court system. The report offers a fresh approach to access to justice. Rather than streamline the existing court system and focus exclusively on dispute resolution, the report recommends a three-tier online court that turns the existing format on its head by focusing on dispute avoidance and dispute containment as well as on dispute resolution.

In the Working Group's model, the route taken by those seeking redress for a problem or grievance is via three stages, although the dispute may be resolved at any of them:

Tier 1 – Dispute avoidance: online evaluation of the problem with the support of interactive aids and information services. This will help people diagnose their issues and identify the best way of resolving them.

Tier 2 – Dispute containment: online facilitation. Trained, experienced facilitators bring an objective eye to the problem and try to help the parties reach agreement on resolving the issue.

Tier 3 – Dispute resolution: online judges. Professional judges will decide suitable cases online, largely on the basis of papers received electronically, but with an option of telephone hearings. The decisions would be as binding and enforceable as court rulings.

An excellent idea. Making it binding is what is needed. Mediation is not binding, hence the failings of it.

The working group also looked at policy and legal issues arising from an online court – such as whether it offers a fair hearing process, and whether it excludes people with no easy access to technology. However, the report also reflects on the realities of the situation – that people are voting with their mice and conducting online transactions and questions whether the court systems are responding sufficiently to this. The report suggests the first phase would be progressed in 2015–16 with an online court system pilot, ahead of an anticipated full roll-out in 2017. It is also understood that the old-style 'Registrars' may be redeployed to take up some of this work – another good idea – especially if it is farmed out to lawyers who are specialists in the particular area of the case. Counsel, for example, could be sent the papers like they would ordinarily and asked to provide an opinion, or judgment, on the same – efficient and fair.

This is to be welcomed. However, the ethos of 'Courts know best' needs to change too. Choice is key for 'consumers' of the Criminal and Civil Justice systems. There is choice in education and in health care, so why not in the Court system?

If you get rid of proportionality, then you can have a choice; a bronze, silver and gold system, for example, with gold for a full hearing, bronze for an online paper determination and silver for something in between. The parties decide which one is applicable. As long as specialist judges are allocated and as long as certain cases have to be gold cases, access to justice could be greatly improved. (see also the report of Briggs LJ.)

Another potential reform relates to the production of lawyers themselves. The bedrock of our justice system has to be quality lawyers – whether it is judges, barristers or solicitors. The birthplaces for such people are university and Bar/law school. The introduction of tuition fees to universities coupled with the high fees for Bar/law school are prohibitive for many people. The pool of good-quality lawyers is ever decreasing. Access to justice is curtailed. There is little justification for such high fees. Such institutions need to become more efficient and provide value for money. Making such courses shorter and therefore cheaper is perhaps one solution.

A level playing field for solicitors and barristers should also be sought. This could include the mandatory requirement that all advocates of the Crown Court and above have the same training and qualifications. This would certainly sort out the wheat from the chaff.

Conclusion

As I arrive back into Chambers from London the tannoy chimes: 'Can you take a call from the pupil, Sir?' I pick up the phone to be met with the anxious words of the pupil who tells me that a Judge of the Crown Court has decided to turn a simple 'mention to fix' a trial date into a trial. The pupil, who just had the trial availability of his pupil master with him, had been given half an hour to read over 1,000 pages of documents. He wondered what he should do. I told him that he must tell the Judge that he is not in a position to proceed (i.e. he is professionally embarrassed). As it turned out, the case did not proceed for other reasons, but therein lies another example of justice being denied in the misguided aim of disposal. For I have no doubt that the Judge wanted the case off his bench so another successful statistic could be created. Keeping cases in the system is not cost-effective for HMCTS.

I conclude this chapter with one simple message: justice requires time, consideration and skill. The obsession of rattling through cases and saving costs is misguided, unjust and perverse. Lawyers are professionals who spend years studying and training and should be afforded proper time and remuneration for their skill and dedication. Equally, parties have spent time, money and turmoil in striving to have their day in Court. Sadly, Government cuts in education and the legal system mean that lawyers and justice is becoming a luxury only for the wealthy. Access to justice is constrained in choice and personal financial circumstances and is now hijacked by austerity measures.

All that being said, England and Wales still have one of the greatest and best criminal and civil justice systems in the world, which must be cherished and preserved. The saving of costs and court time is not the right solution.

I spy 7 o'clock as the bell tower of the old assizes courthouse of Leeds strikes its bells. I endorse my brief and decide that it is time for Louis to meet Julieta.

Statutes

The Children Act 1989
The Civil Procedure Rules 1998
The Youth Justice and Criminal Evidence Act 1999
The Family Procedure Rules 2010
Sentencing and Punishment of Offenders Act 2012
The Criminal Justice and Courts Act 2015
The Prosecution of Offences Act 1985 (Criminal Courts Charge) Regulations 2015

Beliefs about the European Court of Human Rights in the United Kingdom Parliament

Introduction

There is widespread and growing mistrust of the European Court of Human Rights (ECtHR) in the United Kingdom (UK). Recent high-profile judgments against the UK on issues such as the disfranchisement of offenders in prison (*Hirst v the United Kingdom (no. 2)*, 2005) and the irreducibility of 'whole life orders' imposed on prisoners (*Vinter and Others v the United Kingdom*, 2013) have led senior politicians to claim that the ECtHR has 'discredited' and 'distorted' the concept of human rights (David Cameron MP, quoted in BBC News, 2012) in ways that would have the founders of the European Convention on Human Rights (ECHR) 'turning in their graves' (Chris Grayling MP, quoted in Watt and Travis, 2013). This sentiment has found popular support as shown, for example, by 39 per cent of respondents in a survey of UK adults believing that the ECtHR was most responsible for the delay in deporting Abu Qatada (often described as a 'radical Muslim cleric') from the UK (Ipsos MORI, 2012), and a survey by YouGov (2014) showing that 41 per cent of adults favour the withdrawal of the UK from the ECHR. Within this context, the UK used its chairmanship of the Committee of Ministers of the Council of Europe to attempt to limit, with partial success, the scope and function of the ECtHR (European Court of Human Rights, 2012). Since then, the UK Conservative Party (2014) has gone on to propose fundamental changes to the UK's relationship with the ECtHR (which include making ECtHR judgments 'advisory' rather than 'binding') and suggested that if such changes are not agreed by the Council of Europe then a Conservative government would withdraw the UK from the ECHR.

In response to what can be seen as the progressive 'folk deviling' of the ECtHR in the UK (Cohen, 2002; Johnson, 2014), the aim of this chapter is to explore how beliefs about the ECtHR are created and sustained. To achieve this aim, I focus attention on beliefs about the ECtHR that are expressed by members of the UK Parliament (MPs in the House of Commons, and Lords Spiritual and Temporal in the House of Lords). Through an analysis of parliamentary debates, I examine how parliamentarians discursively represent their beliefs about the ECtHR and how these beliefs come to achieve degrees of collective acceptance among MPs and Lords. My primary aim is not to determine whether expressions of belief about the ECtHR are 'true' – although an assessment of the veracity of claims inevitably informs my analysis – but to examine which beliefs are most often expressed and accepted by parliamentarians. Offering an analysis of parliamentary debates is based on the premise that discourse in Parliament has an influence on 'popular' public perceptions and beliefs. While the beliefs of UK citizens about the ECtHR cannot be seen to be influenced in any simple way by discourse in the Westminster Parliament, it is well recognised that parliamentary debates serve as important platforms from which public opinion on key social issues is both shaped and reflected (Epstein et al., 2000). While parliamentary debate is not hermetic and is itself influenced by multiple and competing external interests (from various government departments, lobby groups, commercial interests and private citizens), Parliament, as the theatre of the state (Kyle, 2012), is a key social site from which authoritative ideas are expressed and conveyed. In this sense, as van der Valk argues, 'Parliament is the medium par excellence by which political discourse, via the media, including the televising of parliamentary debates, reaches and influences the public' (2003, p. 316). Therefore, although positivistic claims about a causal relationship between parliamentary debate and broader popular beliefs should be viewed with suspicion, it is incontrovertible that parliamentary discourse influences public opinion to some extent.

The analysis contained in this chapter is of parliamentary debates relating to the enactment of one Act of Parliament: the Marriage (Same Sex Couples) Act 2013. The analysis is divided into three sections, which each consider an aspect of how the ECtHR is represented in parliamentary debates. The first section examines how parliamentarians represent the ECtHR as a source of 'risk' for individuals in the UK and to the sovereignty of the nation as a whole. The second section considers how parliamentarians represent ECtHR jurisprudence and its implications for legislation enacted by Parliament. Finally, the third section assesses the ways in which parliamentarians seek to discredit the ECtHR by representing it as a 'biased' institution. Across all three sections, the analysis demonstrates how parliamentarians articulate beliefs about the ECtHR in order to realise particular legislative ambitions. While many of these ambitions are ultimately unsuccessful, the analysis shows the extent to which expressions of belief about the ECtHR have become common in parliamentary debate and, as a result, how Parliament provides an important platform from which to disseminate beliefs about the ECtHR to a wider public audience.

Representing the ECtHR as a 'risk'

The passage of the Marriage (Same Sex Couples) Act 2013 (MSSCA), which extended marriage to same-sex couples in England and Wales, generated a significant amount of opposition. Much of this opposition was from individuals and organisations opposed to same-sex marriage on religious grounds. As a result of this, when the bill was introduced in Parliament it included extensive provisions designed to ensure that religious organisations that solemnise the marriages of different-sex couples could not be compelled to solemnise the marriages of same-sex couples. The Government described these provisions as a 'quadruple lock' designed to promote 'religious freedom' (Maria Miller MP, HC Debate, 5 February 2013, c.129). The four 'locks' included in the MSSCA ensure that: solemnising same-sex marriage in places of worship or in another place according to religious rites or usages requires a religious organisation to 'opt-in'; no person or religious organisation can be compelled by any means to undertake an 'opt-in activity' or to carry out, attend or take part in solemnising the marriage of a same-sex couple according to religious rites or usages; any person or religious organisation that does not conduct, consent to or otherwise participate in a marriage in a place of worship or in another place according to religious rites or usages, for the reason that it is the marriage of a same-sex couple, does not contravene anti-discrimination law relating to the provision of services and the exercise of public functions; and the Church of England and Church in Wales are unable to opt-in to solemnising same-sex marriage in the same way as other religious organisations (for a full discussion of these provisions, see: Johnson and Vanderbeck, 2014, pp. 136–140).

Parliamentarians opposed to the enactment of the MSSCA focused their opposition almost entirely on what they claimed to be the inadequateness of the religious protections. One of the key ways in which parliamentarians sought to demonstrate this inadequateness was to argue that there was significant potential for the religious protections to be 'overturned' in the ECtHR. A much-repeated assertion was that same-sex couples would make complaints to the ECtHR about religious organisations that refused to solemnise their marriages and that this would result in adverse judgments against the UK. As a consequence, it was argued, religious organisations (and the individuals in them) would be compelled to solemnise the marriages of same-sex couples. At the time the MSSCA was debated, the ECtHR had never upheld a complaint made by a same-sex couple about their inability to marry or enter into any alternative form of legal partnership. In respect of Article 12 of the ECHR, which guarantees men and women of marriageable age the right to marry and to found a family, the ECtHR had explicitly stated that this provision 'does not impose an obligation on [a] Government to grant a same-sex couple ... access to marriage' (*Schalk and Kopf v Austria*, 2010, § 63). Furthermore, the ECtHR had never communicated any complaint by a same-sex couple relating to alleged discrimination by a religious organisation that refused to register a partnership or solemnise a marriage. Nevertheless, parliamentarians repeatedly expressed the belief that a complaint by a same-sex couple about the religious protections in the MSSCA would succeed in the ECtHR and, therefore, that this posed a substantial 'risk' to religious freedom.

From the outset, the government sought to challenge the belief that the ECtHR posed a risk to the religious protections contained in the MSSCA. For example, at second reading of the bill in the House of Commons, Maria Miller MP stated:

> There has been much discussion about the powers of the European Court of Human Rights, but I believe that its case law is clear: the question of whether – and if so, how – to allow same-sex marriage must be left to individual states to decide for themselves ... The belief that the Court would order the UK to require religious organisations to marry same-sex couples in contravention of their religious doctrine relies on a combination of three highly improbable conclusions. The first is that the Court would need to go against its own clear precedent that countries have wide discretion in the matter of same-sex marriage. The second is that the Court would need to decide that the interests of a same-sex couple who wanted a particular religious organisation to marry them outweighed the rights and beliefs of an entire faith and its congregation as a whole. The third is that the Court would need to discount the importance of article 9 of its own convention, which guarantees freedom of thought, conscience and religion. That would be rewriting the rules not just for one religious organisation in England and Wales, but for all religious organisations in all 47 states of the Council of Europe. I believe that such an outcome is inconceivable (HC Debate, 5 February 2013, c.131).

The key point of Miller's argument was to assert her belief that it was 'inconceivable' that a complaint to the ECtHR by a same-sex couple about a religious organisation refusing to solemnise same-sex marriage would succeed. Yvette Cooper MP echoed Miller's belief, arguing that 'it is inconceivable that the European Court would tell a Church or faith group to hold same-sex weddings' (HC Debate, 5 February 2013, c.139).

Despite these strong expressions of belief about the robustness of the religious protections, parliamentarians continued to express the view that the ECtHR did pose a risk to the 'locks' in the MSSCA. However, belief about the extent of the risk posed by the ECtHR differed among MPs and

Lords. For example, some parliamentarians believed with certainty that a complaint about the religious protections contained in the MSSCA would be made to the ECtHR but that there was a reasonable prospect of the legislation withstanding such a challenge. Lord Faulks, for instance, argued that although 'no Government can legislate in complete certainty that a Bill will survive any legal challenge', and '[i]t is almost certain that some litigation will be generated by these provisions', that '[t]he parliamentary draftsmen, by their so-called quadruple lock, seem to have skilfully ensured that the Bill is as Strasbourg-proof as it reasonably can be' (HL Debate, 4 June 2013, c.1067). Other parliamentarians – particularly those who voted against the MSSCA – expressed a different belief about the extent of the risk. For instance, Tony Baldry MP (Second Church Estates Commissioner) argued that 'there is an inevitable degree of risk in all this, given that it would ultimately be for the courts, and in particular the Strasbourg court, to decide whether provisions in the legislation are compatible with the European convention on human rights' and although '[t]he Government believe that this is a risk worth taking', '[t]he Church of England does not' (HC Debate, 5 February 2013, c.144).

Many parliamentarians, who shared Baldry's view that the religious protections in the MSSCA were at risk from successful litigation in the ECtHR by same-sex couples, offered an interpretation of existing ECtHR jurisprudence to support their beliefs. Jim Shannon MP, for example, argued as follows:

> The Minister [Maria Miller MP] has claimed that the quadruple lock will ensure that Europe cannot change. She and everyone else in this House knows that … decisions have been made in Europe that overturned legislation in this country. I have five examples, but I will give only one, because time is against me: Islington council sacked registrar Lillian Ladele for requesting an accommodation of her conscientious objection to same-sex civil partnership, and the European Court confirmed that a public authority could force employees to act against their beliefs on marriage and sack any who resist. That demonstrates that a quadruple lock and any other kind of lock will fall down when it comes to the European Court. (HC Debate, 5 February 2013, c.165–166)

The evidence offered by Shannon, to support his belief that the religious protections in the MSSCA would 'fall down' in the ECtHR, was the failure of the complaint to the ECtHR by Lillian Ladele. Ms Ladele had complained to the ECtHR about being compelled by the local authority for whom she worked to carry out duties associated with her role as a (same-sex) civil partnership registrar, despite her objection to doing so on the grounds that 'same-sex civil partnerships are contrary to God's law' (*Eweida and Others v the United Kingdom*, 2013, § 23). Citing the failure of this complaint in the context of a debate about the religious protections in the MSSCA can be regarded as problematic because Ms Ladele, as a civil partnership registrar, was not involved in performing any religious ceremony or function – since her duties involved carrying out a purely secular function on behalf of a public authority – and Parliament had not enacted any legislation to enable or allow her to refuse to register civil partnerships on the grounds of a religious objection. In this sense, neither Ms Ladele's complaint nor the judgment of the ECtHR are relevant to a consideration of the extent to which religious organisations, and those working in them, are protected from being compelled to solemnise the marriage of a same-sex couple. Shannon's reliance on the ECtHR's judgment in *Eweida and Others v the United Kingdom* to assert the general claim that 'everyone ... knows that ... decisions have been made in Europe that overturned legislation in this country' is therefore problematic because the judgment did not require any change to domestic legislation.

A strong belief that existing ECtHR jurisprudence made religious organisations and individuals vulnerable to litigious same-sex couples was present throughout the MSSCA debates despite the fact that, as I outlined above, the ECtHR had never communicated (let alone upheld) a complaint by a same-sex couple about a religious organisation refusing to register or solemnise a partnership. Such a belief underpinned assertions by MPs that '[t]he matter could be taken to the European Court. Indeed, ... it will be taken to the Court (Graham Brady MP, HC Debate, 5 February 2013, c.172), and that the MSSCA 'is a Pandora's box of endless litigation, offering division in society and setting one group against another. For that reason and for community cohesion, we must resist it' (Stewart Jackson MP, HC Debate, 5 February 2013, c.201). Similarly, in the Lords, while the Archbishop of Canterbury (Justin Welby) – who strongly opposed the MSSCA – expressed the lukewarm belief that the religious protections in the legislation 'may have *some chance* of withstanding legal scrutiny in Europe' (HL Debate, 3 June 2013, c.953, emphasis added), a more common sentiment expressed by their lordships was that they did not 'believe that the protections promised to the religious organisations are valid' (Lord McAvoy, HL Debate, 3 June 2013, c.1006). This strong belief underpinned the repeated dismissal by Lords of reassurances offered by government ministers about the robustness of the religious protections in the MSSCA. For example:

> Government assurances that their lawyers see little likelihood of European human rights legislation being used to force people to act against their consciences inspire little confidence ... It is in reality a measure that could well force many with sincerely held religious and ethical beliefs to either compromise those beliefs or lose their jobs. (Lord Singh of Wimbledon, HL Debate, 3 June 2013, c.1009)

The MSSCA debates therefore demonstrate a widely held belief among legislators that the ECtHR poses a significant risk to people of faith in the UK.

(Mis)representing ECtHR jurisprudence

One of the ways in which parliamentarians attempted to legitimise their beliefs about the ECtHR during the MSSCA debates was through recourse to claims about ECtHR jurisprudence. However, when making such claims, many MPs and Lords frequently represented ECtHR decisions and judgments in ways that might be regarded as inaccurate or misleading. It is not possible to infer from an analysis of Hansard why parliamentarians represent ECtHR jurisprudence in ways that might be regarded as erroneous – in terms of whether, for instance, such representations are accidental (being the result of an ill-informed understanding of ECtHR jurisprudence) or intended to be deliberately misleading – but it is possible to find many examples that raise questions about the veracity of claims made about the ECtHR in Parliament. I provide two examples below, one from the House of Commons and one from the House of Lords.

(Mis)representing the ECtHR in the House of Commons
The first example of how parliamentarians could be seen to misrepresent ECtHR jurisprudence is taken from a debate in the House of Commons Public Bill Committee that considered the MSSCA. It concerns a probing amendment tabled by Kate Green MP to one of the key provisions in the MSSCA that provides individuals and organisations with protection from being compelled to solemnise a marriage of a same-sex couple. The provision in question is contained in S.2(2) of the MSSCA which, when the bill was introduced, provided that
A person may not be compelled –

- (a)   to conduct a relevant marriage,
- (b)   to be present at, carry out, or otherwise participate in, a relevant marriage, or
- (c)   to consent to a relevant marriage being conducted,

where the reason for the person not doing that thing is that the relevant marriage concerns a same sex couple.

Green's proposed amendment, which was eventually withdrawn, would have inserted additional words into the first line of this section to make it read '[a] person may not be compelled by a couple who wish to be married' (HC Committee, 28 February 2013, c.259). The purpose of the amendment was to determine whether S.2(2) of the MSSCA – which provides protection for a person (which also includes a religious organisation) who does not want to conduct, participate in or consent to a 'relevant marriage' (marriage in a place of worship or in another place according to religious rites or usages) – would allow individuals in a religious organisation to refuse to solemnise same-sex marriages if their organisation decided to 'opt-in' to do so. As Green explained, the amendment was designed to consider whether 'the intention is that [individual] ministers should be able to refuse to conduct same-sex marriages even though their overall religious body has decided that it wishes to conduct them' (HC Committee, 28 February 2013, c.260). The government minister in the Committee, Hugh Robertson MP, stated that the amendment was unnecessary because '[i]f the religious organisation governing [a] minister's church were to opt in to same-sex marriages and he were to have an objection to doing them, he would absolutely be protected' (HC Committee, 28 February 2013, c.278). Robertson's explanation could be accepted as a reasonable and accurate interpretation of S.2(2) MSSCA given that the provision was designed to protect individuals who do not want to participate in religious marriage ceremonies and, furthermore, is distinct from a separate provision protecting faith groups from being compelled to opt-in to same-sex marriage at the organisational level (S.2(1) MSSCA).

However, some MPs – particularly those opposed to the MSSCA more generally – took a different view to Robertson's. David Burrowes MP, for example, stated that Green's proposed amendment was helpful because it 'exposes a clear chink in the armour – a flaw in the Government's [commitment to protecting] "religious liberty"' (HC Committee, 28 February 2013, c.267). Burrowes went on to explain as follows:

> It is important to look at the serious prospect that legislating for same-sex marriage and opt-ins for religious organisations, which is at the heart of [the] amendment ..., could lead to an incursion on the religious freedom of individual ministers. Strasbourg would offer no remedy for that. (HC Committee, 28 February 2013, c.267)

The essence of Burrowes's argument was that the effect of the adoption of Green's amendment would be to 'expose individual clergy ... to legally permissible sanctions from their religious organisations ... for refusing to solemnise same-sex marriages' (HC Committee, 28 February 2013, c.267). Although Burrowes also argued that the amendment 'exposed a contradiction' in the MSSCA, because 'it admits that the Bill's quadruple locks and the Equality Act amendment cannot truly protect individual conscientious objectors' (HC Committee, 28 February 2013, c.268), his key concern was that Green's amendment would, as Jim Shannon MP put it, 'have the effect of narrowing the already too narrow protections of the quadruple lock that the Government want to put in place' (HC Committee, 28 February

2013, c.272). A key aspect of Burrowes's argument was the claim that, if the amendment was adopted, the ECtHR would offer 'no legal relief against sanctions imposed by religion on individual ministers who want to opt out' (HC Committee, 28 February 2013, c.268).

To support his claim about the ECtHR, Burrowes invoked the admissibility decision of the former European Commission of Human Rights (EComHR) in *Finska församlingen i Stockholm and Teuvo Hautaniemi v Sweden* (1996). The case concerned a Finnish parish of the Church of Sweden in Stockholm and the chairman of its board who complained about a prohibition of the use of the liturgy of the Finnish Evangelical-Lutheran Church. The prohibition was a consequence of a decision by the Assembly of the Church of Sweden (which is an Evangelical-Lutheran congregation) to adopt a Finnish translation of its liturgy and to revoke an earlier decision to allow the use of the liturgy of the Finnish Evangelical-Lutheran Church in the applicant parish. The adoption of the Finnish translation by the Church of Sweden had been 'considered necessary in view of the large number of Finnish-speaking members of the Church of Sweden and was aimed at harmonising the liturgy used in the Finnish-speaking parishes in the country' (*Finska församlingen i Stockholm and Teuvo Hautaniemi v Sweden*, 1996: 95). The applicants complained, inter alia, that the prohibition of the use of the Finnish Evangelical-Lutheran Church liturgy violated Article 9 of the ECHR (freedom of thought, conscience and religion) because a large majority of the parish members wished to use it and, furthermore, that the prohibition bared visiting Finnish priests from conducting services. The EComHR reached the decision that 'the respondent State cannot be held responsible for the alleged violation of the applicants' freedom of religion resulting from the decision of the Church Assembly', because the state played no part in that decision, and '[t]here has thus been no state interference with that freedom' (*Finska församlingen i Stockholm and Teuvo Hautaniemi v Sweden*, 1996: 97). The Commission further decided that the state had not failed to meet any positive obligation required by Article 9 of the ECHR to protect the applicants' freedom of religion and their freedom to manifest their religion in worship for the following reasons:

> It has not been established that the applicant parish would be prevented from leaving the Church of Sweden if it were unable to accept the liturgy of that Church. Nor can the Commission find any substantiation of the applicants' assertion that the prohibition against the use of the liturgy of the Finnish Church effectively bars Finnish priests from conducting services in the parish. Finally, there is no element indicating that the prohibition, for any other reason, effectively limits the applicants' right to freedom of religion and notably their freedom to manifest their religion in worship. (*Finska församlingen i Stockholm and Teuvo Hautaniemi v Sweden*, 1996: 97)

Burrowes claimed that the EComHR's decision in this case – that there had been no failure on the part of the state to protect the applicants' freedom of religion – showed that the ECtHR would offer no remedy to an individual in England and Wales who, in the absence of any statutory protection by the state, was compelled to participate in a religious marriage ceremony of a same-sex couple.

Burrowes's conclusion – that the EComHR's interpretation of Article 9 of the ECHR, in respect of the Church of Sweden's decision to substitute one version of the Evangelical-Lutheran liturgy with another, definitively establishes that individual ministers would have no protection under Article 9 from being compelled by their employers to participate in the religious solemnisation of same-sex marriages – is highly questionable. This is not least because, in a previous case which the EComHR had declared inadmissible, which concerned a complaint by a minister who had been dismissed for refusing to perform state-related functions in his role as a clergyman within the State–Church system of Norway (including duties related to solemnising different-sex marriage) as a protest to changes in the law on abortion, the EComHR had been careful to note that the applicant's Article 9 rights had not been interfered with because he had not 'been under any pressure to change his views or … prevented from manifesting his religion or belief' (*Knudsen v Norway*, 1985: 258). Given that the ECtHR has long held that '[w]hile religious freedom is primarily a matter of individual conscience, it also implies, inter alia, freedom to "manifest [one's] religion"' and that '[b]earing witness in words and deeds is bound up with the existence of religious convictions' (*Kokkinakis v Greece*, 1993, § 31), it is likely that the case of a religious organisation compelling a minister with a religious objection to same-sex marriage to engage in the 'words and deeds' that comprise a religious marriage ceremony would be viewed by the ECtHR as significantly different to a religious organisation substituting the 'words and deeds' proscribed by one Finnish version of the Evangelical-Lutheran liturgy with another. Although both cases involve the issue of a religious organisation imposing a requirement on its members to participate in a religious practice that they object to, it is possible that the ECtHR would view the scope and nature of each requirement as fundamentally different. It is also possible that the ECtHR would view the absence of employment protection for an individual minister who wished to refuse to solemnise a same-sex marriage to amount to a failure on the part of the state to fulfil its positive obligations under Article 9. Burrowes's emphatic conclusion, based on a selective citation of EComHR jurisprudence, and his representation of the ECtHR, could therefore be understood to be either or both specious or misleading.

(Mis)representing the ECtHR in the House of Lords

The second example of how parliamentarians might be understood to mis-represent ECtHR jurisprudence is taken from debates in the House of Lords Committee that considered the MSSCA. The example relates to an amend-ment moved, and subsequently withdrawn, by Baroness Deech that pro-posed to add a requirement to the provisions in the bill relating to 'review of civil partnership'. At the point that the Lords Committee considered the bill, it contained a clause that placed a requirement on the Secretary of State to arrange 'for the operation and future of the Civil Partnership Act 2004 in England and Wales to be reviewed'. This provision was not originally include in the bill but was inserted at Report Stage in the Commons (HC Debate, 20 May 2013, c.1017) to enable a formal review of whether civil partnership (a form of legal partnership available only to same-sex couples) should be extended to different-sex couples. Deech's amendment proposed to make it a requirement that the review of civil partnership 'must deal with the case for amending the criteria in the Civil Partnership Act 2004 which define the eligibility of people to register as civil partners' and con-sider whether eligibility should be extended to 'unpaid carers and those they care for' as well as 'family members who share a house, who have cohabited for five years or more and are over the age of eighteen' (HL Debate, 24 June 2013, c.524). The stated purpose of Deech's amendment was to address 'the unfair way in which carers and siblings are treated in our law, compared with those in a sexual relationship' (HL Debate, 24 June 2013, c.525).

Deech explained the importance of her proposed amendment by referring to the case of Joyce and Sybil Burden:

> The case to which I refer … is that of Miss Joyce and Miss Sybil Burden, sis-ters, one of whom is now well over 90 and the other approaching 90. They are still alive, to the best of my knowledge, and have lived together for about 85 years. They remain single. They cared for their parents and two aunts to the end and did not allow them to go into a home. On the death of the first sister, inheritance tax was estimated in 2008 to be about £120,000 and may be more now if the value of their house has risen. (HL Debate, 24 June 2013, c. 526)

The Burden sisters had complained to the ECtHR that their ineligibility in respect of an exemption from inheritance tax enjoyed by surviving spouses or civil partners amounted to a violation of Article 1 of Protocol No. 1 (protection of property) taken in conjunction with Article 14 (prohibition of discrimination) of the ECHR. The complaint was considered by a cham-ber of the ECtHR (*Burden and Burden v the United Kingdom*, 2006) and subsequently by the Grand Chamber (*Burden v the United Kingdom*, 2008). In both cases, the ECtHR found that the treatment of the Burden sisters did not amount to a violation of the ECHR. Deech explained the Grand Chamber judgment in the following way:

> The sisters lost their case of discrimination before the Grand Chamber of the European Court of Human Rights. The court held that marriage was different. With respect, the judgment was unsatisfactory not only because of the narrow defeat in court but for the lack of logic. The Government took down the barriers between marriage and other forms of association by enacting advantages for same-sex couples entering a civil partnership and now, shortly, gay marriage. The European Court of Human Rights held that there was discriminatory treatment of the sisters, but that the UK had a wide margin of appreciation afforded to it and could treat benefits differently according to status in pursuit of the aim of promoting stable relationships by providing the survivor with, inter alia, financial security on the death of a spouse or partner. The lines drawn by the court in that case will no longer exist. All will be redrawn by the passage of the Bill. The unions or marriages that the Government seek to bolster will no longer have to be heterosexual, will not have to involve sex or procreation, but need only to be stable, loving and committed. Those are to be the only criteria in future. (HL Debate, 24 June 2013, c.526)

There are a number of problems with Deech's representation of the Grand Chamber judgment, not least that it appears to confuse it with the earlier chamber judgment that it superseded. It was the chamber, not the Grand Chamber, that reached the conclusion that 'to treat differently for tax purposes those who were married or who were parties to a civil partnership from other persons living together, even in a long-term settled relationship, … cannot be said to have exceeded the wide margin of appreciation afforded to [the state] and that the difference of treatment … was reasonably and objectively justified for the purposes of Article 14 of the Convention' (*Burden and Burden v the United Kingdom*, 2006, § 60–61). However, when the Grand Chamber considered the complaint it dismissed the Burden sisters' allegation of discrimination on the ground that, as cohabiting sisters, they could not be compared for the purpose of Article 14 of the ECHR to a married or civil partnership couple. In holding that the sisters were not in a relevantly similar or analogous position to couples who had entered into marriage or civil partnership the Grand Chamber would not proceed, in line with its established practice, to a consideration of whether the difference in treatment amounted to discrimination in violation of the ECHR. The Grand Chamber reasoned that

> the relationship between siblings is qualitatively of a different nature to that between married couples and homosexual civil partners under the United Kingdom's Civil Partnership Act. *The very essence of the connection between siblings is consanguinity, whereas one of the defining characteristics of a*

marriage or Civil Partnership Act union is that it is forbidden to close family members ... The fact that the applicants have chosen to live together all their adult lives, as do many married and Civil Partnership Act couples, does not alter this essential difference between the two types of relationship ... Moreover, the Grand Chamber notes that it has already held that marriage confers a special status on those who enter into it ... As with marriage, the Grand Chamber considers that the legal consequences of civil partnership under the 2004 Act, which couples expressly and deliberately decide to incur, set these types of relationship apart from other forms of cohabitation. *Rather than the length or the supportive nature of the relationship, what is determinative is the existence of a public undertaking, carrying with it a body of rights and obligations of a contractual nature* ... [T]he absence of such a legally binding agreement between the applicants renders their relationship of cohabitation, despite its long duration, fundamentally different to that of a married or civil partnership couple. (*Burden v the United Kingdom*, 2008, § 62–65, emphasis added)

Given the reasoning of the Grand Chamber, it is difficult to understand how Deech could reach the conclusion that '[t]he lines drawn by the court in that case will no longer exist' and 'will be redrawn by the passage of the Bill'. If the 'lines' Deech refers to means the distinction between, on the one hand, married and civil partnership couples and, on the other hand, sibling relationships, then the MSSCA did not 'redraw' this distinction. The MSSCA did not extend marriage to couple relationships based on consanguinity and marriage (and civil partnership) remains forbidden between close family members in England and Wales (S.1 and Sch.1 Marriage Act 1949; S.3 and Pt1 of Sch.1 Civil Partnership Act 2004). Nor did the MSSCA change the nature of marriage as a public undertaking, carrying with it a body of rights and obligations of a contractual nature, that distinguishes it from sibling relationships. In the light of this, Deech's representation of the Grand Chamber judgment could be said to be misleading because it suggests that the extension of marriage to same-sex couples would make the judgment in *Burden v the United Kingdom* (2008) redundant.

Representing the ECtHR as biased

Throughout the MSSCA debates, a belief commonly expressed by parliamentarians about the ECtHR was that it is a court that is inherently biased in respect of certain groups of people and, in particular, people of faith. Parliamentarians repeatedly represented the ECtHR as an institution that is unwilling to protect the rights of religious individuals and groups. For example, Roger Gale MP argued as follows: 'It is abundantly plain to most Conservative Members that the product of this Bill will end up before the courts and before the European Court of Human Rights, and that people of faith will find that faith trampled upon. That, to us, is intolerable'

(HC Debate, 5 February 2013, c.152). Similarly, David Burrowes MP stated: 'When looking at competing rights, such as sexual orientation rights and people's right to manifest their faith, a number of cases have reached the European Court, and it has been the case that the rights of those seeking to manifest their faith have been trumped' (HC Committee, 26 February 2013, c.222).

These claims about the rights of people of faith being 'trampled upon' and 'trumped', in favour of rights relating to (homo)sexual orientation, were often evidenced by references to the ECtHR judgment in respect of complaints made by Lillian Ladele – which were discussed above – and Gary McFarlane (*Eweida and Others v the United Kingdom*, 2013). Mr McFarlane, who held the Bible-based belief that homosexual activity is sinful and that he should do nothing to directly endorse such activity, complained to the ECtHR that disciplinary proceedings brought against him by his private-sector employer, when he refused to commit himself to providing a service (psycho-sexual therapy) to same-sex couples, amounted to a violation of Article 9 alone and in conjunction with Article 14 of the ECHR. The ECtHR accepted that Mr McFarlane's objection was motivated by his Christian beliefs and that his refusal to provide the service to same-sex couples constituted a manifestation of his religion and belief. In this respect, the ECtHR recognised that the national authorities had a positive obligation under Article 9 of the ECHR to secure Mr McFarlane's rights. In its consideration of the merits of the complaint, the ECtHR stated that the most important factor was that Mr McFarlane's employer had acted in order to ensure the provision of a service without discrimination. The ECtHR held that the national authorities had not exceeded the margin of appreciation available to them to decide where to strike the balance between McFarlane's right to manifest his religious belief and the employer's interest in securing the rights of others. The ECtHR reached a similar conclusion in respect of the complaint brought by Ms Ladele, holding that the national authorities had not exceeded the margin of appreciation available to them.

Given the judgment in *Eweida and Others v the United Kingdom* (2013), it is difficult to see how the ECtHR could be understood to have 'trampled upon' or 'trumped' the rights of Ms Ladele or Mr McFarlane. The key feature of the ECtHR's judgment is that it deferred to the discretion of the UK to decide how best to ensure an appropriate balance between competing ECHR rights. In short, the ECtHR played no active part in any detriment suffered by Ms Ladele and Mr McFarlane because of their faith-based objection to homosexuality but, rather, confirmed that it was for the national authorities to determine the extent to which such an objection should be accommodated in a workplace. However, the belief that the ECtHR played an active role in 'overriding' the rights of Ms Ladele and Mr McFarlane, as well as other people of faith, underpinned several attempts by parliamentarians to insert additional religious protections into the MSSCA. For example, Tim Loughton MP attempted in the Public Bill Committee to insert the following bespoke provision into the MSSCA, designed to prohibit sanctions against clergy employed by a public authority:

> No sanction may be imposed upon or discrimination exercised against any member of the clergy who refuses to conduct a same sex marriage who –
>
> (a) is employed as a member of the armed forces;
> (b) is employed as a chaplain in the National Health Service; or
> (c) is employed by any other state institution or organisation. (HC Committee, 12 March 2013, c.477)

Loughton argued that this protection was needed because in complaints to the ECtHR 'where there was a clash between sexual orientation rights and religion and belief rights ... namely in relation to Lillian Ladele and Gary McFarlane, both cases were lost' (HC Committee, 12 March 2013, c.479). Loughton went on as follows:

> I am mindful of the two people whose loss of employment the European Court of Human Rights has recently endorsed, and the fact that two people have already lost their jobs because of their views on same-sex marriage, even before it has become law; those worries are certainly not without foundation. People working for public authorities would clearly be foolish not to hold such concerns. (HC Committee, 12 March 2013, c. 481)

Loughton's claim that the ECtHR 'endorsed' Ms Ladele and Mr McFarlane's loss of employment is problematic because, as I stated above, the ECtHR simply confirmed that the UK had acted within the margin of appreciation available to it to determine how best to secure for everyone the rights and freedoms contained in the ECHR. What the ECtHR 'endorsed', therefore, was not the specific treatment of Ms Ladele and Mr McFarlane but, rather, the discretion available to contracting states which, '[i]n all the circumstances' of these complaints, the UK had not exceeded (*Eweida and Others v the United Kingdom*, 2013, § 106 and 109). However, on the basis of Loughton and others' arguments about the need for additional protection in this area, the Government subsequently introduced an amendment to the bill (HC Debate, 20 May 2013, c.977), which upon enactment provides that a person cannot be held personally liable under the Equality Act 2010 for not conducting, participating in, or consenting to a religious marriage ceremony of a same-sex couple (S.2(5) MSSCA, amending S.110 Equality Act 2010). Expressions of the belief that the ECtHR is a court that 'endorses' people of faith losing their jobs because of an objection to same-sex marriage can be seen to have significantly encouraged the inclusion of this additional protection.

The strong belief among some parliamentarians that the ECtHR would find in favour of a same-sex couple who complained about the refusal of a religious organisation to solemnise their marriage motivated perhaps the most far-reaching proposed amendment to the MSSCA in the House of Lords. The amendment, moved by Lord Stoddart, proposed the insertion of the following clause in the legislation:

> In the event that the provisions of this Act are found by the European Court of Human Rights to be incompatible with the Convention for the Protection of Human Rights and Fundamental Freedoms, the Secretary of State shall act to withdraw the United Kingdom's signature to the Convention. (HL Committee, 24 June 2013, c.628)

Stoddart argued that this provision was necessary because, if the ECtHR decided in future that Article 12 of the ECHR imposed an obligation on a state to allow same-sex couples to marry, 'the so-called quad locks could look pretty obsolete, especially for the Church of England, which, as an emanation of the state, has a duty to marry anyone in the parish' (HL Committee, 24 June 2013, c.629). Stoddart continued as follows:

> Some say that the Article 9 right to freedom of religion would protect religious freedom in any clash with Article 12. However, the recent ruling against the registrar Lillian Ladele shows only too well the European court's unsympathetic approach to religious beliefs about marriage. (HL Committee, 24 June 2013, c.630)

Although Stoddart's proposed amendment was clearly aimed at protecting faith groups and religious individuals from litigation in the ECtHR by same-sex couples it could, had it been adopted, have produced the ironic effect of triggering the withdrawal of the UK from the ECHR as a result of a religious organisation or individual successfully complaining to the ECtHR that the MSSCA interfered with the right to manifest religion guaranteed by Article 9 of the ECHR. Stoddard withdrew his amendment, but its substance found favour with those Lords who held the belief that the ECtHR is a biased organisation. Such a belief underpinned the claim that the 'seismic shift in social customs' underpinning the legalisation of same-sex marriage had been 'accelerated by the European Convention on Human Rights' (Lord Vinson, HL Debate, 4 June 2013, c.1077) and that the reason legislation had been introduced to permit same-sex marriage was that the 'Government have colluded with equal love campaigners and the European Court of Human Rights' and engaged in 'outrageous, behind-the-scenes arm twisting' (Lord Framlingham, HL Debate, 15 July 2013, c.543). For these parliamentarians, a strong belief that the ECtHR is a biased court committed to favouring the rights of one group over another provided a fundamental basis for opposing the MSSCA.

Conclusion

The aim of this chapter has been to demonstrate how beliefs about the ECtHR circulate and become accepted among parliamentarians. Through an analysis of parliamentary debates, I have shown how MPs and Lords discursively deploy their beliefs about the ECtHR in pursuit of particular legislative ambitions. A common feature of parliamentary debates, as the analysis demonstrates, is that parliamentarians frequently deploy and attempt to encourage beliefs about the ECtHR in order to legitimise their political arguments. Such beliefs therefore provide parliamentarians with a powerful discursive 'tool' with which to advance their political objectives. In recent years, the expression of negative and hostile beliefs about the ECtHR has become more prominent in parliamentary debates. As the analysis of the MSSCA debates shows, the ECtHR is depicted as a biased institution that poses a risk to the human rights of large sections of the UK population. If it is accepted that parliamentary discourse has an influence on wider public perceptions and opinions, then the beliefs expressed by parliamentarians that are outlined in this chapter should be of concern to anyone with an interest in encouraging a balanced and informed understanding of the ECtHR among the population of the UK.

List of judgments and decisions of the European Court of Human Rights and former European Commission of Human Rights

Burden and Burden v the United Kingdom, no. 13378/05, 12 December 2006

Burden v the United Kingdom [GC], no. 13378/05, 29 April 2008

Eweida and Others v the United Kingdom, nos. 48420/10, 59842/10, 51671/10 and 36516/10, 15 January 2013

Finska församlingen i Stockholm and Teuvo Hautaniemi v Sweden, no. 24019/94, Commission decision, 11 April 1996, Decisions and Reports 85-A, 94–97

Hirst v the United Kingdom (no. 2) [GC], no. 74025/01, 6 October 2005

Kokkinakis v Greece, no. 14307/88, 25 May 1993

Knudsen v Norway, no. 11045/84, Commission decision, 8 March 1985, Decisions and Reports 42, 247–258

Schalk and Kopf v Austria, no. 30141/04, 24 June 2010

Vinter and Others v the United Kingdom [GC], nos. 66069/09, 130/10 and 3896/10, 9 July 2013

References

BBC News (2012) 'Concept of human rights being distorted, warns Cameron', 25 January. Available at: www.bbc.co.uk/news/uk-politics-16708845. Last accessed 30 August 2016.

Cohen, S. (2002) *Folk Devils and Moral Panics: the Creation of the Mods and Rockers* (3rd edn). Abingdon: Routledge.

Conservative Party (2014) *Protecting Human Rights in the UK: the Conservatives' Proposals for Changing Britain's Human Rights Laws*. London: Conservative Party.

Epstein, D., R. Johnson and D. L. Steinberg (2000) 'Twice told tales: transformation, recuperation and emergence in the age of consent debates 1998', *Sexualities* 3(1), 5–30.

European Court of Human Rights (2012) 'High level conference on the future of the European Court of Human Rights: Brighton declaration'. Strasbourg: Council of Europe.

Ipsos MORI (2012) 'Public blamed ECHR over the Home Secretary for Abu Qatada delays', 14 May. Available at: www.ipsos-mori.com/researchpublications/researcharchive/2964/Public-blamed-ECHR-over-the-Home-Secretary-for-Abu-Qatada-delays.aspx. Last accessed 30 August 2016.

Johnson, P. (2014) 'Turning the European Court of Human Rights into a folk devil: the UK Conservative Party and human rights', *Discover Society*, 14. Available at: www.discoversociety.org/2014/11/04/turning-the-european-court-of-human-rights-into-a-folk-devil-the-uk-conservative-party-and-human-rights-2/. Last accessed 30 August 2016.

Johnson, P. and R. M. Vanderbeck (2014) *Law, Religion and Homosexuality*. Abingdon: Routledge.

Kyle, C. R. (2012) *Theater of State: Parliament and Political Culture in Early Stuart England*. Redwood City, CA: Stanford University Press.

Van der Valk, I. (2003) 'Right-Wing Parliamentary discourse on immigration in France', *Discourse and Society* 14(3), 309–348.

Watt, N. and A. Travis (2013) 'Tory ministers condemn ECHR ruling on whole-life prison sentences', *Guardian*, 9 July. Available at: www.theguardian.com/law/2013/jul/09/whole-life-sentences-david-cameron-human-rights. Last accessed 30 August 2016.

YouGov (2014) 'Scepticism about human rights as well as the ECHR', 20 July. Available at: https://yougov.co.uk/news/2014/07/20/scepticism-about-human-rights-well-echr/. Last accessed 30 August 2016.

Forward! Coding, decoding and recoding law in public art for urban regeneration

Introduction

This contribution explores the coded dimension of public artworks (sculptures or installations), or, better perhaps: the coded dimension *in* large public artworks, particularly as part of urban regeneration efforts. Public space is dotted with such artworks. Some are built on a monumental scale. The focus in this contribution is on the normative codes that are supposed to be embedded in both the material structure and the 'aura' of the works. Indeed, when authorities decide to commission public artworks the brief to artists will often include specifications that pertain not just to the desired visual and expressive effect of the work (the artwork is then supposed to express a particular idea or content) but also to a more normative intention (i.e. the artwork is then required either to tap into or mobilise an existing set of cultural, social or political codes, or indeed consolidate, propagate or even generate them).

An element in the normative coding of public artworks, which this chapter will be focusing on in particular, relates to notions or indeed visions of 'public order' that the works are assumed to radiate and project. Public artworks are often meant to project the following message: 'This is us. Or at least: this is how we ought to be and what we ought to be like. And you, visitor, are now entering a particular space with a particular code. Beware and behave accordingly.' But the question now arises as to whether public artworks are at all able to realise any of their intended effects. Is it not the case that the intended codes embedded in the artwork are bound to be subjected to continuous decoding and recoding? It is on these particular questions and issues that this contribution attempts to shed light. The focus shall be on one particular sculpture, namely, Raymond Mason's (1922–2010) *Forward!*, which stood in Birmingham between 1991 and 2003. Let us begin with a few words on this sculpture.

On 17 April 2003, the statue was actually destroyed. The work, made of fibreglass and polyester resins, burned down in a blaze of smoke and fire at the location – Centenary Square – where it had been standing since 1991. The artwork had been commissioned at the end of the 1980s by the local City Council (then Labour) to form part of a massive city-centre regeneration project, which included Centenary Square itself, and a variety of complexes and buildings such as the International Convention Centre. The statue was emplaced in the square in 1991. After it had been destroyed in 2003, youths, suspected of having had a part in its destruction, were apprehended, but in the arts community though, there are, to this very day, lingering doubts as to who may really have been behind the decision to actually destroy the work (see, e.g., the art historian Sarah Wilson, 2011). Indeed, sheer physics seems to suggest that the destruction of such a huge statue could not have been an accident caused, as the youths maintained, by a stray match.

As noted by Sarah Wilson, the destruction of the sculpture led to remark-ably little discussion and debate in the press and other media. This was highly unusual. Ever since the vehement debates which, during the 1980s, dominated the art world before and after the removal, from the Foley Federal Plaza in Manhattan, of Richard Serra's minimalist sculpture *Tilted Arc*, issues with public artworks usually, if not always, prompt considerable heated debate in a variety of media. There is no space here to explore the intricate debates about public art that were unleashed by the Serra case. Suffice to say here that much in those debates was about the need to democ-ratise in some way public art commissioning procedures. We shall return to these issues in the next section. Here we just note that there was little in the way of upheaval after the burning of *Forward!*

Perhaps that should not come as too much of a surprise, however. The sculpture, the sculptor and the Council had to face a hostile reception from the very start. At the time of the sculpture's emplacement in 1991 the *Spectator*, for example, published an article (Hamilton, 1991) in which petitions are mentioned which suggested that 76 per cent of the wider Birmingham public was against the erection of *Forward!* in Centenary Square. One would, of course, expect a venue such as the *Spectator* to have made a serious attempt at blasting the local Labour council for having commissioned the work. But the hostility towards *Forward!* did not come from conservative corners only. It was quite widespread from the start. The Arts Council did not think the work would have fitted into the environs of Centenary Square and even the artist himself was not quite sure. Birmingham City Council, however, decided to press ahead with *Forward!* regardless of all opposition.

It should be said that many public artworks actually survive initial hostil-ity. Perhaps the most spectacular illustration of this is Anthony Gormley's *Angel of the North* in Gateshead. Erected in 1998 after years of bad press the *Angel* managed to evaporate nearly all hostility almost from the very moment it stretched its wings across the landscape. We shall, below, briefly touch upon some of the differences between *Forward!* and the *Angel of the North* (for a thorough exploration of the intricacies of the case of the *Angel of the North* though one should refer to Lippens, in press). In sharp contrast to artworks such as the *Angel of the North*, Mason's sculpture in Centenary Square remained under a cloud and was quickly dubbed, not too affectionately, the 'Lurpak statue', because of its overall creamy yellowy hues.

The work in a way depicts the modern industrial history of the City of Birmingham. It looks back on the city's industrial past and heritage, with depictions of factories and workshops. Then the work includes a number of figures who seem to be demonstrating artistic, craftsman and workshop skills. This is then followed by scenes of working-class communal life. The sculpture ultimately ends with a number of what appear to be individual citizens, one of whom seeming to wave his hand, as in a greeting, to all that surrounds him in the newly 'regenerated' post-industrial square.

It is often assumed that the open hostility towards the sculpture was owing largely to its 'socialist realism'. There is something in this assumption.

Figure 1 Raymond Mason *Forward!* (1991–2003). Photo © Birmingham Museums Trust.

Some of the figures in the statue do indeed come complete with the stare and the six-pack abdomens that will remind one of the style that once was ubiquitous in a great many places, and not just behind the Berlin Wall. It is also worth noting that the work was conceived, commissioned and built at the exact time when the Berlin Wall was crumbling to pieces and when the Soviet Empire was falling apart. This may have been one of the reasons why Mason himself had second thoughts at the last moment before the work's installation.

The work's alleged 'socialist realism' may not have been, however, the only reason – nor, for that matter, the most important one – explaining its hostile reception and ultimate destruction. There were probably deeper reasons. We shall be exploring those in the third section of this chapter. But let us say something here about the accusation of 'socialist realism'. Mason was not so much a realist (and much less a socialist-realist) as a Romantic, writes Sarah Wilson (2011). Many of his works betray a sense of nostalgia, and express the sculptor's need to record, in public memory, forms of life that have passed. One of his most known works, *The Departure of Fruit and Vegetables from the Heart of Paris* (1969) depicted scenes of the fruit-and-vegetables market that had just been abolished in Paris (Mason lived in Paris). Mason's drive, a Romantic's drive, was to nostalgically record the passing of more 'natural', 'organic' (fruits! vegetables!) ways of life. Mason's works, including *Forward!*, then, are not so much forward looking. In many of his works, Mason is looking back in time, to a more palatable past. Granted, there is something of a socialist-realist form in *Forward!*, but that form probably appeared in the sculpture because of the occasion, that is, the commemoration of Birmingham's past, and that past had to focus on industrial heritage and working-class achievements and cultures. That said, the sculpture seems to have struck the wrong chord – quite persistently so – with the great majority of Birmingham's general public.

The aim of this chapter is threefold. First, an attempt will be made to explore how events such as the one that befell Raymond Mason's *Forward!* could teach us something about the import of public art in urban regeneration projects. Secondly, we shall explore how aspects of moral and public order – however fleeting and fragile perhaps – are crucially important when it comes to the use of public art in urban regeneration attempts. Indeed, such aspects tend to be coded – very often implicitly though – into the artworks which are then supposed to project, or to radiate them outwards into the surroundings. But there – and this is going to be one of the major points in this issue – these codes are bound to be decoded, recoded and sometimes rejected by a variety of audiences and publics. This is particularly the case in an age such as the present; that is, an age when so many harbour almost extreme levels of distrust towards anything that would dare to even suggest or hint at visions or notions of 'order' at all. In the words of the art critic Patrick Wright (1995), who was writing about public art in Britain (including Mason's), we truly live in a thoroughly 'sceptical and relativist age'. Thirdly, we hope to be able to illustrate how such processes of coding, however implicit they may be, often clash with and crumble under the weight of decodings, recodings and even destruction. The destruction of rejected artworks of course remains an exception. As the case of the *Angel of the North* shows, some codings of moral and public order into artworks are such that they seem to be able to capture a wide variety of oftentimes diverse codings and counter-codings, as well as the multiple desires that fuel them, even in a 'sceptical and relativist' age such as ours.

The remainder of this chapter is structured as follows. The next section deals with the issue of urban regeneration, and the role and place of public art in it. The section also includes explorations on the topic of coding, decoding and recoding of visions and notions of moral or public order in works of public art. This is then followed by a close 'reading', or *ekphrasis* (if you wish), of Mason's *Forward!* sculpture. The chapter ends with some concluding remarks.

Public art and urban regeneration

Public art has, particularly since the late 1970s, become a noted tool in urban and regional regeneration attempts in the UK (Selwood, 1995 and, more recently, research undertaken under the auspices of the Arts Council England, as well as *ixia:* www.publicartonline.org.uk). There is a whole literature on what constitutes 'public art', and whether, for example, creative acts of contestation and resistance (e.g. resistance against the colonisation of public space by corporate capital or state authority) are also forms of public art, or whether 'public art' is actually a separate category at all (Deutsche, 1996, is arguably one of the more sophisticated voices in this debate). The answer to all these questions of definition is varied and will depend on one's point of view. This is not the place to rehearse this debate. For the purposes of this essay we consider 'public art' to be a tool of governance. We intend to focus here on 'public art' that is *officially* commissioned, and that, erected in the open air on the initiative or under the auspices of public bodies or authorities, is accessible to the public. Such art usually has a number of aims and goals or justifications – whether explicitly acknowledged or implicit – such as beautification, enhancement of a site's functionality, attracting visitors and tourism, and so on, and is therefore usually 'site-specific' (see Kwon, 1997). Often the construction and emplacement of public artworks form part of a broader regeneration strategy. This is particularly the case in post-industrialising locations. Whether public art in itself is able to actually contribute to urban and regional regeneration, or not, remains to a significant extent unclear. There is some evidence though that public art that succeeds in beautifying particular locations and in attracting more affluent residents and visitors to the area thus contributes to processes of gentrification, albeit quite often to the detriment of less affluent groups for whom residency will have become unaffordable (Deutsche, 1996; Miles 1997; 2005).

The relative success of public art in regeneration efforts is itself not the focus of this section, however. The focus here is on an under-researched theme in and dimension of public art; that is, (a) the extent to which it is meant, explicitly but more often implicitly, to project a particular sense of order onto users of its surrounding space, and, possibly, instil such a sense; and (b) the extent to which users of such spaces attach meaning to the works of art not just in their attempts to make sense of the order in the spaces that they are passing through but also in their desires for and in their attempts to imagine a particular order in their lives, and in the spaces they inhabit. These issues are all the more important in spaces that are going through or that are deemed to be in need of 'regeneration'. Processes of 'regeneration' have a forward momentum and that momentum opens up space (quite literally so) for a variety of often conflicting 'orders' to emerge in images and visions of urban space, as well as in spatial practices, including the production and consumption of public art.

The term 'order' or the phrase 'sense of order' in the above paragraph could be interpreted in a number of ways. For our purposes here, the phrase 'sense of order' (whether explicit or implicit, expressed or projected, experienced or desired) means a sense of *moral* or *public* order (one could even use the phrase *legal* order here) but those terms are used rather loosely here. A moral, public or legal order, for our purposes here, is an often implicit collection of codes about 'how to be', or 'how to behave' and indeed 'how to live'. Art and public art especially, has a place in processes whereby such orders emerge and clash in the production and in the experience of a 'sense' of place. In legal semiotics and in interdisciplinary legal scholarship more broadly, for example, a trend in contemporary culture towards 'iconic control' has been noticed (Moore, 2007). In late modernity, marked by textual instability, but also by ubiquitous consumerism, governance or 'control' operates ever more directly through 'affects' in the aesthetic sphere, that is, in the sphere of sensory experience itself. The production, circulation and consumption of sensory 'icons' together then constitute the late modern form of 'control' par excellence. This is as such no news to art theorists who have described art and art exhibitions as instrumental in processes of governance and in the institution and circulation of particular visions of order (see, e.g., Bennett, 2005). The sensory sphere of 'iconic control' mentioned here is, it should be noted in passing, not just about the visual. All senses are involved in the emergence and clash of 'senses of order'. Moral and legal order can be seen, tasted, smelt, touched or heard in the synaesthetic make-up of a place. And the desire for order can express itself synaesthetically in the production and subsequent experience of space. The 'synaesthetics' of law and legality for example is one of the emerging themes in interdisciplinary research and scholarship. There is no coincidence in the fact that one of the predominant interdisciplinary forums in the field of interdisciplinary socio-legal studies; that is, the *Roundtables for the Semiotics of Law,* scheduled this theme for their fifteenth international conference (in 2015). In this section, however, we focus on the *visual* dimension of public space, and in particular on the place of public art therein. To be precise: the focus shall be on how, and to what extent particular values and cultural codes are designed into and emphasised in the choice and spatial emplacement of 'iconic art', and how and to what extent these very codes are then experienced and decoded by users of the public place that surrounds them (on the spatial import of urban beautification, see also Zieleniec 2007; 2013).

Much if not most of the effort in the literature on public art has hitherto been spent on a number of recurring topics such as the need for public art (whether or not as part of 'regeneration' projects and strategies) to secure a democratic basis through engagement, or collaboration even, with a variety of audiences (e.g. Burk, 2006; Clements, 2008; Hamilton et al., 2001; Jancovich, 2011; Pollock and Paddison, 2010; Sharp et al., 2005). Some of this work is empirical in nature. By that is meant here that research activities included active engagement with, observation of and interviews with art commissioners, and with producers and consumers of public art (e.g. Hamilton et al., 2001; Selwood, 1995; Visconti et al., 2010; it should be noted in passing that the terms 'producer' and 'consumer' are somewhat artificial in that producers, even when traditional public art is concerned, are also consumers, and consumers can be, and very often are, involved in the production process, whether explicitly, or implicitly, or indeed, as a potential 'force to reckon with'). Some focus on the normative aspect of public art has largely been lacking (but see, e.g., Douzinas and Nead, 1999; Lippens, 2000; in press; Young, 2005). Here we hope to be able to contribute to redressing this situation. Indeed the focus here is on the often implicit codes of order (moral, public, or even legal, in the very broad sense of the word) embedded in public art (however imaginary and however contradictory those orders) as well as on the experience and inevitable 'recoding' of such orders by a variety of consumers of said public art works.

This chapter is not about aesthetic experience as such, nor is it about aesthetic judgment. There is an emerging literature available on the experience of art, including public art (e.g. Basdas et al., 2009; Belfiore and Bennett, 2007; Joy and Sherry, 2003; Leder et al., 2004; Visconti et al., 2010). One of the tentative and provisional conclusions that could arguably be drawn from this body of research and literature is not just that aesthetic experience varies considerably depending on cultural or class backgrounds and psychological make-up, but also that the fullness of the experience of art could never be exhausted by the conceptual or linguistic representations that are generated by it. The 'affect' of the image, so to speak, does indeed speak louder than a thousand words. The aesthetic exceeds the representational. This comes as no surprise to philosophers of art (e.g. Davey, 2005) who, depending on their sources of theoretical inspiration, have been aware of the inevitable and insurmountable 'friction' between on the one hand experience and, on the other, representation, for quite some time. But aesthetic experience, representation and aesthetic judgement are, as such, not the focus here. The aim here is to see and explore how, in this age of 'iconic control' (Moore, 2007), particular codes of order are embedded in public works of 're-generational' art, and how a variety of users of public spaces and therefore also of public art engage with those works of art and mobilise or 'recode', in the wake of their experience of them, their own particular visions of order.

Visions of order, whether avowedly expressive or, in their forward momentum, projective, are very rarely explicitly acknowledged in commissions for public art. Indeed, more often than not such visions would appear in the guise of 'mythical' notions (to evoke Doreen Massey and Gillian Rose's report on public art, 2003) such as 'coherent community', or 'common understanding', 'social cohesion', or still, the 'essential' 'identity' of a place, and so on. And when it comes to the experience and impact of art it would be unwise to assume a mechanical causal relationship between, on the one hand, the experience of the artwork, and, on the other, the 'experience' and subsequent expression of any potentially perceived moral or behavioural code in those works of art by those that cross their surrounding space. Indeed, the experience of space, and the experience of works of art in them, is not just the experience of that particular space or that particular artwork. Users of a particular space and the works of art emplaced in it bring a whole intricate biographical complex of experiences, motivations, desires, plans, and so on with them. When they enter a public square, or when they stop and gaze at a particular work of art, this whole intricate web is mobilised in the very process of reading and 'decoding' the artwork and its surrounding space. This mobilisation is then of course immediately implicated in any reading or decoding attempt. But the reverse is also worth noting: in their ongoing attempts to make sense of the moral, public and legal order of their spatial universe (whether actual and lived, or ideal and desired) individuals mobilise earlier and ongoing experiences, readings and attempts to 'decode' space and art; and again: vice versa. There is very little purely mechanical about this process (see again Davey 2005). This process is not so much a question of causal factors and effects, as an ongoing process of 'sense making'. It is about ongoing and indeed unrelenting experience and reflection not just in users of public space and public art but also in planners of public space and art. In order to be able to conceive of why users of public art, for example, would reject a particular work (e.g. Mason's *Forward!*), one would have to have an understanding of the following: (a) elements of users' complex and biographically intricate networks of experiences, motivations, desires, and visions and ideas about what constitutes 'good' order, 'good' codes of life and behaviour, that those very users of public space and public art bring to the public square (quite literally); (b) how some of those elements are then mobilised in and during their experience of those works of art; and (c) how their experience of the works of art and their readings and 'decoding' of it in turn inform their motivations, desires, and visions and ideas about what constitutes 'good' codes of life and behaviour.

Public artworks and public artwork projects are important foci in this regard for very often it is such artworks or projects that are at the heart of attempts to 're-generate' life, activity, and order back into particular localities. This is of course not to deny the obvious fact that 'regeneration' attempts are not just about the emplacement of works of art. Not at all: regeneration attempts manifest themselves in the spatial arrangement, configuration and aesthetic appearance of a whole range of spaces and objects (e.g. architectural features of buildings, lay-out of squares, roads and other traffic arteries, street furniture, parks and greenery, and places of residence). The sculpture *Forward!*, for example, was, as said above, only one element (a minor one at that, one could say) in a much bigger project of inner city rearrangement. In post-industrial regeneration attempts such spatial arrangement, more often than not, tend to project an image of what Phil Hubbard (1996) calls 'entrepreneurial landscapes'. However, in this age of 'iconic control' of ours (Moore, 2007 again), it is artworks in particular that are meant to be sending out particular civic 'messages' (whether those messages were made explicit or whether they remained implicit) to the users of the spaces that surround them (see also Levinson, 1998). Quite often such sculptures tend to have territorial 'ambitions'; indeed they tend to project a particular 'moral' or 'legal' universe onto the surrounding area. It is precisely here where things went wrong for *Forward!* between 1991 and 2003. Let us now have a closer look at that particular sculpture.

Forward!

One of the first things that one notices about the sculpture is its formal linearity. As said, it starts from manufactories, then shows us a number of artisans and workers demonstrating their artistic and craftsman skills, before moving on to depictions of working-class culture scenes, and eventually ends with what looks like individual citizens greeting not just the viewer but also their surrounding space and world. The sculpture seems to be saying something like this:

> Way back in time we had the manufactories. Then we had an explosion of workshop activity, and the many intellectual, artistic and craftsman skills that went hand in hand with it flourished abundantly and built this city. We've subsequently also known a culture of collective life and solidarity. This gave us stability, and a sense of purpose, a sense of stability indeed. All this has ultimately culminated in a shared confidence which now allows each of us, citizens of Birmingham, to look the future, whatever it holds for us, in the eye, and indeed, this confidence allows us to welcome it. And this is good. This is how it was, and this is how it should be. This is how it must be. These are the lines of our heritage. These are the lines of our future.

Those lines are clear and straight, like an arrow's almost, or like the lines around an immovable slab of concrete.

In some of the early press coverage about the sculpture, the work was sometimes derided for being 'uncompromising'. In one of the very few, if not the only academic paper on the sculpture, Tim Hall (1997) disagrees. According to Hall, *Forward!* is full of compromise. It is a compromise between on the one hand a focus on the local and historical roots of Birmingham's uniqueness, and, on the other, a more future-oriented eye on the city's place in a modern globalised economy of opportunity and possibility. But it also compromises, Hall continues, between notions of collective and systemic forms of life (collective production, mechanic processes, manufactories, etc.) on the one hand, and individual citizenship in an emerging market and consumer economy on the other. In fact, if you look closely, Hall writes, you will see that the middle section in the sculpture makes the connection quite aptly. There we have the individual artisans, artists and intellectuals all working industriously in their workshops. It is hard to disagree with Hall here. Mason may have been struck by a bout of naivety when he was working on the sculpture using 'socialist-realist' forms, but a certain amount of thoughtful consideration did find a way into the work.

So why were reactions to the sculpture so negative and unrelentingly hostile until the very end in 2003? There could be a clue in the title of the work. Mason gave it the title *Forward!*, with exclamation mark. Of course, the word 'Forward' (without exclamation mark), one could say, is just the motto of the City of Birmingham, and so we should perhaps not read more into all this. But the added exclamation mark does make a difference. It could be read as an order, as a command. Looking at the sculpture – which *does* come across as a procession that progresses along strict and straight lines – it probably would not take too wide a stretch of the imagination to read the name of the work as a *marching order*.

The whole sculpture is, as has been mentioned, very linear and unidi-rectional. A while ago, in their book on metaphor, *More than Cool Reason* (1987), George Lakoff and Mark Turner explained how it is almost impos-sible, within the human condition, to escape using or thinking through the metaphor of the 'Great Chain of Being'. Human beings cannot but look at the world, and speak about it, through the use of a number of very basic, very fundamental, and always recurring metaphors. The 'Great Chain of Being' metaphor is one of those. The metaphor betrays a belief in a world which is inevitably hierarchically and sequentially connected and struc-tured. There are the low and the high; the unstructured and the structured; the first and the last; the primitive and the evolved; the animal kingdom and human being; the master and the slave; the past and the future; and so forth. And all these elements are connected and structured, hierarchically and sequentially. Or so the belief implies. It is almost impossible for human beings, qua human beings, *not* to think or speak about the world in terms of origins and developments, or causes and effects. Human beings will tend to look at the world as if it were a collection of interconnected processes, quite linear ones at that, each underpinned by origins, ends, aims, goals or purposes. This almost ineradicable human inclination, it should be noted in passing, can and often does carry political undertones. Indeed, if one consid-ers the world to be inherently ordered, hierarchical, sequentially structured, and therefore evolving according to a law, or a set of codes, then the issue invariably becomes, to evoke the words of the late Bill Chambliss: Whose law? What order?

It is here that we may be able to return to *Forward!* The issue with the sculpture was not so much that many may have disagreed with the par-ticular law and the order that Mason, perhaps unwittingly, or implicitly so, had coded into the work. The issue probably was deeper than that. The issue probably was that both Mason and the commissioners were, in 1991, unaware of the fact that the world had moved on and that new cultural sensitivities had crystallised across the broad demographic spectrum. In a 'sceptical and relativist' age (*dixit* Wright) only very few are left that are still willing to accept the very idea of immovable laws and orders. In an age that puts a premium on personal sovereignty (however imaginary or even illusory and paradoxical personal sovereignty will be, of course) very few remain who are able to enjoy the sight, taste and smell of anything that purports to project law, coded order, structure, hierarchy, or inevitable development. In an age of aspiring sovereigns, very few are willing to be part of a Great Chain of Being. Aspiring sovereigns cannot even bear to contemplate the very idea. They cannot bear to look it in the eye. They simply cannot bring themselves to look at it. Mason's sculpture is unbearable to watch in an age of aspiring sovereigns. It is linearity incarnate. It shows origins and futures, unidirectional interconnections, structured sequences and inescapable processes. To add insult to injury, it shouts the command *Forward!* It shouts, 'Follow this law, submit to this law and accept this code. It always was and always will be the path to follow, the thing to do. Do not resist. Follow! Submit! March!' Faced with the sheer linearity of the sculpture, with the unidirectional straight lines of the slab that is called *Forward!*, and with the leaden inertia – all futile suggestion of movement and change notwithstanding – of a lump of Lurpak, the aspiring sovereign retches and moves away in disgust.

One could, of course, say that Mason's sculpture does leave aspiring sovereigns with something worthwhile to admire. As Tim Hall (1997) has noted, one side of the sculpture (i.e. the 'present') depicts what seem to be confident individual citizens emerging from the mass of history. At least, one could argue, this should allow aspiring sovereigns to recognise themselves in those figures, and to identify with them. But that would be missing the point. First of all, and very practically speaking, the sculpture does not really invite to identify with the figures. All figures are glued, or welded, so to speak, to the slab on which they are standing. If Mason had decided to build a sculpture with a number of separate figures viewers might have decided to explore each one of them in detail, and, possibly, identify with some of them. But now there is just the massive 'Lurpak' in which exploration and identification do not come naturally. Also, and not insignificantly, the Great Chain of Being, in *Forward!*, is largely of the white, industrial and mostly working-class variety. In a multicultural city such as the Birmingham of 1991 the sculpture left very little to identify with indeed. But the more fundamental reason why aspiring sovereigns were unlikely to have seen anything in the sculpture that attracted them is because as aspiring sovereigns they actually do not want to explore or identify with anyone or anything at all. In the world of the aspiring sovereign exploration is unnecessary. The aspiring sovereign aspires to be utterly, completely independent. And the last thing that is on the aspiring sovereign's wish list is to identify. Identification means coming second. It is a form of submission, and what is sovereign about that? One could now point to the fact that in this age of ours so many are willingly submitting to and identifying with consumer and celebrity image. But that would do little to alter the fact that at a deeper level sovereign aspiration is more radical. Many are willing to settle, temporarily, for the *faux sovereignty* provided by or in a very pervasive consumer culture, but this willingness is itself fuelled by deeper, more radical aspirations.

At the exact time when Mason was working on his sculpture (i.e. in 1990), the French philosopher Gilles Deleuze wrote a short paper on 'control societies' (published in translation in 1995), which was to become quite influential in socio-legal studies. In the paper, Deleuze reflects on Michel Foucault's oeuvre and concludes that Western societies are no longer disciplinary in nature. They have become mere 'control societies'. Societies no longer operate according to 'order words' that, once, structured life's activities and experiences towards particular end goals. At best, societies are now regulated contextually; that is, through the circulation, adoption and adaptation of a bewildering variety of mere 'passwords' that are made up, invented, applied and then abandoned according to contextual exigencies. There is more to be said, of course, about Deleuze's notions 'password' and 'control society'. For our purposes here, let us just emphasise the idea that in a society of aspiring sovereigns it should not come as too big a surprise to see that strictly ordered discipline is becoming a thing of the past. Aspiring sovereigns no longer want to discipline, or order the world around them. Why would they? Such an effort would only demonstrate their dependency on the world to which they have actually become largely indifferent. But they do not want to be captured by that world either. They no longer want to be disciplined towards or into strict order. What Deleuze had fully grasped in 1990, Mason and the Birmingham commissioners seem to have been completely unaware of. *Forward!* radiates structure and strict order in a Great Chain of Being in which aspiring sovereigns are made to feel that they are dragged down by the weight of history and the force of the 'arrow of time' (to evoke a term from complexity theory), and where those that feel uncertain in a world of aspiring sovereigns are given the command to go *Forward!* and to welcome a brave, new, but unfamiliar and chaotic world. There is little regeneration possible here.

As said, there is a difference to be noted here with Anthony Gormley's *Angel of the North*. The *Angel* too was part of a massive urban and regional regeneration project. Standing 60-feet high on a knoll made of the detritus of Gateshead's industrial past, the *Angel* stretches its wings far and wide across the landscape. The statue is made of weathering steel. Certainly, it refers to the industrial past and heritage of the north-east. And yet, in all its synthetic symbolism, it is also very open. The *Angel* is, at least potentially, all things to all people. Standing in front of it, one is not forced to identify with or submit to anyone or anything. The *Angel* is, or could be, a messenger (that is what all angels are, at heart). But the message is for us to fabricate. The *Angel* is, or could be, a protector, or a guardian. It could be the bird Phoenix, arising from its own historical ashes, making itself, in a very sovereign way, anew. The *Angel* is quite clearly able to suck signs and energies from its soil and from its past, beaming them outwards, through its wings, into the air of the present. Its wings may be able to detect and capture signs and energies from around the globe, and subsequently transmit them through its feet into the local earth. The *Angel* stirs awe into those who behold its steely mass. But at the same time it comes across as a gentle, almost delicate creature. The aspiring sovereign is likely to recognise the *Angel*'s defying stance, but also its being-in-touch with the world. This *Angel* is beyond and before the strictures of this world, but at the same time it is also firmly planted in that very world. It is a force of nature, yet at the same time it is also a delicate contemplation (for more on the Angel, see Lippens, in press). Viewing the *Angel*, the aspiring sovereign is quite likely to abandon all hostility.

Where the *Angel of the North* succeeded in capturing the cultural sensitivities of a new age, Mason's sculpture failed. Not just because its strictures and its linearity are unbearable in the eyes of aspiring sovereigns, but also because to the latter, a weak inert Lurpak blob that commands you to submit to its codes is a contemptible abomination.

Concluding remarks

In what is arguably one of the finest and most insightful books on public art, Rosalyn Deutsche (1996), inspired by writings on radical democracy, argues that all public art brings with it its own evictions. Some things come in, but then at the same time other things will have to go. This applies both to state sanctioned public art and to alternative public art, or even resistance art, alike. Something comes in; other things have to go. You may win some, but you will certainly also lose some. There is no way around it. This, one could say, is a truism. And yet, it is also an inescapable fact of life that is conveniently forgotten each and every time one thinks a solution has been found to a supposed problem, each and every time one thinks regeneration is necessary, each and every time one thinks the key to regeneration has been worked out and worked into a particular regeneration project, each and every time someone thinks that a particular piece of public art will be able to effect regeneration, or each and every time someone thinks a particular act of artistic resistance will, finally, at last, help solve a neighbourhood's problems. And so it will continue. In an age of aspiring sovereigns, this painfully inevitable fact of life is all the more the case.

That said, sometimes works of public art *are* able to keep this sense, or indeed this experience of eviction, at levels that are quite modest. The *Angel of the North* (1998 – present) is arguably one of the works of art that have achieved this, at least to some extent. Raymond Mason's *Forward!* (1991–2003), which was the focus of this chapter, failed quite considerably in this respect. It failed to capture something of the mood of a deeply sceptical age, and what little it did manage to grasp, it then failed to convey in forms that might have connected onto newly emerged cultural sensitivities. Seen from this perspective *Forward!* was almost all eviction. Very little was 'brought in'. Much, if not all, 'had to go', and indeed 'went'. This is of course an untenable situation. At some point something had to give. On 17 April 2003, *Forward!* went up in flames.

References

Basdas, B., M. Degen and G. Rose (2009) 'Learning about how people experience built environments'. Available at: www.ixia-info.com. Last accessed 25 August 2016.

Belfiore, E. and O. Bennett (2007) 'Determinants of impact: towards a better understanding of encounters with the arts', *Cultural Trends* 16(3), 225.

Bennett, T. (2005) 'Civic laboratories. Museums, cultural objecthood and the governance of the social', *Cultural Studies* 19(5), 521.

Burk, A. L. (2006) 'Beneath and before: continuums of publicness in public art', *Social and Cultural Geography* 7(6), 949.

Clements, P. (2008) 'Public art: radical, functional or democratic methodologies?', *Journal of Visual Arts Practice* 7(1), 19.

Davey, N. (2005) 'Aesthetic f(r)iction: the conflicts of visual experience', *Journal of Visual Art Practice* 4(2–3), 135.

Deleuze, G. (1995) 'Post-Script on control societies' in G. Deleuze (ed.), *Negotiations* (pp. 177–182). New York: Columbia University Press.

Deutsche, R. (1996) *Evictions. Art and Spatial Politics*. Cambridge, MA: The MIT Press.

Douzinas, C. and L. Nead (eds) (1999) *Law and the Image. The Authority of Art and the Aesthetics of Law*. Chicago, IL: University of Chicago Press.

Hall, T. (1997) 'Images of industry in the post-industrial city: Raymond Mason and Birmingham', *Cultural Geographies* 4, 46.

Hamilton, J. (1991) 'The culture virus', *Spectator*, August, 34.

Hamilton, J., L. Forsyth and D. De Jongh (2001) 'Public art: a local authority perspective', *Journal of Urban Design* 6(3), 283.

Hubbard, P. (1996) 'Urban design and city regeneration: social representations of entrepreneurial landscapes', *Urban Studies* 33(8), 1441.

Jancovich, L. (2011) 'Great art for everyone? Engagement and participation policy in the arts', *Cultural Trends* 20(3/4), 271.

Joy, A. and J. F. Sherry (2003) 'Speaking of art as embodied imagination: a multisensory approach to understanding aesthetic experience', *Journal of Consumer Research* 30, 259.

Kwon, M. (1997) 'One place after another: notes on site specificity', *October*, 80(Spring), 85.

Lakoff, G. and M. Turner (1987) *More than Cool Reason*. Chicago, IL: Chicago University Press.

Leder, H., B. Belke, A. Oeberst and D. Augustin (2004) 'A model of aesthetic appreciation and aesthetic judgments', *British Journal of Psychology* 95, 489.

Levinson, S. (1998) *Written in Stone. Public Monuments in Changing Societies*. Durham, NC: Duke University Press.

Lippens, R. (2000) 'Greenwich, 1 January 2000. De-inventing the law of Britain in a tent', *International Journal for the Semiotics of Law* 13(3), 305.

Lippens, R. (in press) 'Angels, warriors and beacons. Totemic law, territorial coding and monumental sculpture in post-industrial landscapes', *Semiotica*.

Massey, D. and G. Rose (2003) 'Personal views: public art research project', Artpoint and Milton Keynes Council report.

Miles, M. (1997) *Art, Space and the City. Public Art and Urban Futures*. London: Routledge.

Miles, M. (2005) 'Interruptions: testing the rhetoric of culturally lead development', *Urban Studies* 42(5/6), 889.

Moore, N. (2007) 'Icons of control: Deleuze, signs, law', *International Journal for the Semiotics of Law* 20, 33.

Pollock, V. L. and R. Paddison (2010) 'Embedding public art: practice, policy and problems', *Journal of Urban Design* 15(3), 335.

Selwood, S. (1995) *The Benefits of Public Art. The Polemics of Permanent Art in Public Places*. London: Policy Studies Institute.

Sharp, J., V. Pollock and R. Paddison (2005) 'Just art for a just city: public art and social inclusion in urban generation', *Urban Studies* 42(5/6), 1001.

Visconti, L., J. Sherry Jr., S. Borghini and L. Anderson (2010) 'Street art, sweet art? Reclaiming the 'public' in public space', *Journal of Consumer Research* 57(October), 511.

Wilson, S. (2011) 'Raymond Mason: a last Romantic?', *Sculpture Journal*, 19(2), 248.

Wright, P. (1995) 'In your face', *Guardian*, 25 August.

Young, A. (2005) *Judging the Image: Art, Value, Law*. London: Routledge, 2005.

Zieleniec, A. (2007) *Space and Social Theory*. London: Sage Publications.

Zieleniec, A. (2013) *Park Spaces. Leisure, Culture and Modernity*. Saarbrucken: Scholars Press.

III

PERCEPTION OF THOSE AT THE FRINGE OF SOCIETY

Criminology and the legacies of Clarice Starling

'Oh, Officer Starling, do you think you can dissect me with this blunt little tool?'

The Silence of the Lambs (Harris, 1988, p. 24)

As an academic discipline, criminology has been variously described as: a 'rendezvous subject'; an 'importer discipline'; perhaps less charitably, as a 'lowbrow discipline'; or, more bluntly, as a 'bastard discipline'. Each description probably holds a kernel of truth and criminologists themselves seem to be perpetually worried about the aetiological origins and future direction of the subject (for a general overview, see, most recently, Bosworth and Hoyle, 2011). One of the most commonly associated questions also asked of it as an academic discipline is 'What is criminology for?' To this query we might as well add a whole list of other questions which, at the very least, would include: 'How should we study criminology?' 'What has been criminology's impact?' and 'How has criminology developed over the past few decades?'

This latter question reminds me that what is less commonly commented upon in these rather feverish discussions is the extraordinary popularity of criminology. When I was a student in the 1980s, criminology was seen to be a subject that was studied mainly at postgraduate level and only then if you wanted to become a civil servant. Now criminology is one of, if not the growth courses at British universities, with over 100 offering undergraduate degree courses in criminology as a single option, or as part of a joint honours programme, according to UCAS. These universities range from the Abertay in Scotland and Aberystwyth in Wales to the universities of Winchester and York in England, with all points of the alphabet and compass covered in between. Added to this, we have had a corresponding increase in Master's courses, PhD programmes, criminology journals, monographs and books and a somewhat, albeit patchy, corresponding growth in the numbers of academics actually teaching criminology. My own university now regularly attracts nearly 2,000 applications for about 100 undergraduate places, despite the fact there is no 'feeder' A level that students might have studied at school to have introduced them to the subject. The majority of these 2,000 applications are always from women. And, allied to those questions that I have already posed, should the students who are actually offered a place be taught theoretical, or applied criminology and do they really care if we badge our academic research and teaching as 'Critical criminology', 'Public criminology' or 'Realist criminology'?

These are important questions and ones which are all too often and, seemingly endlessly, debated by Criminologists – all of which might reveal either the growing fragmentation of the discipline, its vitality or indeed its weakness! However, what is rarely investigated, or even questioned, is what is it that has actually prompted this growth in popularity in the subject and in such a relatively short space of time? This chapter is concerned with one possible aspect of what might actually have driven criminology's boom and takes as its focus an American crime novel called *The Silence of the Lambs*. Written by Thomas Harris and published in 1988, the book won the Bram Stoker Award for Best Novel in that year and was the follow-up to Harris's *Red Dragon*, which was published seven years earlier. Both novels feature a serial killing, cannibalistic, psychiatrist called Dr Hannibal Lecter, who is pitted in *Red Dragon* alongside a forensic psychologist called Will Graham and in *The Silence of the Lambs* against an FBI agent called Clarice Starling whom, we are advised, studied criminology and Psychology 'at a good school', which turns out to be the University of Virginia (Harris, 1988, p. 134).

My choice of this American novel to anchor this very British chapter is not quixotic. Quite apart from the book's success, the film adapted from the book and released in 1991 (dir. Jonathan Demme), starring Jodie Foster as Clarice Starling and Anthony Hopkins as Hannibal Lecter, grossed over $270 million from a budget of $19 million; won all five of the leading Academy Awards in that year; and, in 2011, was deemed to be so 'culturally, historically and aesthetically significant' by the US Library of Congress was selected to be preserved in National Film Registry (BBC News Online, '*Silence of the Lambs Added to US Film Archive*,' 28 December 2011). The book and the film were popular throughout the world, especially in Britain where, at the forty-fifth British Academy of Film Awards (BAFTA) both Hopkins and Foster won in the Best Actor categories and the film was nominated for seven other BAFTAs.

These achievements notwithstanding, I first became intrigued by the legacy of the book and the film through an academic administrative task – reading the personal statements of those 2,000 prospective criminology students who were applying to Birmingham City University.

Perhaps because there was no school set text to fall back upon, I soon became aware that for hundreds of these students, 'what first attracted me to criminology was reading *The Silence of the Lambs*', or some such statement. The book was one of three most regularly cited, with the other two being Oliver Sacks's (1985) *The Man Who Mistook His Wife for a Hat* (the 'million copy bestseller', as it says on its cover) and my own *A History of British Serial Killing* (2009), which was perhaps being very consciously and strategically included in these personal statements because of the university that the student was applying to and despite the fact that the book is written from within a completely different academic tradition! The fictional character of Starling emerged as a 'particular heroine of mine' for hundreds of potential students and, wanting to know why, I reread the book having previously read it when it was first published, while I was still working as a prison governor.

What follows is therefore a critical analysis (for a useful, general introduction to the critical analysis of documents, see Jupp, 1996) of *The Silence of the Lambs*, with a particular focus on understanding the appeal of Clarice Starling. Moreover, through this critical analysis the chapter seeks to question more generally the assumptions at the heart of Harris's book, which may very well have prompted and seems to continue to generate interest in criminology but has, it will be argued, left a legacy that is often unhelpful and misleading about individual serial killers in particular and the phenomenon of serial murder more generally.

It is acknowledged that this is a difficult and unusual source for a Criminologist to use as autobiographies, biographies, 'true crime' products, films, documentaries and novels rarely make their way into academic writing about our discipline (for exceptions, see, e.g., Wilson and Groombridge, 2010; Wilson and O'Sullivan, 2004; 2005). However, despite the difficulties that sources such as these pose, we should be minded of cultural criminology's attack on the slender sources that are usually considered within orthodox criminology and the latter's desire to 'consign various cultural artefacts to the intellectual dustbin, deeming them unworthy of serious scholarly analysis' (Ferrell et al., 2008, p. 158). Chief among those sources deemed unworthy were 'comic books and television programmes', even if they 'helped to create public perceptions that underwrite misguided criminal justice policy, or at other times provide a push for social justice' (Ferrell et al., 2008, p. 158). Ferrell, Hayward and Young go as far as to describe the analysis that can be gleaned from accommodating these and other sources as 'dangerous knowledge', partly because it requires the reader to acknowledge new issues, or answer old questions in new ways. 'Dangerous knowledge', in this context, has also the added advantage of actually treating seriously what these future students articulated, rather than dismissing their interest in the novel and in the character of Starling as nonsense. I begin by offering a brief overview of the plot of *The Silence of the Lambs*.

A serial killer thriller

The narrative of *The Silence of the Lambs* is dominated by a triangle of relationships, made up of one young woman and two older men who, in their different ways and for their own reasons, try to become her teacher. This triangle consists of Clarice Starling, Dr Hannibal Lecter and Jack Crawford, the head of a division of the Federal Bureau of Investigation (FBI), which psychologically profiles convicted serial killers. Very quickly the reader learns that Dr Hannibal Lecter – who had been the evil protagonist in Harris's earlier novel *Red Dragon* – has been caught and incarcerated and is now serving nine life sentences in a Maryland asylum, which is run by the unctuous and ambitious Dr Frederick Chilton. However, of note, Will Graham, who had been instrumental in Lecter's arrest, only appears in the narrative of *The Silence of the Lambs* as someone who is referred to, rather than as a character who will drive the plot. He has been quite literally written out of the novel.

Starling is asked by Crawford to present Lecter with a questionnaire – the 'blunt little tool' dismissively referred to at the start of this chapter – but in reality he is using her to discover what Lecter actually knows about a series of unsolved murders by a serial killer who has been dubbed by the media as 'Buffalo Bill'. This killer's modus operandi is to abduct slightly overweight women and then keep them for a number of days, during which time they will be starved. After they have lost a little weight, he then kills these women, skins them (which is why he is known as 'Buffalo Bill') and discards their peeled bodies in nearby rivers. It will later emerge that the killer is a pre-operative transsexual called Jame Gumb – a lover of a former patient of Lecter's called Benjamin Raspail – and that he is skinning his victims so as to literally 'become' a woman, through wearing their skin.

Starling is sent back and forth to Lecter throughout the novel, trying to extract information and, in doing so, they form a strange bond. However, she is also given practical training by Crawford and in one crucial scene, he takes Starling with him to perform an autopsy on Buffalo Bill's sixth victim, who has been found floating in a river in West Virginia. This victim has been scalped – as was predicted by Lecter – and a pupa is found in her throat. The autopsy provides some clues as to the killer's identity and also reveals something of Lecter's knowledge about the killer. However, the narrative of the novel quickly moves on when the media release information that Buffalo Bill's most recent abductee – and therefore someone who will become his seventh victim – is Catherine Martin, the daughter of Senator Ruth Martin of Tennessee, which adds political pressure onto Crawford and Starling to solve the case. Starling is once again dispatched to see Lecter and offer him a deal.

The odious Dr Chilton discovers what has been happening and, seeking advancement for himself, intervenes and makes his own arrangements with Lecter. Lecter insists on being taken in person to see Senator Martin in Tennessee. In effect this ensures that the FBI lose control of Lecter, who is taken out of the asylum, although not before he has revealed some telling details to Starling which makes her realise that he knows the identity of the killer and, crucially, she works out for herself that the killer would have personally known his first victim. The pupa that was found in the throat of the sixth victim turns out to be of the Death's-head Hawkmoth, which stands as a metaphor for the transformation that Gumb would like to make of himself. Thereafter, in a further exchange for information about the killer, Lecter has Starling reveal her worst childhood memory. Starling describes the death of her father – a policeman – who was shot while responding to a robbery when she was ten years of age and of being sent to live with an uncle on a sheep and horse ranch, where she remembers with horror the slaughtering of the spring lambs. She runs away from the ranch and is eventually sent to live in an orphanage.

In the final sections of the book, Lecter inevitably escapes from his non-FBI guards and vows to track down and kill Dr Chilton. Meanwhile, Starling finally locates Buffalo Bill, whom she kills and, as a result, is able to save the Senator's daughter, Catherine Martin. Starling thereafter graduates as an FBI agent – the seeming culmination of her ambition – and receives a telegram from Lecter who, in congratulating her on her success, says that he hopes that 'the lambs have stopped screaming'.

Starling as a character

Two issues dominate and define the character of Starling throughout the novel. First, her gender and, second, but perhaps less often commented upon, in common with a great deal of criminology (Hall, 2012, p. 164), her class. Lecter picks up on this latter issue immediately and reminds her – and therefore the reader – that 'do you know what you look like to me with your good bag and cheap shoes? You look like a rube. You're a well-scrubbed, hustling rube with a little taste. Your eyes are like cheap birth-stones – all surface shine when you stalk some little answer. And you're bright behind them aren't you? Desperate not to be like your mother' (Harris, 1988, p. 25). Harris's use of 'to me' in the first sentence is meant to distance the reader from Lecter's observations but he has said, as it were, what everyone would have noticed if they could have actually encountered Starling; she was a 'rube' – a 'hick' or a 'yokel', of poor Scottish-Irish descent. So too the idea of her distancing herself from her mother not only reminds us of her gender, but also raises the issue of how Starling could achieve that distancing in just one generation. The explanation of her strategy comes towards the end of the book when we are advised that Starling had caught 'brain fever'. In other words, she 'had lived by schools, her weapon the competitive exam' (p. 333) and so through education she 'could be near the top of her class, approved, included, chosen, and not sent away' (p. 334).

This potent mix of education and gender is rather more positively described in the scene in which Crawford takes Starling with him to perform the autopsy on Buffalo Bill's sixth victim, who had been found in rural West Virginia, near the town of Potter. Crawford notices how Starling, while putting on her surgical gloves, takes control of the situation and especially the local, male, police officers who had gathered to watch the autopsy. It was 'In this place Starling was heir to the granny women, to the wise women, the herb healers, the stalwart country women who have always done the needful, who keep the watch and, when the watch is over, wash and dress the country dead' (p. 94). This is a very powerful passage, which links Starling both to the past and to the future. She is the 'heir' to the historic, 'granny women' of the countryside; of working-class women who had solidarity and who conceivably did not see their working-class origins as something to escape from. However, Starling is also connected to the future, which is perhaps best symbolised by her donning her surgical gloves to indicate her new, technocratic, scientific, professionalism. Starling's class and gender intersect, in other words, to create an FBI agent; a new type of 'wise woman'; a classless woman, who has studied both criminology and psychology. This Starling was going to fly.

Indeed, it had been Crawford's lectures in criminology at the University of Virginia that had made Starling want to join the FBI. In this sense Crawford also represents the future and also, incidentally, alludes to differences between how criminology is taught at most British and American universities. The latter, for example, have a much more applied focus while, perhaps over-generalising, the latter are more concerned with sociological or psychological theory. Of note, Lecter is particularly scathing about psychologists and their attempts to interview serial killers, although he makes no specific comment about Criminologists. He argues that the key FBI finding that serial killers can leave crime scenes which are either 'organised' or 'disorganised' – and on which basis you can infer something about the personality of the offender – is 'simplistic' and goes as far as to suggest that 'in fact most psychology is puerile, Officer Starling, and that practised in Behavioural Science is on a level with phrenology' (p. 22). He is just as dismissive about academic psychologists, whom he compares with 'ham-radio enthusiasts and other personality-deficient buffs. Hardly the best brains on campus' (p. 23). In one sense, this is meant by Lecter as a 'come-on' to Starling for he suggests that it is only him who can give her what it is that she most desires. 'What's that Dr Lecter?' asks Starling. 'Advancement of course,' replies Lecter (p. 29).

Fact in the fiction

It is important at this stage to consider to what extent what is being described in *The Silence of the Lambs* actually relates to how the FBI might have gone about profiling a serial killer such as Buffalo Bill in the 1980s. In other words, does the plot have any basis in reality? However, here we should also note that what might constitute a 'serial killer' is never actually defined in the novel, or how therefore a serial killer might be differentiated from a 'spree' or a 'mass murderer'. The issue of definition – or at least its absence – is one which we can use to begin to deconstruct *The Silence of the Lambs* and the assumptions that lie behind its narrative, the characters who drive that narrative and the phenomenon of serial murder more generally. However, perhaps one issue that Harris accurately reflected and, as one academic has recently described, the 1980s, especially in the USA, were 'the golden age of serial killers,' (Howard, 2010, p. 55). We might also add it was also a golden age for those who wrote or taught about them.

Among the North American academics who first wrote about serial murder were James DeBurger, Ronald Holmes, Stephen Holmes, Eric Hickey, Jack Levin, James Fox, Steve Egger, Philip Jenkins and Elliot Leyton. As for defining what constituted serial murder, in their classic book about the subject, for example, Ronald Holmes and Stephen Holmes (1994) suggested, 'A serial killer is defined as someone who murders three persons in more than a thirty-day period. These killings typically involve one victim per episode' (p. 92). So too, a decade later, James Fox and Jack Levin (2005), in their book *Extreme Killing: Understanding Serial and Mass Murder*, were still defining a serial killer as someone who killed three or more victims, and noted that he 'may continue to kill over a period of months or years, often ha[ving] long time lapses between homicides, during which time he maintains a more or less ordinary life, going to work and spending time with family and friends' (p. 17).

These academics found a great deal of support for their work from a number of FBI agents, often located in the Behavioural Science Unit (BSU), as was depicted within *The Silence of the Lambs*. The BSU had been founded in 1972 by an agent called Jack Kirsch and was then run by John Phaff, Roger DePue and, when DePue retired, by John Douglas. The BSU, which was later re-named as the Investigative Support Unit, was based at the FBI's

Academy in Quantico, Virginia and it was this Academy that the fictional characters Will Graham and Clarice Starling were attached to in Harris's novels. The real-life agents most popularly associated with the BSU included Robert Ressler, Ray Hazelwood and John Douglas, each of whom would also later describe themselves as 'profilers'. These agents would gain considerable fame from writing true crime books, appearing on TV and radio and delivering public lectures, as well as writing, or contributing to more academic books.

One such book was their *Crime Classification Manual*, in which Douglas et al. (1992) attempted to create an operational definition for several crimes, and within their classification of homicide was a subcategory of serial murder, which they defined as 'three or more separate events in three or more separate locations with an emotional cooling-off period between homicides. The serial murder is hypothesised to be premeditated, involving offence-related fantasy and detailed planning.' They continue:

> When the time is right for him and he has cooled off from his last homicide, the serial killer selects his next victim, and proceeds with his plan. The cooling-off period can last for days, weeks, or months and is the key feature that distinguishes the serial killer from other multiple murderers. (Douglas et al., pp. 96–97)

Taken together we can therefore detect how some consensus developed about how to define serial murder although, as you may have noticed, the latter definition about the 'cooling-off period' has become somewhat less focused ('days, weeks, or months') over time, even if the numeric threshold for the numbers of victims remains three or more.

At the time that this consensus was developing, Harris was being given extraordinary access to the BSU and was widely acknowledged by both the academic community and by law enforcement as contributing towards the public's understanding of serial murder. For example, Ronald Holmes in the preface to *Serial Murder*, described how 'I have also been fortunate enough to count Thomas Harris among my new friends.' Holmes continues:

> I have shared some meals with Tom, and I look at him and wonder where in his brain resides the characters he brings to the printed page. More than one time in the cases that I have profiled for police departments across the United States, I have uttered words similar to those of Will Graham: 'You had to touch her, didn't you? (Holmes and Holmes, 1994, pp. x–xi).

Perhaps more importantly, Douglas became Harris's model for Jack Crawford in *Red Dragon* and *Silence of the Lambs* and, in his co-written book about the serial killer Dennis Rader – Douglas and Dodd (2007: 8), *Inside the Mind of BTK: The True Story Behind the Thirty-Year Hunt for the* Notorious *Wichita Serial Killer* – Douglas suggests, in a phrase that would not have been out of place in a novel, that 'climbing inside the heads of monsters is my speciality'.

Frankly, it is not too hard to see where Harris had found some of the inspiration for his characters and how those characters in turn began to shape the reality of the people that they were supposedly based upon. In short, fact met fiction and, in turn, fiction became fact. Everyone seemed to benefit from this cosy consensus about serial killers and the phenomenon of serial murder with academics and profilers able to develop their respective careers through book deals, journal articles and increased student numbers; the FBI enhanced its reputation through being seen to be fighting this new type of predator; and Harris's novels became a small industry not only selling millions of books, but also quickly being adapted for film and television. Indeed, as I write, the new series of *Hannibal* has just started on Sky Atlantic, although this reverts to focusing on Will Graham as opposed to Starling.

Dissenting voices

This cosy consensus was challenged, however, by a number of people at the time and thereafter. For example, the most vociferous of the original dissenting voices about serial killing as a phenomenon belongs to Philip Jenkins. Jenkins (1994) argued in *Using Murder: The Social Construction of Serial Homicide* that serial murder accounted for perhaps less than 1 per cent of all American homicides, which would equate to some 200 deaths per year. Nonetheless this phenomenon had been 'exploited by a wide variety of official agencies and interest groups, and the issue has been used as a multifaceted weapon in political debate' (p. 3). He suggested that serial murder had been presented by these various interest groups as novel and unprecedented and that the threats posed by serial murderers was suggested to be all the greater because serial killers were viewed as highly mobile, wandering freely between different states and legal jurisdictions. This latter suggestion therefore gave greater authority to the federal (as opposed to state) Justice Department to claim that it needed to expand its bureaucratic and law enforcement operations, with associated increases in personnel, financial resources and public and political prestige.

The basis for making the claims that the Justice Department promoted was a research programme within the FBI's Behavioural Science Unit – led by Ressler – called the Criminal Personality Research Project. In effect, what the FBI had wanted to do was to find a way to use the wealth of forensic information that they were able to generate from crime scenes and see if from that evidence they could suggest something of the type of offender who had committed the offence. So, in part using their collective experience of investigating multiple murder and sexual assaults and, crucially through carrying out extensive interviews with thirty-six (not thirty-two as suggested in *The Silence of the Lambs*) convicted murderers, twenty-five of whom were serial killers, they began to assert that the personality of an offender – in cases of serial rape or murder – could be gleaned from a consideration of the following five areas: the crime scene; the nature of the attacks them-selves; forensic evidence; a medical examination of the victim; and victim characteristics. These interviews and the analyses that flowed from them, were the beginning of what we have now come to know as 'profiling'.

On the back of this research programme, the FBI made a number of statements which captured the public's attention and also served to gar-ner political support. For example, the Justice Department alleged that as many as 4,000 Americans per year – about 20 per cent of all homicide vic-tims – were murdered by serial killers. Ressler himself suggested that 'serial killing – I think that it's at epidemic proportions. The type of crime we're seeing today did not really occur with any known frequency prior to the fifties. [It] is a relatively new phenomenon in the crime picture of the U.S.' (quoted in Jenkins (1994, p. 67). So, given this 'epidemic' and 'new phenom-enon' the Justice Department lobbied for – and then created – the National Centre for the Analysis of Violent Crime (NCAVC) and the Violent Criminal Apprehension Programme (VICAP), both of which are still in existence.

In 1996, the independent National Criminal Justice Commission (NCJC), in a report that they called *The Real War on Crime,* was able to offer some critical assessment about these various claims and statements about violent crime generally and serial murder in particular. The report claimed that 'a hoax is afoot'; that the FBI had 'hyped' the threats posed by serial killers; and that the true extent of murder that could be attributed to serial killers per year was between fifty and sixty – still quite a large figure, but no where near the terrifying levels of 4,000. Indeed, what the NCJC was able to show was that the figure of 4,000 related to unsolved murders and that all of these had simply been attributed by the FBI to murders committed by serial killers (Donziger, 1996, pp. 2, 76–79).

Here too we should remember that this period also saw the rapid growth of the prison population in the USA. The numbers of people being impris-oned, for example, increased from just under 500,000 in 1980 to just over 1,500,000 by 1994. Some of that growth can be attributed to specific initiatives undertaken within particular states and more nationally, and which were given shape and support by the adoption of a 'right realist' law and order agenda, which had become more strident with the election of Ronald Reagan as President in 1980. These so-called 'get tough' initiatives included, for example, 'zero tolerance' policing; 'truth in sentencing'; and, more famously, 'three strikes and you're out'. Each served to ensure that the prison population increased.

As *The Real War on Crime* explains, however, this series of policies could be characterised as 'bait and switch'. In other words, they appeared to be focused on locking up violent offenders in a fight against crime, but in fact simply filled American prisons with non-violent and petty offenders, who posed no risk to the public and could easily have been managed within the community (Donziger, 1996, p. 18). Within this type of febrile political climate, talk about 'serial killers' helped serve to keep law and order at the top of the policy agenda and, as one recent critic has put it, also 'elevated the members of the FBI's then Behavioural Science Unit to superstar status (Turvey, 2012, p. 608).

Viewed from the present we can now see that there were a variety of industries and individuals who, consciously or not, helped to socially construct the serial killer. This social construction is all too obvious in *The Silence of the Lambs*, with the serial killer – not only in the shape of Lecter but also of Buffalo Bill – portrayed as new and unprecedented, pathological killers, who could only be apprehended by specially trained law enforcement agents. These agents would use newly developed profiling techniques, which had themselves been fashioned through interviewing those serial killers who had been apprehended and imprisoned. Crucial to all of this was to understand the serial killer's motive, as with Jame Gumb in the novel, although it should be acknowledged that I know of no transsexual serial killer. In other words, serial killers would kill because of some inner drive that propelled them ever onwards and discerning that motive was crucial in bringing their killing cycle to an end. All of this is what is sometimes called, more academically, the 'medico-psychological tradition' of analysing the phenomenon of serial murder and *The Silence of the Lambs* can be read entirely from within this tradition. But how helpful has all of this been in terms of truly understanding the phenomenon of serial murder?

Talking with serial killers

We actually know very little about the thirty-six interviews that the FBI conducted and which, in one sense, is what Crawford sends Starling to do to Lecter, armed with her 'blunt little tool'. However, in reality, or so it would seem, John Douglas, in his rather odd (e.g. he compares himself to the fictional six-year-old boy Cole Sear, who saw dead people in the 1999 film *The Sixth Sense*) and co-written 2007 book called *Inside the Mind of BTK: The True Story Behind the Thirty-Year Hunt for the Notorious Wichita Serial Killer*, describes the fact that the FBI's interview protocol involved 'thousands of questions' and ran to fifty-seven pages in length (Douglas and

Dodd, 2007, p. 4). Many of the FBI's questions were aimed at providing some basic information about the killer's motivation, victim selection, and the impact that the murders might have had on the killer. It would also appear that the FBI agents set out to answer whether or not their interviewees were 'born to kill', or whether, for example, some childhood trauma had influenced their behaviour. The fruits of these interviews eventually led to the publication of Ressler, Burgess and Douglas's *Sexual Homicide: Patterns and Motives* in 1988.

Douglas provides a glimpse of how one of these interviews was conducted in 1981 when he visited Attica Correctional Facility in New York with Robert Ressler to interview David Berkowitz – also known as 'The Son of Sam'. Berkowitz is an American serial killer and arsonist who murdered six people and wounded seven others in New York between July 1976 until his arrest in August 1977. Douglas explains that he and Ressler had gone to Attica to 'pry information out of the head of one of the nation's most notorious serial killers.' He continues:

> We'd arrived unannounced, on a fishing expedition of sorts, hoping to convince David Berkowtiz, aka Son of Sam, to help us with our criminal profiling study, which involved a fifty-seven-page interview questionnaire. We wanted answers to such questions as *What was his motive? Was there a trigger that set him off on his murderous spree? What was his early childhood like? How did he select his victims? Did he ever visit the grave sites of his victims? How closely did he follow the press coverage of his crimes?* His answers would help us better understand the killers we were hunting. (Douglas and Dodd, 2007, p. 19, emphasis in original)

Seemingly, Berkowtiz was brought to see Douglas and Ressler who were waiting for him in a tiny interrogation room, although as the following exchange reveals it is clear that Berkowtiz had no idea who Douglas or Ressler were, or what they wanted.

> 'Who are you guys?' he asked the moment he spotted us seated at the far end of the only piece of furniture in the room – a linoleum-covered table. As planned, the guards had quickly exited before Berkowitz had a chance to tell us to take a hike. 'We're FBI agents, David' I told him. 'We'd like to talk to you. We're hoping you might be able to help us … It's like I always say,' I explained, 'if you want to learn how to paint, you don't read about it in a book. You go straight to the artist. And that's what you are, David. You're the artist … you're famous. You're huge. You had all of New York scared shitless. In a hundred years, no one will remember my name. But everybody will still know who the Son of Sam was. (Douglas and Dodd, 2007, pp. 19–20)

This flattery seems to have worked, for Douglas suggests that Berkowitz became 'putty in our hands' and over the course of the next five hours 'he walked us through every dark, twisted corner of his sad life, sharing details he'd never told anyone' (Douglas and Dodd, 2007, p. 20).

Douglas does not tell the reader what these details might have been and so there is no way of validating this claim and nor is it revealed if Berkowtiz actually completed the fifty-seven-page questionnaire that formed the basis of Douglas and Ressler's research. Indeed, they seem to have simply chatted for a number of hours. However, there are more worrying issues that this account reveals, if this is indeed an accurate depiction of the interview(s). Ignoring the (absence of) ethics of the origin and conduct of the interview, for example, let us simply consider how credulous Douglas and Ressler seem to have been when they interviewed Berkowitz. After all, Berkowitz, at the time of this interview three years into a 365-year sentence, might have had a variety of reasons for agreeing to be interviewed, after he realised that was in fact why he had been taken to the interrogation room, rather than simply falling for Douglas's flattery.

Should we not also consider whether serial killers necessarily tell an interviewer the truth? Might they attempt to confuse, or alternatively be over-eager in the hope of getting some sort of favour such as parole, a better work detail, or simply a more favourable cell allocation? That Douglas, Ressler and the other FBI agents interviewed serial killers who were caught may suggest something about this small sample and their offending behaviour, but all of this might have been very different from those offenders who remained at large and who might have used other approaches – approaches which allowed them to remain at large.

Even so, the FBI's central finding was that it was possible to determine through what became known as 'crime scene analysis' whether that crime scene was 'organised' or 'disorganised' and that this dichotomy could be used to suggest something about the offender's personality in his everyday life. For example, an 'organised' offender would be of above-average intelligence, sexually and socially competent and living with a partner. On the other hand, a disorganised offender would typically be someone who lived alone, sexually and socially inadequate and who would live quite close to the crime scene.

There have been and continue to be a number of criticisms of the FBI's approach – some of which have already been alluded to. Of the remainder, we should note the current and lively debates that continue to be discussed about what is known as the 'homology assumption' and the 'behavioural consistency hypothesis'. The former implies that different offenders who perform the same types of crimes will have similar personal traits or characteristics; the latter hypothesis suggests that the offender's personality will not change over time and therefore he will continue to commit crimes in a roughly similar way. Research on these assumptions has generally shown that the homological assumption cannot really be sustained, although there is evidence to suggest that, by and large, an offender will continue to offend in a similar way and so the crime scene will contain behavioural clues that may be identified as the 'signature' of that offender.

The structural tradition

One way of coming to a better critical understanding of all of this, is to consider the phenomenon of serial murder from what academics describe as the 'structural tradition'. The structural tradition can be viewed as attempting to answer a different set of questions from those which dominate the medico-psychological tradition. It is less interested in, for example, the micro-dynamics of the pathology of individual serial killers and with analysing crime scene patterns, and more concerned with macro questions about which groups most regularly fall victim to serial murder; the periods in history when there were more (or less) serial killers; and which countries seem to produce more serial murderers than others. In essence it champions the idea that wider social forces may drive people in a particular direction even if that direction will be viewed as 'pathological' by the majority. This approach can find its roots in the work of the French sociologist Émile Durkheim (1858–1917), who, for example, pointed to a more societal explanation for what had been regarded until then as the individualistic act of suicide.

As with the medico-psychological tradition, there are also a set of assumptions underlying the structural tradition. Chief among these is the belief that at any given time there will always be a small number of people (for various reasons) who will want to repeatedly kill. If this reality is constant why should it be only at some times, in some societies, that serial killing becomes an issue? It therefore considers how this small number of offenders gets access to their victims, and how they use that access to create the opportunity to kill. Only then are researchers in this tradition interested in what might have motivated the serial killer to kill. Finally, it is suggested that if we want to reduce the incidence of serial murder, rather than focusing on the pathology of individual serial murderers, we should instead concentrate on what it is that creates the vulnerabilities in the groups that are targeted by this type of offender and ameliorate or eradicate that vulnerability.

The Canadian anthropologist Professor Elliot Leyton (1986) in his seminal book *Hunting Humans: The Rise of the Modern Multiple Murderer* was perhaps one of the first academics to argue that, in order to understand the phenomenon of serial killing, factors beyond the medico-psychological tradition needed to be analysed. And, using evidence of North American serial killing since the end of the Second World War, his central thesis was that serial murder should be viewed as a form of 'homicidal protest' by frustrated members of the upper working and lower middle classes, who tend to kill victims from the middle classes in a period he labels as 'Modern'. Leyton does acknowledge that: 'Occasionally ... they (serial killers) continue a metaphor from the earlier era and discipline unruly [*sic*] prostitutes and runaways' (1986, p. 297), although he goes on, 'Much more commonly ... they punish those above them in the system – preying on unambiguously middle-class figures such as university women' (p. 297).

Leyton argued that the during the 'Industrial Era', which he roughly placed as starting in the late nineteenth century and lasting until the end of the Second World War, was one 'in which middle class functionaries – doctors, teachers, professors, civil servants, who belonged to the class created to serve the needs of the new triumphant bourgeoisie, preyed on members of the lower orders, especially prostitutes and housemaids' (1986, p. 276). In this era, Leyton suggests that the crimes of serial killers were a symbolic extension of the need for industrial discipline. In other words, serial killers were taking to their most heinous conclusion the unprecedented control demanded by the cash-nexus of industrial capitalism. Serial killers removed those who lived outside the new moral order, which demanded the maximum extraction of value from the industrial proletariat: 'In killing the failures and the unruly renegades from the system ... they acted as enforcers of the new moral order' (p. 276).

Widening the analysis – serial murder in Britain

Does the type of analysis provided by Leyton apply to Britain? A number of academics have attempted to consider whether British serial murder should be viewed as a form of 'homicidal protest', as described by Leyton, including Chris Grover and Keith Soothill (1997) and David Wilson (2006; 2009). Using Harold Shipman – who largely murdered elderly women and some elderly men – as their example, Grover and Soothill suggest that by widening the focus of social relations beyond class relations to include other social relations, such as patriarchy, it is still possible that 'homicidal protest' has some conceptual value in the British context. In their article, they suggest that 'widening the analysis in this way provides scope for being able to classify a greater variety of serial killers' (Grover and Soothill, 1997, n.p.). They also maintain that there is evidence that among some British serial killers a degree of socio-economic frustration may have existed. However, they claim that it would be both bold and inappropriate to identify socio-economic frustration as either a necessary or sufficient condition for serial killing.

Equally, they claim that as a result of Leyton's failure to consider social relations other than those of capitalism (class), Leyton cannot easily explain why the victims of British serial killers tend to be females, children, young people, gay men and pensioners. In short, they argue that we need to locate serial murder within power relations that go beyond those of class. Only then can 'homicidal protest' remain understandable as a form of revenge, but a revenge that is wreaked upon relatively powerless groups in society.

This argument has found support from feminist commentators, who have argued with both fervour and conviction that it needs to be recognised that Britain is both a capitalist and a patriarchal society. Violence against women and children is thus seen as being reflective of patriarchal relations through which men maintain power over women and children. Hence, recognising patriarchal relations, it becomes clearer as to why serial killers often murder women and children. It is an expression of power through which men are able to dominate and oppress women and children.

Wilson (2006; 2009) has developed this analysis further. For example, he views the murder of gay men and the elderly by serial killers as an extension of the homophobia present in British society and also the more general powerlessness and invisibility of older people in our culture. It is this powerlessness, Wilson argues, that has contributed to this latter group being most regularly attacked by serial murderers, such as Harold Shipman. In short the structural tradition has suggested that to truly understand why serial killers kill we need to investigate the very nature of the social structure – the society – that has created these people whom we define and label as serial killers. And, as is implicit in this analysis, it also suggests that the responsibility for serial killing therefore does not lie so much with the individual serial killer, but can be better found within the social and economic structure of the country which does not reward the efforts of all, and in particular has marginalised large sections of society. It therefore should come as no surprise that the victims of British serial killers have been almost exclusively confined to certain marginalised groups in our culture – the elderly, gay men, sex workers, babies and infants, and young people moving home and finding their feet elsewhere in the country, and that women make up a significant number in all but one of these categories.

Clarice's legacy and some personal statements

All of this seems to have taken us quite far from Clarice and *The Silence of the Lambs*. However, in essence, Starling, the book and the film of the book, and now the TV series too, created an understanding that serial murder was a new and pressing phenomenon; that serial killers themselves were pathological in some way and what might be motivating them to kill could be determined from within a medico-psychological tradition; that the FBI were especially trained at catching this type of perpetrator; and that the tool that they had at their disposal was 'profiling'. As I have argued, all of these issues should be subject to much more critical scrutiny and, moreover, do not necessarily reflect the reality of working on a police investigation related to a linked series of crimes, and certainly do not reflect my own personal experiences of talking to, or managing serial killers after their arrest and incarceration (Wilson, 2006).

However, these objections notwithstanding, Clarice Starling has endured and seems to retain an appeal to students who want to study criminology, whether I like it or not and despite all criminological evidence to the contrary that is presented in *The Silence of the Lambs*. That appeal is probably related both to her gender and to her class. She is a working-class woman, struggling to make her way in an essentially male-dominated world and is able to achieve what she has achieved – and will continue to achieve – through her intelligence; through her ability to pass exams. All of this is surely inspirational to potential students, even if I continue to remind them that if we really want to reduce the incidence of serial murder in our society we should tackle homophobia, reconsider how we police sex work, and do something to reduce the isolation, vulnerability and powerlessness of the elderly. This might all be less immediately attractive to students, but would nonetheless contribute significantly to reducing the number of people who will fall victim to a serial killer.

Let me end by describing another administrative, academic task which once more suggests the hold that Clarice and *The Silence of the Lambs* continues to have on prospective students. At one of our recent open days at the University, I gave my standard introductory lecture about serial murder, pointing out the differences between the medico-psychological and structural traditions, and describing a little of my applied work with serial killers. One student put up her hand to ask a question. 'This is all very interesting Professor Wilson, but I'm squeamish!' 'I don't understand,' I replied. 'Well,' she continued, 'how many dead bodies do I have to see in my first year?'

References

Bosworth, M. and C. Hoyle (eds) (2011) *What Is Criminology?* Oxford: Oxford University Press.

Donziger, S. R. (ed.) (1996) *The Real War on Crime: The Report of the National Justice Commission.* New York: Harper Perennial.

Douglas, J. E., A. W. Burgess and R. K. Ressler (1992) *Crime Classification Manual: A Standard System for Investigating and Classifying Violent Crime.* New York: Simon & Schuster.

Douglas, J. E. and J. Dodd (2007) *Inside the Mind of BTK: the True Story Behind the Thirty-Year Hunt for the Notorious Wichita Serial Killer.* San Francisco, CA: Jossey-Bass.

Ferrell, J. K. Hayward and J. Young (2008) *Cultural Criminology: an Invitation.* London: SAGE Publications.

Fox, J. A. and J. Levin (2005) *Extreme Killing: Understanding Serial and Mass Murder.* Thousand Oaks, CA: SAGE Publications.

Grover, C. and K. Soothill (1997) 'British serial killing: towards a structural explanation', in *The British Criminology Conferences: Selected Proceedings,* Vol. II. Available at: www.lboro.ac.uk/departments/ss/bccsp/vol02/08GROVEHTM. Last accessed 20 June 2014.

Hall, S. (2012) *Theorizing Crime and Deviance: a New Perspective.* London: SAGE Publications.

Harris, T. (1988) *The Silence of the Lambs.* London: Arrow Books.

Holmes, R., and S. Holmes (1994) *Serial Murder.* Thousand Oaks, CA: SAGE Publications.

Howard, A. (2010) 'Serial killers as practical moral skeptics: a historical survey with interviews' in S. Waller (ed.), *Serial Killers: Philosophy for Everyone* (pp. 51–65). Oxford: Wiley-Blackwell.

Jenkins, P. (1994) *Using Murder: the Social Construction of Serial Homicide.* New York: Transaction.

Jupp, V. (1996), 'Documents and critical research' in R. Sapsford and V. Jupp (eds), *Data Collection and Analysis* (p. 298). London: SAGE Publications.

Leyton, E. (1986) *Hunting Humans: the Rise of the Modern Multiple Murderer.* Toronto: McClelland and Stewart.

Sacks, O. (1985) *The Man Who Mistook His Wife for a Hat.* London: Gerald Duckworth.

Soothill, K. and D. Wilson (2005) 'Theorising the puzzle that is Harold Shipman', *Journal of Forensic Psychiatry and Psychology* 16(4), 658.

Turvey, B. E. (2012) *Criminal Profiling: an Introduction to Behavioral Evidence Analysis.* Amsterdam: Elsevier.

Wilson, D. (2006) *Serial Killers: Hunting Britons and their Victims, 1960–2006.* Winchester: Waterside Press.

Wilson, D. (2009) *A History of British Serial Killing.* London: Sphere.

Wilson, D. and N. Groombridge (2010) 'I'm making a TV programme here!: Reality TV's *Banged Up* and public criminology,' *The Howard Journal of Criminal Justice,* 49(1): 1.

Wilson, D. and S. O'Sullivan (2004) *Images of Incarceration: Representations of Prison in Film and TV Drama.* Winchester: Waterside Press.

Wilson, D. and S. O'Sullivan (2005) 'Re-theorizing the penal reform function of the prison film: revelation, humanization, empathy and benchmarking', *Theoretical Criminology* 9(4), 471.

Letters to Casey Anthony, a woman accused of murder

In July 2011, Casey Anthony of Orlando, Florida was acquitted of the murder of her two-year-old daughter, Caylee. The case had been in the public eye for three years, ever since Caylee's grandmother, Cindy, reported her as missing to the police. A 'media frenzy' ensued, with news outlets under pressure to regularly update their websites with the latest developments (Pafundi, 2010, p. 228). Facebook pages, Twitter accounts and websites dedicated to the story proliferated. Clips of Casey both playing with her daughter and on nights out with friends were posted on YouTube (Fuhrman, 2009). This intensive media interest turned Casey Anthony into a celebrity. A Casey Anthony 'voodoo doll' was sold on eBay and a Caylee doll was available online (Fuhrman, 2009).The *New York Times* commented that the case had been a media sensation, 'widely reported in real time through Twitter and cable television' (Alvarez, 2011) and *Time* dubbed it 'the first major murder trial of the social media age' (Cloud, 2011).

The interest in the case was sustained and fed by Florida's exceptionally liberal media law, which decrees that all evidence exchanged between the prosecution and defence is a public document (Gabriel, 2011). Thousands of pages of documents were released in response to public records requests (Pafundi, 2010), meaning that documents later ruled inadmissible in court appeared on websites well before the trial was underway (Gabriel, 2011). Whole episodes of tabloid-style cable news shows such as *Nancy Grace* and *On the Record with Greta van Susteren* were devoted to the release of records related to the case. The exchange of information included material such as photographs of Casey Anthony out on the town with her friends after Caylee had disappeared, entries from her journal and screenshots of her mother Cindy's Myspace page (Pafundi, 2010). As part of the release of documents, the Florida's state attorney's office made over 5,000 pages of letters public in July 2010. These were mainly letters exchanged between

Casey Anthony, relatives, friends and penfriends. However, also included were fifty-one letters to Casey from unconnected members of the public. An analysis of these letters (which are listed numerically at the end of this chapter) forms the basis of this chapter.

I first became aware of the existence of these letters after reading 'Dear Casey', an article on Harper's Magazine website containing quotes from them. Its resonance with my main research interests - gender representations of women who kill (Seal, 2010), the 'transgressive imagination' (O'Neill and Seal, 2012) and public responses to crime and punishment conveyed in letters (Seal, 2011; 2014) – immediately struck me. The value of personal documents such as these is in learning how individuals not only interpret widespread media coverage, but how they can identify with a woman thrust into the spotlight after being accused of murdering her child and interweave her story with their own. Such sources help us to discover, as advised by Ewick and Silbey (1998, p. 33), how 'people experience and interpret law in the context of their daily lives' and to unearth popular understandings and interpretations of criminal cases. These understandings and interpretations can include personally and emotionally meaningful reactions. This chimes with cultural criminology's imperative to prioritise lived experiences and pay attention to the emotional meanings of transgression (Aspden and Hayward, 2015). The letters are part of the 'debris of everyday life' that Presdee (2000, p. 15) contended were the 'data' of the cultural criminologist – examples of how individuals 'make sense' of their lives (p. 21).Cultural criminology analyses how crime is imagined through its 'symbols, images and meanings' in the media (O'Neill and Seal, 2012: 11). Media portrayals construct criminality, transgression and victimisation, although it is difficult to untangle how they relate to popular consciousness (Greer, 2003). Most analyses of media and crime, including those by cultural criminologists, focus on the kinds of meaning transmitted by media portrayals rather than their interpretation by members of the audience. This is beginning to take place in relation to responses articulated via social media (see Salter, 2013; Horeck, 2014). The letters to Casey Anthony also offer the potential to examine audience interpretation. The form of the letter encourages personal reflection and identification, the construction of narrative and engagement in identity work. Although reactions to the case were prominent on social media, the letters offer different, more considered and more personal responses to Casey Anthony as a woman accused of murder. They enable appreciation of how a high profile case 'is imbued with personal meaning by people at a micro level' (Innes, 2004: 351). I have previously explored how portrayals of such cases are windows onto wider cultural understandings (Seal, 2010). Here, I consider how individuals incorporate high profile cases into the fabric of their everyday lives and use them to develop understanding of their own identities.

The case

Caylee Anthony was last seen leaving her grandparents' house, which was her home, in August 2008. She was not reported missing until thirty-one days later, when Cindy Anthony informed the police that she had not seen Caylee for weeks and that the car belonging to Casey Anthony, her daughter and Caylee's mother, smelt as if it had had a dead body in it. Casey claimed that her daughter had been kidnapped by a babysitter, although it soon appeared that the babysitter did not actually exist. In October 2008, Casey was indicted on charges of murder and aggravated manslaughter. Caylee's remains were found in a wooded area near the Anthony home in December of that year. Casey's trial began in May 2011. Her defence to the prosecution's case that she had suffocated her daughter and then dumped her was that George Anthony, her father and Caylee's grandfather, had disposed of Caylee's body after she accidentally drowned in the family swimming pool. The prosecution sought the death penalty and alleged Casey's motive for murdering her daughter was that she got in the way of her partying lifestyle. However, its case was not supported by forensic evidence or witness testimony of Casey mistreating Caylee. Casey was acquitted of murder and manslaughter and found guilty on four counts of providing false information to the authorities. She received a four-year sentence but was released from prison shortly after her trial owing to the time served and good behaviour.

Casey Anthony's acquittal caused a sensation, with much of the American media portraying it as a 'wrongful exoneration' (Battaglia, 2012). This will not be explored further here as the letters that form the dataset were sent between January and July 2009, well before the trial began. The salient events shaping their content were Casey's imprisonment, the discovery of Caylee's body, the revelation in January that George Anthony was suicidal, and a memorial service that was held for Caylee in February. This was attended by hundreds of strangers, some of whom had travelled long distances, and was streamed live on HLN (Pafundi, 2010), a cable channel with programming largely focused on crime stories, forensics and court trials. This includes *Nancy Grace*, which describes itself as 'television's only justice themed interview/debate show' (hlntv.com, 2014), and which maintained a close interest in the disappearance and death of Caylee Anthony, to the advantage of its ratings (Gabriel, 2011; Battaglia, 2012). Titular presenter, Grace, referred to

Casey by the moniker 'tot mom' and vociferously insisted on her guilt (Seidel, 2013).

The 'bad mother' narrative

The increasing appetite of social media and cable news shows for material cannot alone explain why the disappearance and death of Caylee Anthony became a sensation. Although treated as 'rare and spectacular' in the news media, nearly one child per day is killed by their own parent in the USA, and these homicides are evenly divided between mothers and fathers (Barnett, 2006, p. 413). The vast majority are not newsworthy. The Anthony case was distinguished by several factors that enhanced its attraction to the media. First of all, the focus was a white, middle-class family. Casey's father was a retired homicide detective and her mother was a nurse. Casey was only twenty-two years old when Caylee disappeared, and was conventionally attractive and telegenic (Furhman, 2009). She looked like other young women who receive intensive media coverage (although for different reasons). In addition to these social factors, the nature of the events was also relevant. Caylee's disappearance was originally reported as a possible child abduction and subsequently became a story about whether her mother had killed her. It therefore had a strong element of mystery – first of all, what had happened to Caylee and then whether, how and why she had been murdered by Casey. As Barnett (2006) argues, in nearly all cases of child homicide by mothers, there is no doubt over whether she killed the child, rather the mystery is to determine why she did it.

Once Casey had been charged with murder, media coverage employed the well-established 'bad mother' narrative. Bad mothers are cold, callous and evil – willing to be violent and hurt their children, which makes them unnatural (Meyer and Oberman, 2001; Naylor, 2001). They are also 'promiscuous, ungovernable and negligent' (Cavaglion, 2008, p. 274). By contrast, the idealised good mother is self-sacrificing (Naylor, 2001). Women who kill their children are frequently represented as deeply flawed mothers, who have failed at their caretaking tasks. As good motherhood is presumed to be a natural female attribute, flawed mothering requires explanation through the 'mad or bad' dichotomy (Barnett, 2006). The 'bad mother' narrative reflects underlying cultural anxieties about mothers – that they are excessively powerful and to be feared, possessing both the capacity to be all loving but also all destroying (Barnett, 2005; Naylor, 2001). There is a myth of motherhood as the fulfilment of women's ultimate role. Cases of women harming or killing their children uncomfortably reveal maternal ambivalence – the conflicted feelings of love and hate that many women have for their children, undermining this myth (Barnett, 2005). Casey Anthony was fitted into the well-worn bad mother narrative. She was portrayed as a sexually promiscuous party girl who found her daughter an encumbrance. Much was made of the fact that she got a new tattoo that read 'Bella Vita' only two days after Caylee disappeared, a seeming indication that she was relieved to be free of motherhood. Coverage also emphasised that Casey was unsure as to Caylee's paternity. The bad mother narrative was a pre-existing media narrative that could be utilised in relation to Casey Anthony and was made more compelling by her white, middle-class background. This is the normative standard of motherhood so deviation from 'good motherhood' is more newsworthy in relation to a white, middle-class woman.

Casey Anthony as a celebrity

Intensive media coverage from the reporting of Caylee's disappearance onwards turned Casey Anthony into a celebrity. Turner's (2004) definition of celebrity is what happens when the media switches from reporting the public role of a public figure to investigating the details of their private life. In this sense, Casey was a celebrity as soon as she emerged into the public eye as the details of her private life were a constituent part of the story from the beginning. As a woman accused of murder, she fulfilled Penfold-Mounce's (2009) 'notorious' category of celebrity, which is association with illegal or deviant behaviour. Other telegenic young women accused of murder have been catapulted into celebrity. For example, Simkin (2013: 33) explores the intense interest in the case of Amanda Knox and the media's 'steady gaze on [her] character and personal history'. Along with her former boyfriend, Raffaele Sollecito, Knox was found guilty in 2009 of murdering British exchange student, Meredith Kercher, in Italy in 2007 and successfully appealed against this conviction in 2011, when she returned to her native USA. She was reconvicted by Italy's highest court in 2014, but was acquitted in September 2015.

Celebrities have been integrated into the cultural processes of everyday life, becoming foci for the interrogation and elaboration of cultural identity (Turner, 2004). There are specific points of cultural reference through which audiences can decode celebrities. In relation to Amanda Knox, the reference point was the 'femme fatale' trope (Simkin, 2013) and as discussed, for Casey Anthony it was the 'bad mother' narrative. The integration of celebrities into everyday lives means that they also become available as symbols for personal identity work on the part of the audience. In relation to mourning the death of Diana, Princess of Wales, Johnson (1999, p. 31) explores how members of the public 'defined their own identities in relation to her'. This was both through points of similarity and points of difference. Emotional investment in Diana's public representation meant that she became the object of transferred feelings, which 'had little to do with her own life and death, and everything to do with lives of members of her public' (p. 31).

Turner (2004: 91) describes this use by the public of famous individuals as a resource for identity work and the construction of meaning as the generation of celebrity 'from below'. Although the production of celebrity is tied to the media, it is also actively generated by the audience. This boundary between the media and the audience has become increasingly blurred with the advent of social media. Penfold-Mounce (2009) examines the related concept of resonance, a connection with the audience that stimulates a response or interaction, which can be positive or negative. Resonance requires the public to be an active audience. This discussion of the active audience and celebrity from below is highly relevant to the analysis of letters sent to Casey Anthony by members of the public. As people who had never met her face-to-face, their identification with her relied on integrating her and her story into their everyday lives. She resonated with them. This is also especially pertinent to the letter as a form and its role as a medium for the identity work of the author.

Letters and letter writing

Letters are 'documents of life' in the sense that they are human and personal (Plummer, 2001) and are one of the most prevalent forms of life writing (Stanley, 2004). Although letter writing can be regarded as a 'dying art' due to shifts to electronic forms of communication (Plummer, 2001), letters to those in prison represent a continuing use of and need for the form (Maybin, 2000). Letters offer accounts of individual experience and 'present the subjective point of view' of the author (Plummer, 2001, p. 18), meaning that the author's personal characteristics are expressed. They are a 'surprisingly powerful channel for self expression and for pursuing relationships' (Maybin, 2000, p. 151). Plummer (2001, p. 235) argues that letters speak of the writer's world 'but also of the writer's perceptions of the recipient'. This makes the letters that members of the public sent to Casey Anthony particularly significant as they provide glimpses of how she resonated with them and how they integrated their perceptions of her into their everyday lives. One of the advantages of analysing letters as life writing is that they are 'not occasioned, structured or their content filled by researcher determined concerns' (Stanley, 2004, p. 203).

Letters offer the possibility for pursuing imaginary relationships, something Maybin (2006) explores in her research into letters written by British penfriends to condemned prisoners on death row in the United States. As such, they enable imaginative and creative self-presentation. Letters involve the performance of self by the writer (Jolly and Stanley, 2005; Stanley, 2004), and authors are free to rewrite their personal history and rework their sense of identity (Maybin, 2000). The 'subtle interchange between fantasy, writing and relationship' (Jolly and Stanley, 2005, p. 93) that personal letter writing entails exemplifies how letters can be vehicles for the kind of identity work that members of the public can undertake in relation to celebrities. Throsby's (2004) study of letters sent to the poet, Lord Byron, by female admirers examines how the women created an imagined intimacy with the poet and also experimented with different identities. They perceived an emotional affinity with Byron and wrote as if they knew him personally.

Casey Anthony is quite a different figure from Lord Byron, but there are historical precedents for emotional identification with those accused or convicted of high-profile murders. Wood (2012) analyses how letter writers emotionally identified with Beatrice Pace, a British woman tried and acquitted of the murder of her husband in 1928. I have examined how letter writers empathised with Ruth Ellis, who in 1955 became the last British woman to be hanged, in letters that were sent to the Home Secretary to ask for a reprieve (Seal, 2011). Although this was not strictly 'personal' correspondence, many of the authors included details about their lives and relationships in order to express their affinity with Ellis. More recent comparisons can be found in relation to Amanda Knox – Simkin (2013) notes that the letters sent to her demonstrate her status as a celebrity – and Ted Kaczynski, otherwise known as the 'Unabomber'. Kaczynski killed three people (and injured others) with home-made bombs in the course of a nearly twenty-year long campaign against modern technology. The correspondence that he received in prison was of a personal nature, although it was from people who had never met him. Herrada (2003) explains that many wrote as if they were old friends of his and discussed their personal problems.

The letters to Casey Anthony display the features of personal identification, identity work and the construction of an imagined relationship discussed above. The fifty-one letters were sent by forty-seven different members of the public and the writer's gender can be determined for forty-five of them, out of which there is an even split of twenty-three men and twenty-two women. Eleven of the authors are from Florida, Casey's home state. The others are from a variety of different states and one is Canadian. Letters released as part of the case have been uploaded to a website, caseyanthonyisinnocent.com, and are freely accessible at the time of writing. The names and addresses of their authors have not been redacted by the website, although I have anonymised quotes in this chapter and provided only the state of residency rather than a full address. The letters' release was also covered by news stories, some of which quoted directly from a small selection sent from members of the public and included the writers' full names (Associated Press, 2010; *Harper's Magazine*, 2010).

This collection is unlikely to represent all the letters to Casey Anthony from members of the public. Some authors included two letters in one envelope, explaining that their first was returned, for example because they did not include their name on the return address [I counted these as one letter rather than two separate ones]. Others alluded to previous letters they had sent, copies of which are not among those released. It is possible that these never reached Casey Anthony if the sender did not use the correct address. There may also be others that were not released to the public. Although the collection contains love letters, none are sexually explicit and this perhaps indicates that rather than being non-existent these were not made public. These uncertainties should not be regarded as problematic, however. As Stanley (2004) argues, letter writing is by nature fragmentary and dispersed. Letters are not always retained (or delivered) and therefore aiming to access a complete set either written by or sent to an individual is unlikely to be possible.

The rest of the chapter analyses how the letter writers interacted with perceptions of Casey Anthony as a woman accused of murdering her child and as a celebrity. The quotes used retain the original grammar, spelling and punctuation employed by their authors. The reaction to the media coverage of the case and its investigation of Casey's private life is an important and frequent element of the content of the letters. Both identification and disidentification with Casey can be strongly discerned, with many writers conducting a hopeful imagined relationship of friendship, or romantic attachment. Many of the letters also contain fragments of the life story of their author and in this sense are autobiographical. This relates back to identification with Casey and takes place in particular in relation to motherhood and also the experience of imprisonment.

Reactions to media coverage

The letters analysed in this chapter were from people who did not know Casey Anthony personally and who had therefore gained their information about the case from the media. In this sense, their missives were a response to the media coverage (see Bruckweh, 2006 and Wood, 2009 on historical cases where letters could be interpreted as a form of reader response to newspaper articles). Several authors explained how closely they followed the case in the media and that this made them feel a connection with Casey. A Californian woman began her letter 'Let me start by stating that I have seen, listened and read just about everything that has to do with this case' (39) and a man from Colorado had 'been watching your case unfold day by day' (12). Another Californian woman, who had followed the coverage 'since the get-go', explained that 'in a lot of ways I don't feel like you're a stranger cause of everything thats been going on with you and your situation in the news media' (4). A Floridian woman expressed her support by stating 'Casey, I've read all the magazines, all the tabloids, newspaper ads, watched your mom and dad on larry king, and the whole time your story has been the same' (2). Assurances that 'Im not buying the trash on Nancy Grace' (26) and 'I don't buy that garbage' (32) distanced letter writers from the coverage they consumed and allowed them to perform the identity of sceptical and discerning consumers of the news media.

Correspondents were concerned that intensive media coverage was unfair and unduly negative, and expressed empathy with the difficulties this must cause. A man from Missouri commented 'Most of the coverage is bias and one sided. I don't see how you will be able to get a fair trial' (5). Releasing tapes of Casey meeting with her parents 'seems so intrusive of your privacy and very unfair' (27) according to a man from Alabama, who also felt that the media was reporting 'cruel, prejudicial, and insulting things'. A male author from Texas believed that the actions of the prosecution were wrong as 'they seem to leak everything to the press' (25). A man from Florida lamented that 'The media will take a little sentence and turn it into what they want to. They make everybody out to be bad' (41). Media attention meant 'your parents and your brother are under a great deal of stress and pressure' (42).

Demonstrating an awareness of the media as a malign force was an important way for letter writers to strike an empathic tone with Casey, as well as to establish themselves as sophisticated viewers by refuting stereotyped or exaggerated portrayals. In particular, many responded to the sensationalised coverage offered by Nancy Grace and were sure to reject her interpretation. This show was 'the worst' (2 and 5) and Nancy Grace herself was 'really something else. She like other demons, thrive of[f] of the pain and suffering of others' (50). A daily viewer of the show was 'sorry to tell you that I watch that woman put you down day after day' (12). A Floridian man was disgusted that 'certain TV hosts have an agenda and continue to pick on you and yours' (10) and a male correspondent from Missouri disapproved of the way Grace 'twists everything to make you a demon' (5). A woman from California was troubled that Casey was being judged by 'Nancy Grace Fanatics' rather than fair people and that '[t]he media has glorified you as 'Tot Mom' and 'Baby Killer' and even having small children holding signs outside of your home' (38). A female letter writer from North Carolina warned that 'people like Nancy Grace ... want to see you go to death row' (51). Authors were explicit in their disapproval of Nancy Grace. A man from Indiana stated pithily 'I despise Nancy Grace. We'll leave it at that' (3) and a woman from Minnesota hoped that once Casey had been cleared, she would appear on *Nancy Grace* so that she could look the presenter 'in the face and tell her to fly a kite and keep on flying it' (30).

These correspondents had presumably watched *Nancy Grace* and gleaned some of their information about the case from it. Seidel (2013) argues that the show can be understood as an example of what Berlant (2008) conceptualises as an 'intimate public sphere'. This is where a feeling of intimacy is cultivated among viewers or readers of a genre, despite the fact that the vast majority of the audience does not share a face-to-face relationship. *Nancy Grace* is about crime but at the same time it concerns love and intimacy, placing an emphasis on feeling over action. According to Seidel (2013), the Casey Anthony story either gave the audience the opportunity to feel self-righteous – the tone adopted by Grace herself – or to feel sorry for Casey. Both options enabled audience members to feel better about themselves. Letter writers who took Casey's side against Nancy Grace perhaps felt better about themselves by doing so, although as the discussion will show, many of them identified and empathised with Casey rather than simply feeling sorry for her. Feeling and intimacy were clearly important to these reactions, which were formed against rather than through the show. In rejecting the *Nancy Grace* portrayals, letter writers disavowed associated stereotypes of female criminality exemplified by the label 'tot mom'.

Imagined relationships

Letters are an especially suitable form for the pursuit of imagined relationships (Maybin, 2006; Jolly and Stanley, 2005). Many correspondents described their motivation for writing as wishing to offer support and friendship. A man from Indiana wanted to 'reach out to you'(3) and a woman from California wanted to show 'someone else besides your love ones cares & wants the best for you' (7). A man from Colorado 'just wanted to lend my support and let you know not everyone hates or thinks you are some monster' (12). For a man from Florida who wanted to help, '[t]he only thing I know is to write you letters' (41). That letter writers imagined the potential for a relationship between themselves and Casey was borne out by explicit offers of friendship, such as a woman from Florida who wanted to be a companion (47) and a Canadian man who stated '[m]y friendship is unconditional, I will be on your side no matter what' (8). Several expressed assurances that their offers were genuine. A Floridian woman did 'not want to be part of those assholes out their who are trying to make money from your pain' (22) and a man from Michigan was 'not any kind of Casey Anthony fan; or, anything like that at all' (28). A male author from Tennessee explained that he was gay and consequently '[m]y letters aren't to start a relationship or to exploit you in anyway' (24).

In offering support and friendship, many correspondents wanted to establish an ongoing relationship with Casey by receiving letters back from her. A man from South Carolina was 'here for you to write to' (1) and a woman from Florida hoped that 'you will write to me and tell me about yourself' (2), which she explained meant topics such Casey's favourite colour, food, music and songs. Several directly requested that Casey became their penfriend. A man from Missouri had 'never tried writing to someone that I didn't know' but 'thought maybe you would like a pen-pal to pass some time with. Someone who won't judge you and won't ask anything about your pending case' (43). Offers to be penfriends were accompanied by other offers, such as of visits, prayers, money or books and magazines. Wanting to hear back from Casey demonstrated how, in addition to offering support and friendship, letter writers hoped for something in return. A male author from Florida 'would like to hear back from you if possible' (13) and a man from Canada finished his letter with 'Please write me back' (8). Another man from Florida hoped she would respond as he was 'anxious to hear from you' (48).

Several expressed their disappointment that they had not received a reply, or acknowledged that they understood why this had not happened. A woman from Michigan stated that she had written twice before but volume of mail probably meant 'it is impossible to answer all the letters' (19). More plaintively, a Floridian man opined 'Why you don't write, I'm not sure' (10). Others acknowledged that they were perhaps not worthy of Casey's attention. Due to the 'millions of letters a day' she must receive, a male author would be 'stoked' if she read his letter (13). A woman from Minnesota knew that Casey might 'throw this immediately away, I am no one special' (30). A man from Ohio who wished to 'stand beside you no matter the out come' was aware that Casey did not 'really write to many people … and you may never write to me' (44). However, even for these individuals there was clearly the hope that Casey might respond and therefore a relationship could be established.

Offers of 'unconditional friendship' demonstrated that, even without receiving a reply from her, letter writers imagined a kinship with Casey – that she was someone they could be friends with. Some male correspondents hoped for a romantic connection and included compliments in their letters, such as 'I hear nothing but my own thoughts of how beautiful you are' (32) and 'I really do think you are *such* a beautiful woman!!' (13). A couple of these men interpreted their feelings in a way that constructed an imagined romantic relationship. A man from Ohio included a picture of himself and commented that his girlfriend probably would not like him writing to Casey (32) and a man from Mississippi related how when his girlfriend had found his photos of Casey 'she clowned, wanted me to tear them up' (45). For this author, being able to follow Casey on the television was an important means of sustaining his relationship with her. Writing in June 2009, he expressed his frustration that Michael Jackson's death had pushed her case out of the news. He lamented, 'I miss you Casey, and I wish they would Quite [*sic*] talking about Michael Jackson and start talking about you' (45).

Personal identification and autobiography

Personal identification and emotional affinity with celebrities can be expressed in letters (Throsby, 2004), and writing letters provides the opportunity to engage in identity work (Maybin, 2000). Letter writers both identified and disidentified with Casey, finding points of similarity and distance. Unsurprisingly, disidentification was related to a firm belief in her guilt. A woman from Utah wrote 'I hate you and I hope you get whats [*sic*] coming to you … You are a monster' (18). It is interesting to note that this woman included her email address in her letter, indicating an imagined relationship with Casey, even if it was one of antagonism. A female author from New York stated 'I know you killed her!! We all know!!' and also threatened 'You are lucky I cant come visit you, why because I would want to strangle you' (9). These reactions, which were in keeping with the tenor of broadcast media such as *Nancy Grace*, and were frequently expressed in social media, are rare in the letters. This no doubt relates to the form of the letter, which inclines towards imagined relationships and personal identification – as well as to identity work on behalf of the author.

Authors who positively identified with Casey expressed belief in her innocence. Sentiments such as 'I do not believe you are responsible' (8) and 'I don't think a woman like yourself deserves to be in the place you're in' (7) further developed the care and concern that letter writers conveyed when they offered friendship and support. However, the empathy that correspondents expressed, and the imagined relationships that they invested in Casey Anthony, were not dependent on a belief in her innocence. This was demonstrated by a man from Missouri who stated, 'Whether you are guilty or not your day to day life must be hell. If you are guilty you have to live with that everyday. If you are not guilty your life was ripped from you for no reason' (5). A male writer from Indiana was candid that he did not 'even care if you screwed up or not' (3). Others communicated ambivalence, such as a Floridian man who expressed his wish to keep writing to Casey but admitted 'since the evidence points to you, I don't know what to think' (42). A man from Colorado explained 'I don't think you did it … And I also pray to god that you didn't' (12). A woman from North Carolina wanted to 'fight' those who believed Casey deserved the death penalty and advised that Casey needed to win the sympathy of the jury, or should plead insanity if she was in fact guilty (51). This was based on her conviction that 'the Lord does not want this [death penalty] for you'.

In personally identifying with Casey, correspondents wrote about themselves and related fragments of their autobiography, making clear the letters' status as life writing (Plummer, 2001; Stanley, 2004). Establishing their own identities was part of the imagined relationship that they pursued. Several letters established the author's identity: 'I am a 33 year old mother of two girls' (2), 'I am a 50 year old mwf, from Nebraska, a mother of 3 grown sons, and a grandmother' (33). A woman from Minnesota described herself as a single parent with four children and a 'domestic abuse survivor' (50). In addition to situating themselves in relation to social identity, authors also painted a picture of their everyday lives. A man from Texas related that his grandchildren had, variously, suffered from croup and missed school because of a snow day. He also listed his favourite films as *The Ten Commandments* and *JFK* (25). A man from Mississippi who had expressed romantic interest in Casey stated that he was a big wrestling fan and had been to see some wrestling with his girlfriend (45).

Others articulated emotional experiences that offered the potential for connection with Casey. A woman from Michigan assured 'Do I know what it feels like to be depressed – of course I do. If you have any of those feelings, I can definitely relate' (19). She also explained that she felt Casey would not judge her as '[p]eople are probably judging you based on what they hear or read', indicating that in Casey she perceived the chance of an empathic correspondent. In expressing why she wished to be a pen pal, a Floridian woman stated that she was lonely when her husband committed suicide and '[l]etters made me feel just a little better' (22).

For female authors, motherhood was a major source of personal identification with Casey. This could be straightforwardly affirmative, such as the Floridian woman who assured 'See, as a mom I can safely say that you are a good person, a loving mom, and very intelligent' (2), or candidly damning, such as the woman from New York who stated 'I have a son 1yrs old and can't image [*sic*] hurting him. you are a bad mother and caylee didn't deserve you' (9). There were others who were more ambivalent. A Californian mother of two daughters 'wouldn't let time go by if they went missing' and thought that 'a loving, worried, upset, frighten [*sic*] mother who doesn't know where her daughter is could never have done what you did' (4). This was the same woman, quoted further above, who proclaimed that she did not feel like Casey was a 'stranger'. A mother of two children from North Carolina found Casey's story of abduction 'unbelievable'. She 'was a single mother also, and I knew then and now, that the party was over the minute I found out I was having a baby' but wanted Casey to know 'that I know what it was like being all alone as a mother' (17). For these women, writing letters to Casey Anthony enabled them to perform and explore their identities as mothers, and the kinds of mothers that they thought they were or wanted to be. The writer from North Carolina clearly felt a resonant identification with Casey even though she did not believe her account of what happened, reflecting ambivalence about mothering and its difficulties. The resonance of Casey as a mother, despite the predominant bad mother narrative in the media, is striking. As a story of motherhood in the extreme, the case inspired discussion of mothering identities in respondents' letters.

For some male authors, experience of imprisonment was an important source of affinity with Casey and formed the basis for identity work that related to personal biography. A man from Colorado had 'been to jail myself and know it sucks trying to cope with outside family issues' (12). Writing letters to Casey offered the chance to confess to mistakes made and to emotions that men in prison would usually need to hide or suppress. A man from Tennessee claimed to 'know how you feel sitting in jail not knowing how long you're gonna have to be in there. I got charged with forgery in 2006. I messed my life up. I used to be a Nurse' (24). A man writing from a prison in Michigan had been there for five years. He related parts of his life story as an explanation for his present situation. He had grown up alone with his father and from the age of ten 'sex, drugs and rock-n-roll were my life'. He also had a five-year-old daughter who 'reminds me so much of Caylee' (28). A Floridian man who had briefly spent time in prison confided, 'When I was in jail, when you have to go through orientation in jail, when I was sitting on the bed in my cell, I started crying. I'm sure you did that too' (42). A thirty-four-year-old man held in a Missouri prison had been incarcerated since he was seventeen. He no longer had any friends left on the outside and his mother was the only family member with whom he was in contact. Having seen Casey on the television, he thought she looked 'shocked and scared' in the courtroom and explained he knew 'what its like having no one to talk to while being in here'. Men who had experienced imprisonment could therefore perform vulnerable identities in their letters, which they would not necessarily otherwise express and which spoke of fear and loss.

Implications for cultural criminology

In previous work, I have examined the construction of discourses of femininity in relation to women who kill as 'killing by women violates norms of femininity, such as nurturance, gentleness and social conformity' (Seal, 2010, p. 1). I have assessed both how these discourses play a role in the regulation of femininity and how they reflect and contribute to wider cultural meanings (Seal, 2010). As a high-profile case, the Casey Anthony story was a symbol for important social and cultural issues, such as family life and what it should be and the meanings attached to normative young woman-hood. This chapter has undertaken a different type of analysis. Via a close examination of letters sent to Casey Anthony, a woman accused of murder, it has aimed instead to understand how individuals reacted to her story and how they incorporated their images of her into their everyday lives. Inevitably, letter writers drew on media portrayals for their information about Casey, which were predominantly representations of female deviance. However, for the majority an important part of their identity work in the letters was to reject sensationalised representations and to offer empathy and understanding instead. This signalled a desire to be perceived as discern-ing consumers of news who could distinguish themselves from those more easily manipulated by the media, but also to be seen as potential sources of support for Casey.

The creation of imagined relationships with Casey in the letters shows how the form enabled authors to express perceived affinity with her and to offer friendship or even romantic involvement. These imagined relation-ships sprang from personal identification, especially in relation to specific shared experiences such as motherhood or imprisonment. In order to articu-late identification (and to build imagined relationships), letter writers related aspects of their life story and also engaged in identity work, reflecting on significant experiences and associated emotions. As Johnson (1999) argues, such identity work has more to do with the lives of members of the public as individuals than it does with the celebrity it is associated with. The letters were a chance for their authors to reflect on who they were in relation to their perception of Casey Anthony, especially as her case was endowed with symbolic significance.

This analysis of the letters that members of the public sent to Casey Anthony has implications for cultural criminology, which studies mean-ings and narratives associated with crime, deviance and transgression as aspects of everyday life (O'Neill and Seal, 2012; Presdee, 2004) and pays close attention to the emotions of crime (Ferrell, 2006). Penfold-Mounce (2009) has employed cultural criminology to explore celebrity culture and crime, particularly in relation to the pleasure of transgression. Her previ-ously discussed concept of resonance – the connection with a celebrity which stimulates response or interaction – is clearly relevant to strangers' moti-vation for writing to Casey Anthony. Penfold-Mounce (2009, pp. 65–66) explains that 'resonance with celebrity can be a result of relating and inter-acting with the publicised version of the self or rather what we would like it to be'. Perceived connection with celebrity criminals can be a means of resisting dominant discourses of law and conformity through celebrating transgression. Examples include the legend associated with mid-twentieth-century London gangsters, the Krays, and romanticised versions of celebrity bandits, Bonnie and Clyde. Resonance can also involve negative emotions of 'disgusted and fearful pleasure', by which notorious criminals, such as serial killers, are constructed as 'monsters' (Penfold-Mounce, 2009, p. 73).

The letters to Casey Anthony demonstrate that resonance with a figure whose celebrity is rooted in notoriety is not necessarily indicative of joy in transgression, but rather can exemplify the kind of emotional invest-ment, personal identification and transferred feelings that Johnson (1999) explores in relation to Diana, Princess of Wales. This potentially opens up a greater variety of everyday meanings that are associated with celebrity and criminality and has an important methodological implication relat-ing to the nature of the sources analysed. The collection of letters is not 'representative' of public responses to Casey Anthony but shows how the form of the letter can facilitate the creation of imagined relationships and the expression of fragments of autobiography. Although a couple of let-ters stemmed from negative emotions, the rest derived from more posi-tive, although sometimes ambivalent, personal identification. Other ways of responding to the case, such as through tweets or leaving comments at the bottom of a news story or blogpost, do not lend themselves to the kind of reflexive identification exhibited in the letters. This demonstrates the importance of considering the form of a response as well as the meanings or discourses it conveys. As criminology increasingly turns its attention to narrative as an 'avenue for the imaginative rendering of the self' (Aspden and Hayward, 2015, p. 236), it is important for cultural criminologists to interpret not only 'offender narratives', but also those from the audiences of high profile crimes. This further illuminates how crime and law live in the everyday.

Cultural criminology must interrogate how the celebration of transgres-sion, deviance and rebellion is gendered (O'Neill and Seal, 2012). Celebratory cultural representations of violent women – real and fictional – can be found, for example female avengers such as the Lisbeth Salander charac-ter from Stieg Larsson's Millennium trilogy (see O'Neill and Seal, 2012), or romanticised versions of Bonnie Parker, as mentioned above. However, joy in the transgression of a woman suspected of killing her child remains cul-turally taboo in a way that fascination with or pleasure in the violent crimes of male criminals such as the Krays does not. The letters to Casey Anthony do not celebrate her for the crime of which she was accused. Rather, they show that the creation of celebrity 'from below', the integration of celebri-ties into people's everyday lives and the role of celebrity in the elaboration of cultural and personal identity can take place in relation to a woman accused of murder. This is even when, or perhaps because, she has been the object of othering discourses and further highlights the symbolic potency of female murder. It is tempting to conclude that, particularly in relation to transferred feelings and the expression of empathy, this is more likely in relation to cases involving women rather than men. While women's identifications around motherhood or men's admissions of feelings of vulnerability in prison do seem more likely to be communicated through an imagined relationship with a woman, Herrada's (2003, p. 40) discovery that people wrote to Ted Kaczynski as if they were old friends 'discussing their personal problems' indicates that this type of personal resonance is not restricted to responses to female cases.

Letters cited:

1. Male, South Carolina, 20.1.09
2. Female, Florida, 19.1.09
3. Male, Indiana, 19.1.09
4. Female, California, 2.2.09
5. Male, Missouri, 2.2.09
7. Female, California, 3.2.09
8. Male, Alberta, undated
9. Female, New York, 21.1.09
10. Male, Florida, 2.2.09
12. Male, Colorado, 3.2.09
13. Male, Florida, 3.2.09
17. Female, North Carolina, 29.1.09
18. Female, Utah, 21.1.09
19. Female, Michigan, 30.1.09
22. Female, Florida, 31.1.09
24. Male, Tennessee, 30.1.09
25. Male, Texas, undated
26. Male, Minnesota, 27.1.09
27. Male, Alabama, 29.1.09
28. Male, Michigan, 14.1.09
30. Female, Minnesota, 2.4.09
32. Male, Ohio, 6.4.09
33. Female, Nebraska, 25.3.09
38. Female, California, 22.5.09
39. Female, Texas, 21.5.09
41. Male, Florida, 21.5.09
42. Male, Florida, 25.6.09
43. Male, Missouri, 1.7.09
44. Male, Ohio, 27.6.09
45. Male, Mississippi, 28.6.09

47. Female, Florida, 30.6.09
48. Male, Florida, 5.7.09
50. Female, Minnesota, 28.5.09
51. Female, North Carolina, 28.6.09

References

Alvarez, L. (2011) 'Casey Anthony not guilty in slaying daughter', *New York Times*, 5 July. Available at: www.nytimes.com/2011/07/06/us/06casey.html?pagewanted=all&_r=1. Last accessed 11 May 2014.

Aspden, K. and Hayward, K. J. (2015) 'Narrative criminology and cultural criminology: Shared biographies, different lives?', in L. Presser and S. Sandberg (eds) *Narrative Criminology: Understanding Stories of Crime*, New York: New York University Press, pp. 235–59.

Associated Press (2010) 'Letters to Casey Anthony include Bible quotes, marriage proposals from fans and haters', *Fox News*, 25 June. Available at: www.foxnews.com/us/2010/06/25/letters-jailed-casey-anthony-include-bible-quotes-marriage-proposals-fans/. Last accessed 8 August 2014.

Barnett, B. (2005) 'Perfect mother or artist of obscenity? Narrative and myth in a qualitative analysis of press coverage of the Angela Yates murders', *Journal of Communication Inquiry* 29(1), 9–29.

Barnett, B. (2006) 'Medea in the media: narratives and myth in newspaper coverage of women who kill their children', *Journalism* 7(4), 411–432.

Battaglia, N. A. (2012) 'The Casey Anthony trial and wrongful exonerations', *Albany Law Review* 75(3), 1579–1611.

Berlant, L. (2008) *The Female Complaint: the Unfinished Business of Sentimentality in American Culture*. Durham, NC: Duke University Press.

Bruckweh, K. (2006) 'Fantasies of violence: German citizens expressing their concepts of violence and ideas about democracy in letters referring to the case of the serial killer Jurgen Bartsch (1966–71)', *Crime, History and Societies* 10(2), 53–82.

Cavaglion, G. (2008) 'Bad, mad or sad? Mothers who kill and press coverage in Israel', *Crime, Media, Culture* 4(2), 271–278.

Cloud, J. (2011) 'How the Casey Anthony murder case became the social media trial of the century', *Time*, June 16. Available at: http://content.time.com/time/nation/article/0,8599,2077969-1,00.html. Last accessed 12 August 2014.

'Dear Casey' (2010) *Harper's Magazine*, October. Available at: http://harpers.org/archive/2010/10/dear-casey/. Last accessed 20 July 2011.

Ewick, P. and Silbey, S. (1998) *The Common Place of Law: Stories from Everyday Life*, Chicago: University of Chicago Press.

Ferrell, J. (2006) *Empire of Scrounge*. New York: New York University Press.

Fuhrman, M. (2009) *The Murder Business*. Washington DC: Regnery.

Gabriel, R. (2011) 'American justice or American idol? Two trials and two verdicts in the Casey Anthony case', *The Jury Expert* 28(4), 1–7.

Greer, C. (2003) *Sex Crime and the Media*, Abingdon: Routledge.

Herrada, J. (2003) 'Letters to the Unabomber: a case study and some reflections', *Archival Issues* 28(1), 35–46.

Horeck, T. (2014) '"A film that will rock you to your core": Emotion and affect in Dear Zachary and the real crime documentary', Crime, Media, Culture 10:2, 151–67. Innes, M. (2004) 'Signal crimes and signal disorders: notes on deviance as communicative actions', British Journal of Sociology 55:3, 335–55.

Johnson, R. (1999) 'Exemplary differences: meaning (and not mourning) a princess', in A. Kear and D.L. Steinberg (eds), *Mourning Diana: Nation, Culture and the Performance of Grief* (pp. 15–39). London: Routledge.

Jolly, M. and L. Stanley (2005) 'Letters as/not a Genre', *Life Writing* 2(2), 91–118.

Kohm, S. A. (2009) 'Naming, shaming and criminal justice: Mass-mediated humiliation as entertainment and punishment', *Crime, Media, Culture,* 5:2, 188–205.

Maybin, J. (2000) 'Death row penfriends: some effects of letter writing on identity and relationships', in D. Barton and N. Hall (eds) *Letter Writing as Social Practice* (pp. 151–177). John Benjamins BV: Amsterdam.

Maybin, J. (2006) 'Death row penfriends: configuring time, space and selves', *Auto/ Biography Studies* 21(1), 58–69.

Meyer, C. and M. Oberman (2001) *Mothers Who Kill Their Children.* New York: New York University Press.

'Nancy Grace' (2014) *HLNtv.com.* Available at: http://www.hlntv.com/shows/ nancy-grace. Last accessed 12 August 2014.

Naylor, B. (2001) 'The "bad" mother in media and legal texts', *Social Semiotics* 11(2), 155–176.

O'Neill, M. and L. Seal (2012) *Transgressive Imaginations: Crime, Deviance and Culture.* Basingstoke: Palgrave.

Pafundi, B. (2010) 'Public access to criminal discovery records', *University of Florida Journal of Law and Public Policy* 21(2), 227–272.

Penfold-Mounce, R. (2009) *Celebrity Culture and Crime.* Basingstoke: Palgrave.

Plummer, K. (2001) *Documents of Life 2: An Invitation to a Critical Humanism.* London: SAGE Publications.

Presdee, M. (2004) *Cultural Criminology: the Long and Winding Road.* London: SAGE Publications.

Seal, L. (2010) *Women, Murder and Femininity: Gender Representations of Women Who Kill.* Basingstoke: Palgrave.

Seal, L. (2011) 'Ruth Ellis and public contestation of the death penalty', *The Howard Journal* 50(5), 492–504.

Seal, L. (2013) 'Pussy Riot and feminist cultural criminology: A new Femininity in Dissent?', Contemporary Justice Review 16:2, 293–303.

Seal, L. (2014) 'Imagined communities and the death penalty in Britain, 1930–65', British Journal of Criminology 54:5, 908–27.

Seidel, L. (2013) *Mediated Maternity: Contemporary American Portrayals of Bad Mothers in Literature and Popular Culture.* Lanham, MD: Lexington Books.

Simkin, S. (2013) '"Actually evil not high school evil": Amanda Knox, sex and celebrity crime', *Celebrity Studies* 4(1), 33–45.

Stanley, L. (2004) 'The Epistolarium: on theorizing letters and correspondences', *Auto/Biography* 12(3), 201–235.

Throsby, C. (2004) 'Flirting with fame: Byron's anonymous female fans', *Byron Journal* 32(2), 115–123.

Turner, G. (2004) *Understanding Celebrity*. London: SAGE Publications.

Wood, J. (2009) '"Those who have had trouble can sympathise with you": press writing, reader response and a murder trial in interwar Britain', *Journal of Social History* 43(2), 439–462.

Wood, J. (2012) *The Most Remarkable Woman in England: Poison, Celebrity and the Trials of Beatrice Pace*. Manchester: Manchester University Press.

10   *Robert Jago*[1]

The gypsy's lot: myth and reality

Gypsies are 'the jewel in the European crown ... if the non Roma/Gypsy peoples of Europe can come to terms with their willful hatred, persecution and discrimination of the Roma/Gypsies, then the peoples of Europe together as a mixed, but racially unified society, will be well equipped to face the new and challenging social and racial demands of globalism.'
(Ivatts, 2005, quoted in Richardson and Ryder, 2013, p. 221)

Introduction

Nowhere is the relationship between law and popular belief better demonstrated than in the case of the gypsy. Whether the law regulates and recognises the status of a gypsy as a race or ethnic group,[2] regulates their everyday behaviour[3] or regulates their nomadic lifestyle,[4] it is clear that the law impacts significantly on their everyday lives. However, it is not just the law that has an impact, as evidence suggests that the lived experiences of gypsies are also affected by popular belief. This popular belief treats them as 'less than equals' (Coxhead, 2007, p. 26), where they suffer routine discrimination and vilification, facing regular social stigma and power imbalance. It is the task of this chapter to explore the gypsy's lot. That is the lived experience of gypsies who find themselves subject to different legal provisions depending on their circumstances (an ethnic group in equality legislation deserving of protection but a relatively powerless group when it comes to planning law). Coupled with these legal provisions are the myths that tend to inflame and encourage the social stigma that follows. This tends to morph into both the formal and informal controls over the gypsy's life, which unlike other marginalised groups within society have not improved over time (Richardson, 2006, p. 133).

Who is the 'gypsy'?

When considering this group of 'gypsies' it is important to note that the term, although historically pejorative, is a broad term, which for the purposes of this chapter will include Romany English Gypsies, Irish Travellers, Welsh Gypsies and Scottish Gypsies, as well new Roma migrants from Eastern Europe (Richardson and Ryder, 2013, p. 5). While Coxhead (2007, p. 24) warns against such conflation for fear of oversimplifying the historical experience of these groups, Quarmby (2013, pp. xiv–xv) decides that such conflation is acceptable on the basis that:

> 'artists, activists, academics and community members continue to debate which word they prefer to this day. A number of internationally renowned artists have now 'reclaimed' the word 'Gypsys' as they say it describes an international identity better than the words 'Rom' or 'Roma'. This is not for me to judge.'

Equally, it is important for the purposes of simplicity (Pogany, 2004, p. 21) to use the term 'gypsy' interchangeably while using the other terms (gipsy, Roma, Romani, traveller) when other sources refer to these terms.

The notion of a gypsy as a conniving beggar or a cunning peddlar is one that has been perpetuated for many centuries. As far back as the fifteenth century, they were variously described as 'creatures' (Tuetcy, 1881) or 'vagabonds' (Gronemeyer, 1987). Even today there is a sense that gypsies are an entirely separate people who exist outside 'normal' British society and follow their own rules and customs with little regard for national legislation or societal norms. This is an issue for gypsy communities across Europe, not just in Britain. The European Court of Human Rights (ECtHR) has formally described the Roma as a disadvantaged and vulnerable minority[5] and the case law of ECtHR demonstrates a string of violations relating to (among other things) educational segregation and forced sterilisation (ECHR, 2013).

Despite the protections from the ECtHR, the Equality Act 2010 and other legislation, the perception of 'gypsies' still seems to be one fraught with prejudice and lack of knowledge. There is little understanding of a culture that tends to use and display wealth immediately rather than saving. There is often a misconception of wealth. Equally, there can be misconceptions about neediness. Perhaps because gypsy culture and history is not widely known and understood, people seem to be both intrigued and afraid of gypsies; torn between a romantic ideal of handsome wandering naturalists with painted caravans and an uneasy distrust of dirty, untrustworthy outsiders with no respect for private property. Overall the law's response to gypsies has been characterised as one of: 'expulsion, repression, discrimination and uneasy tolerance of a group which is ethnically distinctive, socially and economically non-conformist' (Barnett, 1995, p. 133).

Myth and the 'gypsy'

In order to understand law in popular belief in this context, it is important to explore a number of the myths that have emerged over centuries when considering gypsies. This exploration enables us to understand the 'lot', or lived experience, of gypsies and helps us to measure these myths against relevant realities. Cupitt (1982, 29) has argued that myth, in the context of ancient Greece, is 'typically a traditional sacred story of anonymous authorship and archetypal or universal significance which is recounted in a certain community and often linked with a ritual.'

Segal (2015) confirms that, at its core, myth is 'a story' and as a story it can be used 'broadly as a credo and a conviction' (Segal, 2015, p. 3). This becomes important because Segal argues that the function of myth can differ according to those who are employing it and it can be used both positively[6] and negatively[7] depending on who is undertaking its employment. Although not wishing to commit himself to confirming the function of myth Segal proposes that myth 'accomplishes something significant for adherents' (Segal, 2015, p. 5). For Segal one such adherent is Rubinstein who argues that 'myth is a conviction, false yet tenacious'.[8]

Having established myth to be a story, it then becomes important to consider how true that story may be. Stories can also be 'tales', 'narratives', 'accounts', 'yarns', 'legends' and 'anecdotes'. Such labels may not always equate to truth. Coupe (1997, p. 108) explains that when interpreting myth 'all myths presuppose a previous narrative, and in turn form the model for future narratives'. When evolving into new myths the 'premature finality of realism is the death of myth' (Coupe, 1997, p. 110). This suggests that myths can and will be either recycled or their exposure under a realist lens, where possible, can signal their death. This will become significant later when we look forward, but for now it can be argued that although myths may reinvent themselves over time their relationship with truth is posited against this notion of realism. Much of what has been written about myth has considered its plight when faced with the realities of the natural sciences (Segal, 1999) but here we are not considering the existence or not of God(s), or of the prowess of Achilles or Pegasus.[9] Here we are considering the myths presented as truth about an existing group within society: gypsies.

Using the work of Segal and Rubinstein, this chapter aims to explore some key myths relating to gypsies. Firstly some historically romantic positive myths will be considered. The chapter will then consider three key negative myths that currently face gypsies. These negative myths are gypsies as 'child snatchers', gypsies as 'thieves' and related to that myth is gypsies as 'land grabbers'. It will be shown that although realism continues to challenge these myths they have in some instances reinvented themselves in new narratives over the centuries. Importantly these myths will be shown to be stories, which have captured popular belief, and in this exploration the role of law will become apparent in its either endorsing or colluding in the construction of the gypsy's lot.

A romantic figure?

Myths concerning gypsies are not a new phenomenon. In fact, historically there were some positive representations of gypsies. White (2008, p. 305) explains that an examination of literature from the fifteenth century onwards shows that gypsies became 'transfigured by the literary imagination into a collective troupe'. This troupe appeared to embrace freedom and escape from the trappings of everyday life. They were seen to be exotic, foreign and capable of fortune telling. By the nineteenth century gypsies were very much part of the romantic imagination where they regularly appeared 'in the familiar guise of exotic, dark-skinned, nomadic and romantically alluring rural nomads' (Mayall, 2004, p. 139). In *Wuthering Heights* (1847), Emily Brontë suggests that Heathcliff's parentage is linked to possible gypsy blood and the character of Will Ladislaw in George Eliot's *Middlemarch* (1871) is thought to have gypsy parentage, which accounts for his reckless character. In *The Mill on the Floss* (1860) George Eliot has the protagonist Maggie Tulliver running away to the gypsies but this is only after being upset because everyone told her she was a 'wild gypsy'. It is interesting to note, however, that such romantic myths were very much particular to the artists and writers who deployed them. White uses the work of Espuglas (1999) to explain that during this time of romantic presentation gypsies were in fact shunned and much of this was due to their being seen as a 'degenerate' breed of humankind who refused to conform to the regular economic system.

This difference between the romance and the reality is confirmed by Hancock (1976), who identifies that some young women between the ages of sixteen and twenty-six (some forty-three identified from a range of organisations in the USA, Canada and the UK) wished to make contact with gypsies, during the 1970s as they were desperate to affiliate themselves with gypsies to such an extent that gypsy-related organisations referred to the emergence of 'fantasy correspondence', where the young women claimed to have Romani heritage as a way of forming a connection with existing gypsy communities. In spite of this, Hancock (1976, p. 1) confirms that the gap between the image of the gypsy in the 1970s and the gypsy in real life remained significant. This apparent dichotomy between myth and reality for the Gypsy is therefore nothing new. It could, however, be argued that such romanticism has declined over the past forty years.

Indeed, Jack Straw, Home Secretary from 1997 to 2001, controversially indicated in 1999 that 'There are relatively few real Romany gypsies left, who seem to mind their own business and don't cause real trouble to other people, and then there are a lot more people who masquerade as travellers or gypsies, who trade on the sentiment of people.'[10] This proved a controversial claim because first of all it underlined a shift in view of gypsies, but secondly Straw refers to the 'sentiment of people' as if this is somehow a romantic strand of tolerance that had always existed with gypsies. The reality would appear to have been very different. Espuglas's work (1999) paints a rather different picture.

Myth 1: 'Gypsy as child snatcher'

> I was stolen by the gypsies.
> My parents stole me right back. Then
> the gypsies stole me again.
> This went on for a long time.
> Charles Simic (1989), 'I Was Stolen by the Gypsies'

The myth of gypsies routinely stealing children can be traced back to the fifteenth century. During this time the German Reichstag accused gypsies of child stealing[11] (Walker, 2013). In Scotland it was alleged that gypsies kidnapped Adam Smith in the eighteenth century only to be returned to his family (White, 2008). The gypsies, it was said, stole children, so they could become slaves. These children could become unpaid workers who were too vulnerable to resist such expectations. Such stories were often key plot devices in nineteenth-century literature, which while sometimes proposing romantic images of the gypsy lifestyle were also keen to represent the horror of child snatching. The most notable examples can be seen in Victor Hugo's *The Hunchback of Notre Dame* (1831) and Wilkie Collins's *Armadale* (1866). White (2008, p. 308) argues that this child snatching was often used as an 'ancient device of romance where a child is sold or stolen by a group of outsiders.'[12]

The narrative, or myth, of outsiders is evident from two key historic examples of apparent abduction, which is then attributed to the gypsies (Walker, 2013). In 1904 the body of a young boy was found in a deserted house less than a mile from a local Gypsy camp in Pennsylvania. A young man George Wahl claims to have seen the gypsies taking the child. Five men were then arrested. It transpires that George Wahl himself was the murderer of the child. In 1915, a young boy disappeared again in Pennsylvania. This time a travelling carnival was in town with gypsies taking part in fortune telling. There is no evidence the boy had been snatched by the gypsies beyond their local presence. It transpired that years later the remains of the dead boy were found some two miles away from the site of his disappearance and the authorities concluded that he simply wandered off.

These accounts perhaps appear, on first glance, to have been consigned to the annals of history. However, a more recent example remind us of how strong the myth of gypsy as child snatcher remains. In 2013, a child with blonde hair and blue eyes, called by the press 'Maria', was found to be living with a Roma couple in Greece who were not her real parents (Walker, 2013). She was dubbed the 'blonde angel', and it was at this point that the myth of the gypsy as child snatcher surfaced once more. DNA testing confirmed that the girl had not been born to the couple that had been caring for her. However, there was equally no record of any such child having been abducted and no sign of any entry onto the Interpol missing persons list. The popular press jumped to condemn the couple even though they claimed that although they were not the real parents of 'Maria', they were in fact looking after her for a Bulgarian woman who had left 'Maria' in their custody.

The popular press (Turvill, 2013) was keen to point out that 'Maria' had been discovered during a raid on the Roma camp where it was alleged arms had been kept. The press also ignored the fact that very often in these camps it is the community that raises children. At this stage, it was thought 'Maria' could have been American (Spencer, 2013) and 'Maria' could have been found at a camp where a young British boy (Ben Needham) who went missing twenty-four years previously, could also have been (Murphy, 2013). Suddenly, it seemed the Roma were responsible for historic crimes as well as this latest offence. It transpired that 'Maria's' biological mother was Bulgarian and she corroborated the Roma couple's story. At this point the mother was presumed to have sold her child to the Roma couple (BBC News, 2013). It was then alleged 'Maria's' mother was on the run for child trafficking (Rossington, 2013). Once it was established that the Roma couple may have been telling the truth the popular press decided that 'Maria' could have been 'groomed to be a child bride' (Spencer, 2013) and it was finally reported that 'Maria' was now going to be raised by a Greek children's charity (Wareing, 2014). Thereby justifying their hostile reporting from the outset.

The Roma couple and the mother of 'Maria' were not universally criticised in the press. It was felt by some that the whole incident permitted old attitudes against the Roma to resurface (Sarvaricas, 2013). The incident appeared to feed into age-old stereotypes (Borev, 2013) and it was noted that while 'Maria' the 'Blonde Angel' had captured the imagination of the world, the plight of Roma children was highlighted as one of 'exclusion' where 'Maria' will have to 'navigate her way through life suffering illiteracy, unemployment and segregation' (Jovanovic, 2013). It would appear that even the sympathetic press would be relieved that 'Maria' is now being cared for by a children's charity. After all, children taken into care are all well looked after.

Just as news of the case of 'Maria' broke, so two further examples emerged which provided something of a 'perfect storm' for the myth of gypsy as child snatcher. Days after the case of 'Maria' emerged, it was announced that there had been three arrests on the island of Lesvos in Greece where it was alleged that three gypsies tried to register the birth of a two-month-old blond boy as their own. The gypsies lacked the relevant documentation and so suspicions were raised. (Turvill, 2013). Then, in Ireland, two other blonde-haired children were removed from their Roma parents following an anonymous tip off to the police. This removal of the children was based on the colour of their hair and eyes. In the Irish cases, both children were returned to their parents. Although they had provided the relevant documentation to police at the time the children were taken away the children were not returned before the police had undertaken DNA testing, which proved the couple's parenthood. While the popular press explained factually that the 'Two blond children returned to their Roma parents in Ireland as police are accused of racism' (Nolan, 2013) other press coverage suggested 'Embarrassing U-turn comes after DNA tests prove that girl put into care, 7, is biological daughter of Dublin couple' (McDonald, 2013).

These cases demonstrate that the myth of gypsy as child snatcher is alive and well in society today and it could be argued that this myth influences the police in their initial suspicion. It may, of course, be the case that some gypsies are involved in some child kidnapping in the same way that other members of the population are, but as Walker (2013) correctly concludes: 'Has a Gypsy ever kidnapped a child? Undoubtedly: There are criminals in every ethnic group.' The key though is how effectively the myth, based in some occasional truth, mutates into something much larger and all of a sudden the world believes that all gypsies are child snatchers involved in human trafficking in ways far beyond any actual evidence-based conclusion.

Myth 2: 'Gypsy as thief'

'They come. They steal. They go.' (Swiss slogan, 2012)

A common myth associated with gypsies is that they are all thieves. In folk lore the statement 'as thick as thieves' which indicates a group of people who are close and stick together is often attributed to represent, in part, gypsies (*A New Dictionary of the Terms Ancient and Modern of the Canting Crew*, 1698). Historically Locke (1974) claimed that gypsy life in Shropshire in the early twentieth century involved 'fraud, poaching and petty thievery in farmers fields'. The key with this representation is that it could equally be applied to all poor people in a predominantly agrarian society rather than just being levelled at gypsies. Where the myth extends to gypsies usually comes in the activities of 'charmers and healers' (Nixon, 2000) Low-level theft and fraud in society generally appears to have been extended to gypsies. Indeed Cher, in her now infamous song, 'Gypsies, Tramps and Thieves' (1971) indicated: 'Papa would do whatever he could, preach a little gospel, sell a couple of bottles of doctor good.'

By 2010, it appeared that the myth of gypsies being thieves had developed into a more organised and less opportunistic arrangement. It was reported that since Romania had become a member state of the European Union in 2007 there was an example of a Romanian gipsy gang snatching children from poor families and bringing them to Britain to pick pockets (Bloxham, 2010). The case against the gipsy gang was being heard at a court in Romania where some twenty-six men were accused of trafficking. The report talks of the men being members of a 'mafia style gang' but there is nothing, beyond the headline, to explain how these men were gypsies. There is a reference to the men grooming the children into a modern-day version of Fagin's urchins. Charles Dickens's Fagin from *Oliver Twist* was, of course, a Jew, but still the account makes reference to gypsies. It is interesting to note that the trial was later dropped through lack of evidence but the popular press chose not report on this development.

Barnett (2013, p. 58) states that 'One of the stereotypes many people have in their minds is that all gypsies are thieves. Some Roma and Travellers certainly are thieves – but it is patently absurd to extend this to all of them. And of course, there are many more thieves who are not Romanies.' This myth does have some truth to it, arguably much more than the earlier myth concerning child stealing. However, to label all gypsies as thieves is in itself corrosive and further discriminates against those who may already believe the law is heavily weighted against them. Barnett (2013) has argued that gypsies may, in some instances, have to turn to low-level theft to counter the decline of their own industries (such as horse trading and basket making). Again if this were the case, it would be the case for all groups who have found their way of earning money reduced by economic developments within society. What is clear is that gypsies are over represented in the prison population in England and Wales. They currently make up 5 per cent of that population when it is estimated they only account for 0.1 per cent of the overall population (Cotterell-Boyce, 2014). We must consider these statistics carefully though as we do not know whether these numbers show higher rates in criminality or rather higher rates in law enforcement. It may be that further empirical research (e.g. into the numbers of police arrests) would be helpful in this instance. After all, we already consider other ethnic groups within the prison population who are over-represented.

Myth 3: 'Gypsy as land grabber' – national wars and local battles

> They are scum, and I use the word advisedly. People who do what these people have done do not deserve the same human rights as decent constituents going about their everyday lives. (MacKay, 2002)

The final myth to be considered in this chapter is that of 'Gypsy as land grabber'. In many ways this has, certainly in the UK, been the most prevalent myth in recent years, in part owing to the well-documented events at Dale Farm (Quarmby, 2013). It certainly helps us to understand the 'gypsy's lot'. Not just in terms of their lived experience but also their current rights of land ownership in law. However, in order to understand the context within which the notion of 'land grabber' emerges, it is important to consider how gypsies have historically undertaken their nomadic lives. Recent relevant legislation has governed the gypsy way of life, at least in England and Wales. After a history of subjugation and deportation, it was hoped by the 1960s that a more liberal understanding of the gypsy way of life would emerge. Barnett (1995) explores the historic legal position for gypsies and their rights over land. What has become apparent is that the past sixty years have caused extensive problems for the courts and the legislature in terms of deciding when their occupation of land will be legalised.

The Highways Act 1959 offered no definition of 'gypsy'. It referred to a 'gypsy', 'hawker' or 'other itinerant trader' and stated that any person would be guilty of an offence if they encamped on a highway. The Caravan Sites Act 1968 decided that 'gypsies' would be broad in definition as it is clear that 'gypsies do not constitute a cohesive and separate group within our society' (Barnett, 1995, p. 142). The courts pointed to a 'nomadic lifestyle' as being the hallmark of any person labelled 'gypsy'. This wide definition of 'gypsy' proved to be a boon and an encumbrance because under s16 Caravan Sites Act 1968 local authorities were required to make site provision for all nomadic peoples. A series of cases[13] saw the courts wrestle extensively with local authority decisions to take possession of land, which had been inhabited by gypsies. Barnett (1995, p. 147) argues that these decisions generally show that attempts to distinguish between 'real' gypsies and others who appear to have been living nomadic lifestyles ensured restrictive practices could be exercised. The statutory duty was therefore limited in providing relevant sites. The restrictions continued with section 6 of the Caravan Sites Act 1968, which imposed a duty on the local authority to provide appropriate accommodation for gypsies. However the use of the term 'so far as may be necessary' meant the duty did not 'apply uniformly to all authorities' (Barnett, 1995, p. 149). The aim here was to ensure that gypsies could travel from place to place with relative freedom, thus embracing and supporting the nomadic lifestyle. In reality, the legislation ensured a significant shortfall in lawful sites provide for gypsies.

The duty to provide suitable accommodation for gypsies, so far as is necessary, was subsequently repealed by the Criminal Justice and Public Order Act 1994.[14] The other important move came under section 61 of the 1994 Act, which gave powers to the police to move gypsies on from were deemed to be 'unauthorised encampments'. Richardson (2006, p. 15) argues that the criteria to move gypsies on were quite easy to meet. In the first place, two or more people needed to be trespassing on the land. Secondly, the purpose of the trespassing was to reside on the land. Thirdly, the owner of the land had to have asked the gypsies to move. Finally, either damage had been done to the land or property on the land or abusive and threatening language had been used or there were more than six vehicles on the land. In practice, some areas appeared more accepting of 'unauthorised encampments' unless actual physical damage had been done to the land.

At the same time as the Criminal Justice and Public Order Act 1994 tried to make the nomadic life more difficult, Circular 1/94 issued by the Department of the Environment and Welsh Office adopts a rather punitive tone. It confirms that gypsies wanting a nomadic existence should be permitted on but this must be within the confines of the law. The legislation and the accompanying circular have then been seen to have 'ideological and political' implications for gypsies (Richardson, 2006, p. 15). Crawley (2004, p. 19) explains that ideologically the 1994 Act (as amended by the Anti-Social Behaviour Act 2003) was committed to private enterprise with a view that gypsies should be encouraged to purchase land with which to build their own sites. This was seen as a form of 'self-help' but naturally planning law needed to accommodate this shift. The problem here was that just as occupation of the land was controversial and could lead to gypsies being moved on, so obtaining the land with the correct planning permission was also problematic.

A series of cases came before the courts, which have clearly informed any debate concerning the place of law and popular belief in this area. The conjoined appeals in *Wrexham County Borough Council v National Assembly for Wales and Berry* (2003); *South Bucks District Council v Porter and Another* (2003) *and Chichester District Council v Searle and Others* (2003)[15] saw the House of Lords reject the requests for injunctions by the district councils in favour of the gypsies. Not only favour but a real concern about the effectiveness of requiring gypsies to submit to the planning system. To be effective their lordships argued there must be some real prospect of success:

> In the case of Gypsies, the problem [i]s compounded by the features peculiar to them: their characteristic [nomadic] lifestyle debarred them from access to conventional sources of housing provision. Their attempts to obtain planning permission almost always met with failure: statistics quoted by the European Court ... [found that] 90% of applications made by Gypsies had been refused whereas 80% of all applications had been granted. But for many years the capacity of sites authorised for Gypsies had fallen far short of that needed.

While the use of the courts was proving, in some cases, to be helpful to the gypsy, another unprecedented case emerged which would further undermine the position of the gypsy. The events at Dale Farm have arguably had the most significant impact in recent years and have put the gypsy cause back by some years. The Dale Farm protests in 2011 involved the residents of Dale Farm in Basildon, Essex. Home (2012, pp. 178–188) explores the foundations of this dispute and the legal arguments around this forced eviction. Dale Farm is a site of around 2.5 hectares. English gypsies had lived in the area of Dale Farm for many years. In 1987, one of these families obtained planning permission on the site known as Oak Lane. When a scrap metal dealer lost his permission to continue his business, he then sold his land to gypsies. This took place and Irish travellers arrived in 1998. Dale Farm itself was then purchased by the travellers and subdivided into plots. A planning application was refused for there to be twenty plots on the site and in 2003 a public local inquiry was held. Residents were given two years to find alternative accommodation. No alternatives were found and the plots had now grown to fifty. At one stage, Dale Farm housed over 1,000 people. The local council attempted to secure compliance with the enforcement notices but was unsuccessful. By 2011, the council finally succeeded in clearing the site. Ninety families were to be cleared in September 2011 and by October the clearance was complete. These clearances were an unedifying spectacle. There were riot police sent in to clear gypsies from the site they had called home for at least ten years. The gypsies had lost their battle at Dale Farm but polarised opinion at the same time.

Smith and Greenfields (2013, pp. 27–29) use the canonical study of Sibley (1981) to understand events at Dale Farm. Sibley explains that the urbanisation of gypsies has occurred over time on the basis of two key propositions. In the first place, all societies adopt policies that aim to either exclude or incorporate outsider groups into the mainstream, and, secondly, as society becomes more industrialised so power becomes more centralised and this in itself ensures that land use must provide some contribution to the productive process. At Dale Farm the refusal of the gypsies to accept the Council's offer of alternative accommodation was met with shock in the media and yet this demonstrated the Council's desire to suppress and forcibly assimilate the gypsies into conventional accommodation. As Sibley

(1981, p. 182) has long indicated: 'The discriminatory nature of these policies is masked by the emphasis of the higher standards that will enable the minority to enjoy the lifestyle of the majority, and it is easy to appeal to a sense of social justice in providing a deprived ethnic group with bathrooms or electric lighting.'

Similarly, Quarmby (2013) published a largely moving and supportive account of the lives of gypsies and travellers in response to the events at Dale Farm. Quarmby (2013, p. 286) reminds the reader that gypsies were subject to extermination during the Second World War by the Nazis and they also fought against the Nazis alongside the Allied Forces. They wanted a place to call home but she concludes by referencing the work of Delaine Le Bas that 'There is a space for everyone ... Not just for the chosen few.'

Politicians and the popular press provided a more conventional perspective against the gypsies at Dale Farm. Commenting on the events at Dale Farm, the then-Prime Minister David Cameron suggested:[16]

> What I would say is that it is a basic issue of fairness; everyone in this country has to obey the law including the law about planning permission and about building on green belt land. Where this has been done without permission it is an illegal development and those people should move away.

Meanwhile, the popular press decided that gypsies had cynically used their children as 'shields to protect them against eviction' (Platell, 2011) and focused on the cost of clearing the sight which ran to £22 million (Sawer and Ljunggren, 2011).

Home (2012, p. 187) suggests that the events at Dale Farm saw a further shift of opinion against gypsies with a view to enabling local authorities to be far more resolute in the upholding of their planning laws against this minority group. The result was a worldwide spectacle of minorities being removed by riot police and the majority supporting this action. If there was any apparent sympathy for gypsies at this stage the events at Dale Farm will have undermined this.

Events around the country at this time demonstrated that Dale Farm was not the only case concerning land rights for gypsies. A further dimension here in this area of 'gypsy as land grabber' came in the case of *Buckland v UK* (2012),[17] in which the European Court of Human Rights decided that Mrs Buckland's eviction in Wales was deemed disproportionate. This was after both the High Court and the Court of Appeal decided the eviction was lawful. The decision is important, not just for considering the procedural safeguards required in these decisions but also in the backlash that followed. The popular press balked at the European Court's decision deciding that the judgment 'could now pave the way for other traveller families to use human rights grounds to fight eviction notices' (Doughty, 2012), and it further reinforced the view that gypsies had all rights, which were recognised by a European Court at the expense of the landowners.

While these high-profile cases demonstrate how the myth works at a national level, it is useful to focus on events in a local area as foci for discussion to see whether since Dale Farm and *Buckland v UK* (2012) things have improved for the gypsy By looking at the county of Surrey, it is possible to explore a typical local response to unauthorised encampments.

Tesco in Guildford, Surrey

In August 2013, an unauthorised traveller encampment was set up outside a Tesco shop on Bannister's Field in Guildford. Local reports in the paper showed 'bemused' onlookers watching as the caravans arrived and reported that the travellers intended to stay for ten weeks because the site was close to shops and a playground (Harris, 2013). However, subsequent reports noted that, although some derogatory comments about the travellers had been posted on Facebook, many people in Surrey take a more balanced view of transient gypsy encampments (Giles, 2013).[18] It was evidence that after the ten weeks had passed, the council sought to move the encampment on and to discourage damage to shrubs as the caravans accessed the site, although it did provide refuse and recycling bins. Evidently, in its 2013 Traveller Accommodation Assessment Consultation Document, Guildford Borough Council explained that the travellers had not chosen to camp by Tesco because of a lack of transitory pitches but because they wanted to be close to the hospital while travelling to work at the Appleby Fair in Cumbria (Guildford Borough Council, 2013, pp. 40–41). This example demonstrates a typical local response to an unauthorised encampment. Surrey is an affluent part of the UK and although there was some evidence of tolerance within that community the press response continued to suggest that a widespread misconception remains that gypsies are dirty and that they do not wash or clean their caravans. (Giles, 2013).

Planning applications, Surrey

It is clearly not just transient encampments, which face difficulties. Local newspapers frequently carry reports of planning applications and disputes about unauthorised building work in relation to private caravan or mobile home pitches (often in rural areas on or abutting the Green Belt or designated areas of outstanding natural beauty). Although many applications are opposed (both by individuals and by parish councils), many are approved. In June 2014, Guildford Borough Council published an updated Traveller Strategic Housing Land Availability Assessment (Traveller SHLAA, 2014). Among other things, this document records that sixteen new permanent traveller pitches have been approved since June 2012 and a further sixteen pitches have been given temporary planning permission because of an absence of a five-year supply of deliverable land for traveller accommodation. Almost all of this land is Green Belt and/or in Areas of Outstanding Natural Beauty and the applications tend to be granted under a rural exception policy.

Guildford Borough Council would appear to have been to promote integration between gypsies and local residents (although it is not clear whether this is something that either the gypsies or local residents are keen to foster). It also expressed a desire to avoid large sites and stand-alone gypsy accommodation. As is consistent with national policy the Council appeared keen to encourage bricks and mortar accommodation for gypsies but in a traveller style. Clearly the Council would prefer all travellers owning land in the borough to have static homes rather than caravan pitches as these would arguably look nicer and it maybe considered as a further attempt at assimilation. This may also, in part, inform its apparent reluctance to provide additional temporary pitches and promote once more a more conventional way of living.

Normandy village
The 2014 SHLAA identifies a number of gypsy/traveller-owned properties within Guildford Borough where planning applications have been granted. In Normandy, for example, there is a mix of settled and transient travelling communities. One site is in Wood Street Village, where it was noted that there was substantial opposition from local residents despite the fact that the site is recorded as being 'well established and exceptionally well kept'. In part, this opposition arose because the land is question is situated within the Green Belt and therefore being used 'inappropriately'. This meant that the Council had to determine whether harm to the Green Belt would be outweighed by harm caused to the gypsies because of a lack of available land for gypsy and traveller accommodation.

This conflict between 'preserving' Green Belt land and providing gypsy pitches is not unusual and is confirmed in the popular media (Watkins, 2013). Local residents who had opposed the application accused the local authority of letting them down. Denying suggestions of 'nimbyism', these residents however suggested that allowing more traveller sites in Normandy would 'change the nature of the village'. Subsequently, the Normandy Action Group received the support of MP Jonathan Lord for a petition alleging that the local authority had failed in its duty to protect the Green Belt. The group stated its support for a decision by the then Secretary for State for Communities and Local Government, Eric Pickles, to call in all planning appeals in order to ensure that they followed his robust guidance about the criteria necessary to justify Green Belt development. It is interesting to note that, in January 2015, the High Court[19] determined that the decision by Mr

Pickles to call in all planning applications breached the 2010 Equality Act and violated Article 6 of the ECHR because it resulted in a disproportionate delay to gypsy and traveller applications (Baker, 2015).

Charmaine Valler

The case of Charmaine Valler provides a salutary reminder of the power of the popular media and the concerns raised by the House of Lords in *Wrexham County Borough Council v National Assembly for Wales and Berry* (2003); *South Bucks District Council v Porter and Another* (2003) *and Chichester District Council v Searle and Others* (2003).[20] Ms Valler is a member of the gypsy community and worked with a community organisation supporting this community, which was funded by Guildford Borough Council. In this capacity she attended numerous council meetings and participated in Guildford Borough Council's consultation about the provision of accommodation for gypsies, travellers and show people. She also gave talks to local parish councils about gypsy and traveller culture and intra-community engagement.

Charmaine Valler and her brother both bought land in West Byfleet. Although located within the Green Belt, the property was bought legitimately. In 2013, Charmaine Valler's sister-in-law applied for planning permission to alter her site to allow for mobile homes to be pitched there and for sewerage. An administrative error caused the application to be submitted twice but it was only considered once. Charmaine Valler's property – which was opposite that of her brother and sister-in-law – was not included within the application. The application were made according to planning law and duly considered by Woking Borough Council. However, local residents vehemently opposed the applications and alleged a conspiracy because they did not discover the application until a few days before the closing date for comments. Local residents subsequently organised demonstrations, sold T-shirts and attended a Woking Borough Council meeting in order to raise concerns about both the applications specifically and use of the Green Belt generally.

Numerous letters objecting to application became very personal and displayed prejudicial assumptions about both the Vallers themselves and the gypsy traveller way of life. A supporting letter from Richard Lingard, formerly Guildford Borough Solicitor emphasised that these perceptions were not accurate but his voice was in a clear minority and a petition demanding the withdrawal of the application apparently received more than 2,000 signatures. At an open meeting in July 2013, planning officers rejected the Vallers's application but there was also criticism of the behaviour of those who had objected to the plans. During the planning process, Charmaine Valler (whose land was not included in the application) was subjected to abuse because of complaints about, among other things, 'pig odours and bonfires'. One reason stated for objections to the planning permission was the fact that local Byfleet residents had been used to using a path through the land to reach the countryside and that this path was frequently blocked by herds of goats. By August 2013, Charmaine Valler was telling reporters that she felt that she had no option but to leave West Byfleet and was offering to sell her land to the local Residents Association. Even the Council's planning officers had criticised the behaviour of those opposing the Vallers's application but no other action appears to have been taken about it.

In October 2013, the Vallers lodged an appeal against Woking Borough Council's refusal of the application and local media described the move as a thickening plot. However, Mrs Valler's application was submitted at around the time Mr Pickles was calling in all such planning appeals and appears to have subsequently been withdrawn. Matters deteriorated further in 2014 when, having obtained planning permission to remove some trees on her own land, Charmaine Valler discovered that two of her pet goats had been hanged. This story was reported in both local and national media, along with graphic photographs of the goats. At this stage, it should be noted that a planning application for a scout hut in Murrays Lane was approved in September 2014 (following a previous rejection) and that, in its Local Plan, Woking Borough Council is considering further development of the Green Belt – both for bricks and mortar homes and for traveller pitches. It was also noted on Twitter that proposals to build a new housing estate in Byfleet did not attract nearly as much vitriol as the Vallers's application.

More recently, another tragic development has emerged in this arena. In October 2015, a fire swept through a travellers' site in Dublin, Ireland and killed ten people. The casualties were largely from two families, the Connors and the Lynches, who had lived on the site for eight years. At the time, Ireland was shocked and the Irish President, Michael D. Higgins said: 'It's such an unspeakable tragedy to have an entire family wiped out in a horrific inferno' (BBC, 2015). In response to the fire there was an 'Outpouring of sympathy from political and civic leaders; contributions of food and clothing from local people and businesses; the laying of flowers and toys at the site; and money into a fund for the surviving members of the family who now had nowhere to go' (Joyce, 2015).

This response of sympathy, however, did not last long and 'as the days passed, the veneer of sympathy slipped away' (Joyce, 2015). Invoking emergency powers, the local council attempted to utilise an existing piece of land nearby for the remaining travellers during a period of grief. This land was equipped for travellers and had running water and mains sewage. The response of the local community demonstrated once more the concerns surrounding gypsies and their use of land. Some of the local residents set up a blockade and this prevented access for the survivors of the fire to enter the site. Joyce (2015) recognises this response to be typical in Ireland where: 'the protestors are not unique; they fought and won a battle that has been fought and won, year in, year out, for as long as anyone can remember.' The local council eventually gave in and housed the travellers elsewhere in an area which did not have running water and mains sewage. Joyce reminds us though that although these travellers are part of a particular group within Irish society they are still Irish travellers and there is a call to 'treat our own outcasts with decency.' It appears the local community were worried about these people living nearby. They were clearly worried about further land grabbing in this instance.

Throughout the discussion of the myth of 'gypsy as land grabber', it has become clear that the legal framework has ebbed and flowed. From the largely progressive legislation of the 1960s through to the much more restrictive response in the 1990s, it is clear that the law has not always been sure as to how to respond to the perceived problem of the gypsy. On the one hand, the legislature and courts have paid lip service to providing for this, and other nomadic forms of life, but in practical terms this has not always been possible. The tide is turning slowly with the Human Rights Act 1998 ensuring a proportionality requirement when it comes to evictions, but ironically events at Dale Farm and the perceived protections of the Human Rights Act 1998 could result in repeal and stronger measures to ensure evictions from illegal camps take place efficiently (Dominiczak, 2015). Experience locally is mixed although the message is still one of 'accommodation, if we must'. Charmaine Valler's experience and that of the Connors and Lynch family are all too common in the current climate. As a coda the actual victory at Dale Farm for the authorities may have been a pyrrhic one because a gypsy site has now sprung up very close by (Robinson, 2014) but the damage may have been far greater in terms of the public imagination. The myth of 'gypsy as land grabber' is cemented now.

Conclusion

Article 27 of the International Covenant on Civil and Political Rights 1966 states that

> In the States in which ethnic, religious or linguistic minorities exist, persons belonging to such minorities shall not be denied the right, in community with other members of their group, to enjoy their own culture, to profess and practice their own religion, or to use their own language.

Given the operations of the law and the myths that inform popular belief, it would appear that this requirement of the state is currently left wanting when it comes to gypsies. Faced with distrust by society at large, with popular belief seeing them as 'child snatchers', the 'thieves' and 'land grab-bers' tend to undermine their ability to engage in their own way of life. Stewart (1997, 84) suggests this is, however, nothing new and

> Every age, ours as much as its predecessors, believes that it will be the law to be blessed (and cursed) by the presence of the Gypsies. Well-wishers and hostile commentators, romantics and cynics alike after of fixed opinion that the 'wanderers of the world' have at last been 'domesticated', their way of life finally out moded and that that 'the time of the Gypsies' has run out.

It is unlikely that the time of the gypsy has run out. The Human Rights Act 1998 may still assist the gypsy in their battle for a home and although the gypsy adapts and remains in spite of extensive hostility, the myths concern-ing their lifestyle remain. In this instance, myths (i.e. stories), born in some instances from truth and in other instances from fear, can have some utility. As Warner (1994) argues:

> Myths offer a lens which can be used to see human identity in its social and cultural context – they can lock us up in stock reactions, bigotry and fear, but they're not immutable, and by unpicking them the stories can lead to others. Myths convey values and expectations that are always evolving, in the process of being formed, but – and this is fortunate – never set so hard they cannot be changed again.

It can only be hoped that the current stasis, when it comes to the myths sur-rounding gypsies can evolve once more to provide a calmer and more settled experience for the gypsies. On the basis of current evidence, this period of calm is not coming any time soon.

Notes

1 Particular thanks to Katy Peters for her excellent research assistance and to the editors for their forbearance. All errors remain my own.
2 The Race Relations Act 1976 has now been replaced by the Equality Act 2010 for this purpose.
3 The criminal law regulates the behaviour of gypsies in the way other groups are regulated.
4 Criminal Justice and Public Order Act 1994 as amended by the Anti-Social Behaviour Act 2003.
5 DH & Ors –v– Czech Republic application n° 57325/00, Grand Chamber judg-ment of 13 November 2007, § 182.
6 A useful example here would be the myth of 'rags to riches' that Segal explores.
7 Here Segal looks at the work of Rubinstein (1997) who explored the myth that many Jewish victims of the Nazis could have been saved if the Allies had cared.
8 Rubinstein's view is explored in Segal (2015, p. 5).

9 See Segal (1999) where he considers whether myth has a future in light of its chief modern challenge, the natural sciences. Segal argues that myth has also been subject to modern intellectual, religious or political challenge but such challenges are not merely modern. He looks to Plato's rejection of the Homer myth as an example from the Classical world.

10 Millar, S. 'Straw's travellers gaffe misconstrued.' *Guardian* [Online] 20 August 1999 (last accessed 10 September 2015).

11 At this time the age-old blood libel legend was also in place, which concerned another much vilified minority: the Jew.

12 This motif can be traced back to the story of Joseph being sold to the Ishmaelites in the Old Testament.

13 *Greenwich London Borough Council v Powell* [1959] 1 AC 995; *Horsham District Council v Secretary of State for the Environment* (1989) *Guardian*, 31 October; *R v Shropshire County Council ex p Bungay* [1990] 23 HLR 195; *R v South Hams District Council ex p. Gibb and others* [1993] EGCS 179

14 Section 80 of the 1994 Act repealed the 1968 Act.

15 2 WLR 1547.

16 Hansard HC vol. 532 col. 353.

17 App. No. 40060/08.

18 See, for example, articles on the 'Guildford Dragon' website: www.guildford-dragon.com (last accessed 12 September 2015)., including a report on 2 September 2013, for example, was sympathetic towards the travellers and noted that two women amongst the group were seeking antenatal care at the Royal Surrey County Hospital that the group as a whole were keen to dispel perceptions that they or their caravans were dirty.

19 *Moore and Another v Secretary of State for Communities and Local Government and Others* [2015] EWHC 44.

20 2 WLR 1547.

References

Baker, K. (2015) 'Eric Pickles "unlawfully discriminated" against gipsies who wanted to pitch on Green Belt land, High Court Rules', Mail Online, 21 January. Available at: www.dailymail.co.uk/news/article-2920629/Eric-Pickles-unlawfully-discriminated-against-gipsies-wanted-pitch-Green-Belt-land-High-Court-rules.html. Last accessed 3 June 2015.

Barnett, H. (1995) 'The end of the road for gypsies', *Anglo American Law Review* 24(2), pp. 133–168.

Barnett, R. (2013) *Jews and Gypsies: Myth and Reality.* Amazon: Ruth Barnett.

BBC News (2013) 'Mystery girl Maria's parents found in Bulgaria by DNA' *BBC News* [Online] 25 October. Available at: www.bbc.co.uk/news/world-europe-24673804. Last accessed 2 July 2015.

BBC News (2015) 'County Dublin fire: ten people die in blaze at travellers' site', *BBC News* [Online], 10 October. Available at: http://www.bbc.co.uk/news/world-europe-34495331. Last accessed 20 November 2015.

Bloxham, A. (2010) 'Romanian gipsy child-snatchers stole almost 200 poor children from their families and brought them to Britain to pick pockets.' *The Telegraph* [Online], 27 September. Available at: www.telegraph.co.uk/news/worldnews/europe/romania/8027694/Romanian-gipsy-gang-snatched-200-children-from-homes-to-use-them-as-beggars.html. Last accessed 4 July 2015.

Borev, F. (2013) 'I was a pale Roma baby – it's always been a family joke that I was stolen.' *Guardian* [Online] 25 October. Available at: www.theguardian.com/commentisfree/2013/oct/25/pale-roma-baby-blond-maria. Last accessed 3 July 2015.

Cotterell-Boyce, J. (2014) 'Too many Gypsies and Travellers end up in prison – this must be addressed.' *Guardian* [Online] 12 March. Available at: www.theguardian.com/commentisfree/2014/mar/12/too-many-gypsies-travellers-prison-education. Last accessed 10 July 2015.

Coupe, L. (1997) *Myth*. London: Routledge.

Coxhead, J. (2007) *The Last Bastion of Racism: Gypsies, Travellers and Policing*. Stoke: Trentham Books.

Crawley, H. (2004) *Moving Forward, the Provision of Accommodation for Travellers and Gypsies*. London: Institute of Public Policy Research.

Cupitt, L. (1982) *The World to Come*. London: SCM Press.

Dominczak, P. (2015) 'Gypsy caravans in England increase by a third in 10 years', *Telegraph* [Online], 18 June. Available at: www.telegraph.co.uk/news/politics/11676045/Gypsy-caravans-in-England-increase-by-a-third-in-10-years.html. Last accessed 5 July 2015.

Doughty, S. (2012) 'Gipsy wins human rights case against campsite that threw her out for causing very substantial nuisance.' *Mail Online* [Online], 18 September. Available at: www.dailymail.co.uk/news/article-2205311/Gipsy-wins-human-rights-case-campsite-threw-causing-substantial-nuisance.html. Last accessed 8 July 2015.

ECHR Factsheet (2013) *Roma and Travellers, European Court of Human Rights Press Releases*, October. Available at: www.echr.coe.int/Documents/FS_Roma_ENG.pdf. Last accessed 22 July 2015.

Espuglass, C. (1999) 'Gypsy women in English life and literature. The foreign woman in Button', in M. D. and T. Reed (eds), *The Foreign Woman in British Literature: Exotics, Aliens, and Outsiders* (pp. 145–158). Westport, CT: Greenwood Press.

Giles, M. (2013) 'Opinion: How should Guildford treat travellers?', *Guildford Dragon* [Online], 22 August. Available at: www.guildford-dragon.com/2013/08/22/opinion-travellers/. Last accessed 9 June 2015.

Gronemeyer, R. (ed.) (1987) Zigeuner in Spiegel Frueher Chroniken und Abhandlungen quellen can is bis zum is Jahmdert, Giesen (p. 15); quoted in Stauber R. and Vago R. (2007) *Roma: a Minority in Europe*. Budapest: Central European University Press.

Guildford Borough Council, Guildford Borough Council Traveller Accommodation Assessment Consultation Record (2013, September) Available at: www.guildford.gov.uk/media/15381/Guildford-Borough-Traveller-Accommodation-Assessment-Consultation-Record/pdf/TAA_Consultation_Statement.pdf. Last accessed 2 June 2015.

Hancock, I. (1976) 'Romance vs. reality: popular notions of the gypsy', *Roma* 2(1), pp. 7–23.

Harris, T. (2013) 'Traveller caravans arrive in field next to Guildford Tesco', *Surrey Advertiser* [Online], 16 August. Available at: www.getsurrey.co.uk/news/local-news/traveller-caravans-arrive-field-next-5740427. Last accessed 1 June 2015.

Home, R. (2012) 'Forced eviction and planning enforcement: the Dale Farm gypsies', *International Journal of Law in the Built Environment* 4(3), 178–188.

Jovanovic, Z. (2013) 'Maria is Roma – so now she will become invisible once more', *Guardian* [Online], 25 October. Available at: www.theguardian.com/commentisfree/2013/oct/28/maria-roma-invisible. Last accessed 4 July 2015.

Joyce, J. (2015) 'We Irish proclaim moral superiority but look at how we treat our outcasts', *Guardian* [Online], 25 October. Available at: www.theguardian.com/commentisfree/2015/oct/25/dublin-fire-we-irish-treat-travellers-as-outcasts-joe-joyce. Last accessed 25 November 2015.

Locke, J. (1974) 'Gypsy life in Shropshire – as it was and as it is', *Journal of the Gypsy Lore Society* 1, 14–21.

McDonald, H. 'Irish police return blonde girl to Roma parents', *Guardian* [Online], 24 October. Available at: www.theguardian.com/world/2013/oct/24/blonde-girl-roma-parents-returned-dna. Last accessed 4 July 2015.

MacKay, A. (2002) *House of Commons Hansard Debates*, Part 5, 15 January, Available at: www.publications.parliament.uk/pa/cm200102/cmhansrd/vo020115/halltext/20115h05.htm. Last accessed 15 July 2015.

Mayall, D. (2004) *Gypsy Identities 1500–2000 From Egyptians and Moon-men to the Ethnic Romany.* London: Routledge.

Miller, S. (2015) 'Straw's travellers gaffe misconstrued.' *Guardian* [Online], 20 August. Available at: www.theguardian.com/world/1999/aug/20/race.political-news. Last accessed 10 September 2015.

Murphy, S. (2013) 'Was missing Ben Needham at the same gypsy camp as 'Maria'? Police probe claims that abducted British boy was seen at site where blonde girl, four, had been found', *Mail on Sunday* [Online], 20 October. Available at: www.dailymail.co.uk/news/article-2468431/Police-probe-claims-Ben-Needham-spotted-gypsy-camp-Maria.html. Last accessed 3 July 2015.

Nixon, P. (2000) 'Life patterns, hazards, and ascendancies: gypsies, tinkers and travellers in Great Britain and Ireland' in M. P. Baumann. (ed.), *Music, Language and Literature of the Roma and Sinti* (pp. 453–460). Berlin: Verlag fur Wissenschaft und Bildung.

Nolan, S. (2013) 'Two blond children returned to their Roma parents in Ireland as police are accused of racism', *Mail Online* [Online], 24 October. Available at: www.dailymail.co.uk/news/article-2474834/Two-blond-children-returned-Roma-parents-Ireland-police-accused-racism.html. Last accessed 4 July 2015.

Platell, A. (2011) 'The REAL victims of the illegal gipsy camp.' *Mail Online* [Online], 22 October. Available at: www.dailymail.co.uk/debate/article-2052073/Dale-Farm-eviction-The-REAL-victims-illegal-gipsy-camp.html. Last accessed 12 July 2015.

Pogany, I. (2004) *The Roma Café.* London: Pluto Press.

Quarmby, K. (2013) *No Place To Call Home*, London: Oneworld.

Richardson, J. (2006) *The Gypsy Debate? Can discourse control?* Exeter: Imprint-Academic-Com.

Richardson, J. and A. Ryder, A. (eds) (2013) *Gypsies and Travellers: Empowerment and Inclusion in British Society*. Bristol: The Policy Press.

Robinson, J. (2014) 'Travellers return to Dale Farm: council attacked for spending £7m to evict residents who have moved just 50ft down the road', *The Telegraph* [Online], October 22. Available at: www.dailymail.co.uk/news/article-2802841/travellers-return-dale-farm-council-attacked-spending-7m-evict-residents-moved-just-50ft-road.html. Last accessed 14 July 2015.

Rossington, B. (2013) 'Greece's girl Maria's mum on run after being told she cannot have her back despite DNA match', *Mirror* [Online], 26 October. Available at: www.mirror.co.uk/news/world-news/greece-girl-marias-mum-sasha-2592009. Last accessed 3 July 2015.

Rubinstein, W. (1997) *The Myth of Rescue: Why the Democracies Could Not Have Saved More Jews from the Nazis*. London: Routledge.

Sarvaricas, N. (2013) 'Old attitudes resurface in Greece: inside the Roma camp where Maria the "blonde angel" lived', *Independent* [Online], 23 October. Available at: www.independent.co.uk/news/world/europe/old-attitudes-resurface-in-greece-inside-the-roma-camp-where-maria-the-blonde-angel-lived-8897530.html. Last accessed 4 July 2015.

Sawer, P. and H. Ljunggren (2011) 'The £22 million cost of evicting the Dale Farm travellers', *Telegraph* [Online], 2 October. Available at: www.telegraph.co.uk/news/uknews/law-and-order/8800962/The-22-million-cost-of-evicting-the-Dale-Farm-travellers.html. Last accessed 7 July 2015.

Segal, R. A. (1999) *Theorizing About Myth*. Boston, MA: University of Massachusetts Press.

Segal, R. A. (2015) *Myth: a Very Short Introduction*. Oxford: Oxford University Press.

Sibley, D. (1981) *Outsiders in Urban Society*. New York: St Martin's Press.

Smith, D. M. and M. Greenfields (2013) *Gypsies and Travellers in Housing: The Decline of Nomadism*. Bristol: The Policy Press.

Spencer, B. (2013a) 'Pictured: Couple who "snatched Maria and held her in a Gypsy camp in Greece" as half the promising leads about her real identity come from the US – suggesting she could be American', *Mail Online* [Online], 21 October. Available at: www.dailymail.co.uk/news/article-2469776/Is-Maria-AMERICAN-Half-promising-leads-identifying-little-blonde-girl-saved-Greek-gypsy-camp-US.html. Last accessed 3 July 2015.

Spencer, B. (2013b) 'Maria "was groomed to be a child bride": Police claim girl found in gipsy camp was set to be married off at the age of 12 by couple who adopted her', *Mail Online* [Online], 23 October. Available at: www.dailymail.co.uk/news/article-2474417/Maria-groomed-child-bride-Roma-Gypsy-couple.html. Last accessed 3 July 2015.

Stewart, M. (1997) 'The puzzle of Roma persistence: group identity without a nation' in D. Anderson and G. Mullen (eds), *Romani Culture and Gypsy Identity* (pp. 82–96). Herts: University of Hertfordshire Press.

Traveller SHLAA (2014) Available at: www.guildford.gov.uk/newlocalplan/travel-lershlaa. Last accessed 5 July 2015.

Tuetcy A. (2007) *Journal d'un Bourgeois de Paris 1400 – 1499*. Paris, 1881, 219–221; quoted in Stauber R. and R. Vago *Roma: A Minority in Europe*, Budapest: Central European University Press.

Turvill, W. (2013) 'Three Roma arrested after ANOTHER unidentified child is found kidnapped in Greece', *Mail Online* [Online], 23 October. Available from: www. dailymail.co.uk/news/article-2473971/3-Roma-Gypsies-arrested-ANOTHER-child-kidnapped-Greece.html. Last accessed 3 July 2015.

Wareing, C. (2014) 'Greek Girl "Maria" found in Roma Gypsy camp to be raised by children's charity, court rules', *Mirror* [Online], 3 June. Available at: www.mirror. co.uk/news/world-news/greek-girl-maria-found-roma-3639707. Last accessed 3 July 2015.

Walker, J. (2013) 'The legend of the child-snatching gypsies', *Reason.Com* [Online], 30 October. Available at: http://reason.com/archives/2013/10/30/the-legend-of-the-child-snatching. Last accessed 2 July 2015.

Warner, M. (1994) *Managing Monsters: Six Myths of Our Time*. London: Vintage.

Watkins J. (2013) 'Three year approval for Gypsy pitch', *Surrey Advertiser* [Online], 5 August. Available at: www.getsurrey.co.uk/news/three-year-approval-green-belt-gypsy-5396820. Last accessed 1 June 2015.

White, L. M. (2008) 'Beyond the romantic Gypsy: narrative disruptions and ironies in Austen's Emma', *Papers on Language and Literature* 44(3), 305–327.

Index

EU authorised representative for GPSR:
Easy Access System Europe, Mustamäe tee 50,
10621 Tallinn, Estonia
gpsr.requests@easproject.com

www.ingramcontent.com/pod-product-compliance
Lightning Source LLC
Chambersburg PA
CBHW052004270326
41929CB00015B/2785